twins!

2ND EDITION

*Pregancy, Birth, and the
First Year of Life*

Connie L. Agnew, M.D., Alan H. Klein, M.D.,
and Jill Alison Ganon

ILLUSTRATIONS BY VICTOR ROBERT

Collins
An Imprint of HarperCollinsPublishers

Pages 330–34, American College of Obstetricians and
Gynecologists. Immunization During Pregnancy.
ACOG Committee Opinion No. 282. Washington, DC
© ACOG, 2003

HarperCollins books may be purchased for educational,
business, or sales promotional use. For information, please
write: Special Markets Department, HarperCollins
Publishers, 10 East 53rd Street, New York, NY 10022.

Designed by Jennifer Ann Daddio

Library of Congress Cataloging-in-Publication Data

Agnew, Connie L., 1957–
    Twins! pregnanacy, birth, and the first year of life /
Connie L. Agnew, Alan H. Klein, and Jill Alison
Ganon ; illustrations by Victor Robert.—2nd ed.
        p.   cm.
    Includes index.
    ISBN-10: 0-06-074219-4
    ISBN-13: 978-0-06-074219-5
    1. Twins.   I. Klein, Alan H., 1946–   II. Ganon, Jill
Alison, 1952–   III. Title.

RG525.A34   2005
649'.143—dc22
                                          2005045585

09 RRD 10 9 8

This book is dedicated to:

My parents; my husband, William Brien; and my children,
WIlliam Jr., Brent, Kelly, and Ashley

—CONNIE L. AGNEW

The memories of my parents, Lois and Don Klein;
my daughters, Laura Klein-Danilov and Rachael Klein;
and my wife, Rabbi Toba August

—ALAN H. KLEIN

My husband, David Arnay; my son, Miles;
and my wish for a bright future for children everywhere

—JILL ALISON GANON

contents

two: the first year of life

acknowledgments

The authors gratefully acknowledge the following families for their wisdom, humor, and the generous gift of their time in the preparation of this book:

The Copsis family—Judy, Peter, John, and Henry

The King family—Julie, Curt, Kevin, and Steven

The Mandel family—Nidia, Harold, Max, and David

The Meizensahl family—Annie, Paul, Ben, Emily, Molly, and Jeff

The Moffat family—Donald, Samantha, Michael, and the memories of Brian and the children's mother, Susan

The Prince family—Janet, Christopher, William, and Langston

The Timiraos family—Carol, Vince, Alex, and Nick

The Varblow family—Paula, Larry, Paul, and Robert

Once again, we want to thank our agent, Angela Rinaldi, for her great instincts, faith in this project, and hard work on our behalf. We are happy to have completed round two! As always, we thank you for bringing us together for this book, others we've completed, and those yet to come.

To Julie Julie Tupler, RN, for sharing with us her knowledge and passionate concern for maternal fitness.

To Netty Levine, MS, RD and Marlene Clark, RD for enriching our book with their years of experience teaching pregnant women about healthful eating.

To Cheryl Baker, A.A.H.C.C., C.D. for her support of our project.

To Patty Leasure at HarperCollins, thank you for looking at our original proposal and seeing a book there.

To Greg Chaput, who took the reins from Tricia Medved, our editor for the original edition of this book, and saw this new edition through to its birth.

To our illustrator, Victor Roberts, thank you for your beautiful and imaginative drawings.

To Kathy Jessee for transcribing the tapes that were so important to the revision of this book.

Dr. Agnew and Dr. Klein want to thank all their patients for helping them to continue to grow as physicians.

Introduction

our fascination with twins

As we prepare this revised edition of TWINS!, twins, triplets, and higher-order multiples now account for approximately 3 percent of all pregnancies—a percentage point higher than it was when this book was first published in 1997. Society's interest in multiple birth remains keen, yet we grow increasingly familiar with twins in our children's classrooms, on their sports teams, and for some of us, in our immediate or extended families. Scientists continue to study twins, obstetricians and pediatricians all over the country grow more familiar with the particular medical and health concerns that may apply to some twins, and the marketplace is increasingly engaged with supplying products for twins. We are happy to have had the opportunity to update and expand this book to support the needs of loving parents as they prepare to welcome their twins into the world.

As the Roman myth comes to us, Romulus and Remus were born to Mars, the God of War, and Rhea Silvia, one of the Vestal Virgins. After the birth of her two healthy boys, Rhea Silvia's wicked uncle Amulius had them placed in a basket and thrown into the Tiber River, so as to remove any potential threat to his throne. The twins were rescued and nursed by a she-wolf on the slope of the Palatine Hill and later discovered by the shepherd Faustulus and reared by his wife. When the brothers grew to manhood, they deposed Amulius and placed their grandfather Numitor on the throne. Then they decided to build the great city that we know today as Rome.

Romulus and Remus, Castor and Pollux—stories of twins and their unique positions in society appear in Greek and Roman mythology as well as in the literature of the Old Testament. Even before there was any written documentation about the miracle of twinning, there were drawings of twins and twin births. We have ancient evidence of an incredible range of cultural responses to the phenomenon of twinning, as well as equally seasoned documentation of exceptional behavior attributed to twins.

Every culture has its own unique relationship with this phenomenon. It is the structure of each society, from its day-to-day function to its most profound view of life and death, that ultimately informs attitudes toward twinning. Economic conditions undoubtedly influence custom. Anthropologists tell us that in a well-supported economy, twins pose no threat to the survival of the family. But if poverty—with its devastating lack of adequate nutrition and shelter—is more prevalent, twins may represent an unbearable burden to the struggling family.

As we'll discuss later on, there is a racial component to the incidence of twinning. Twinning is most common among the black population. Outside Lagos, Nigeria, there is a temple dedicated to twin deities. Members of the Ibex tribe of Africa erect a statue to honor a twin who died at birth. The statue is carved and raised to watch over its twin. The surviving twin cares for the statue and lives in close proximity to it, reminded forever of the absent brother or sister. The Mojave Indians of North America believe a twin represents the return of some beloved and highly esteemed family member who is honoring them with a reincarnation here on earth. For the Indians of British Columbia, Canada, the birth of a twin into the tribe heralds plentiful hunting and fishing in the year to come. Interestingly, in Asia, where the incidence of twinning is lowest, twins have not traditionally been welcomed. In modern China, there are strict rules governing a family's limit to have only one child. Certainly the birth of twins is not viewed positively by the state.

The significance of birth carries implications in every culture. In some societies, twins have been viewed as an aberration, a punishment for some known or unknown wrongdoing on the part of the mother, father, or both. There are examples in primitive cultures of the community, bewildered by the question of twin paternity—This unfaithful woman has lain with another man!—making outcasts of the mothers of twins. While it is unlikely to be the source of this belief, there is a very rare phenomenon in twinning that can be the result of two different fathers. This extraordinary event can occur if a woman ovulates two eggs that are fertilized within a short period of time by sperm from two men. These are not your everyday twins.

We seem to have an abiding fascination with the miracle of twin birth. Apparently there is no end of curiosity regarding the laws of nature as they apply to multiple births. Media coverage of high-order multiple pregnancies is relentless. Every year, thousands of twins congregate for a Twins Day Festival in Twinsburg, Ohio, where they revel in one another's company and pick and choose from among the many researchers who vie for their attention. Scientists have long been interested in exploiting the uniqueness of twins in an attempt to differentiate between the influence of genetic and environmental factors as they apply to our health and emotional well-being. There is fascinating data confirming our suspicion that we have a lot to learn about twins. From medical journals to television talk shows, there are demonstrations of uncanny similarities in the lives and habits of twins raised apart since earliest childhood. Social anthropologists, psychologists, and educators view twins as a sort of miraculous living laboratory—an invaluable tool for the examination of the effects of environment, parenting, and shared genetic material. Researchers have used twins to study the impact of certain pollutants when one identical twin has been exposed and the other has not. The perception that twins share some special ability to communicate has been noted since primitive times. Identical twins, more rare by far than fraternal twins, hold an even firmer grip on our collective intellect and imagination, holding a mirror up to the face of society and asking us to explore the very idea of identity, and to what degree (if any) our genetic information figures into the development of the individual psyche.

But for a parent, discovering that you are pregnant with twins is like being an explorer at the mouth of a beautiful, unexplored river. There is the shock of discovery, quickly followed by speculation about the unknown. Will the river be wild at times? Is your craft sturdy enough to navigate this uncharted territory? How about your crew . . . and supplies? Can you afford to take the voyage? If the rich, miraculous experience of parents who have already begun their expeditions is any measure, you can't afford not to. So, safe travels to you and your unborn twins. You're starting out on a truly epic journey.

pregnancy
and
birth

what are twins?

fraternal and identical twinning

The miracle of conception takes place when an egg is fertilized by a sperm and becomes an embryo. Twins are defined as the simultaneous development of two embryos in a woman's uterus. After fertilization takes place, the fertilized ova enter the uterine cavity and implantation occurs. This phenomenon results in early differentiation of cells in each embryo: some develop into the extraordinary organ we know as the placenta, and other cells form the membranous, two-layered sacs that will house each embryo. (On rare occasions, both embryos will reside in one sac.) The outer layer of the membrane is the chorion, and the inner layer is the amnion, as is the case in singleton as well as multiple pregnancy. Sounds pretty straightforward, right? But this is just the beginning. This book will talk about the two types of twinning: fraternal and identical.

Scientists refer to fraternal twins as dizygotic, involving the union of two eggs with two sperm to

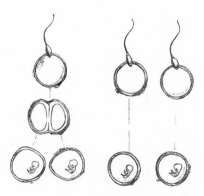

LEFT: *monozygotic (identical) twins occur when one egg is fertilized by one sperm.*

RIGHT: *dizygotic (fraternal) twins occur when two eggs are fertilized by two sperm.*

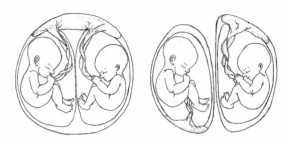

LEFT: *diamnionic/monochorionic twins with one placenta (fused placenta)*

RIGHT: *diamnionic/dichorionic twins with separate placentas*

create two embryos. Dizygotic twins are by far the more common form of twinning, and are two completely separate individuals who are as genetically similar as any siblings born at any time to the same parents.

Identical, or monozygotic, twins are the result of one egg that has been fertilized by one sperm. At some point in the very early stages of cell division, the developing cell group splits in two and develops as two separate embryos. This rare and remarkable twinning creates two embryos that share the complete complement of each other's genetic information; their DNA is identical. The point at which the split occurs will determine which of four possible developmental scenarios will take place.

This is a good time to talk about the difficulties in diagnosing identical twins. Contrary to what you may have heard, it is possible for two embryos to appear to be completely independent of each other within the uterus and still be genetically identical. In the majority of twin pregnancies, the embryos develop with a minimal amount of shared placenta, and that is the best scenario you and your practitioner can hope for. The placenta is magnificently suited to supply your twins with everything they need throughout their gestation. Under the best of circumstances it generously provides for the transfer of oxygen, water, and nutrients from the mother to each of her developing fetuses. There are

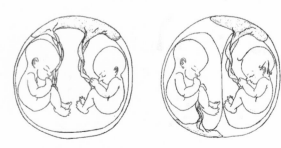

LEFT: *monoamnionic/monochorionic twins with one placenta*

RIGHT: *diamnionic/monochorionic twins with separate placentas*

rare situations in which the placenta appears to provide a preferential supply of nutrition to one fetus over the other. This can result in discordancy and while it may be very subtle, it can often be identified early, allowing practitioners to optimize outcomes for both babies.

It is interesting to note that the prevalence of twins occurring at conception is substantially higher than the birth rate would indicate, but due to a phenomenon called vanishing twin syndrome, one of the embryos may fail to develop and be resorbed by the body even before the diagnosis of pregnancy is made. We'll discuss that in more detail later on in this book.

the factors that influence twinning

The first thing that captures our interest when we discuss twins is the incidence of twinning itself. Naturally, when we look at birth rates, the occurrence of twinning falls within a limited range. But if you look at the most recent data in the medical journals, the frequency of fraternal twinning in the overall population is about 3 percent of all pregnancies. Interestingly, identical twins make their rare and thrilling appearance without regard to any of the factors that impact the incidence of their fraternal counterparts. Identical twinning occurs quite randomly throughout the population, but we are able to isolate and examine several variables that factor into the likelihood of a couple having fraternal twins:

• *Race*

Many people are amazed to learn that there is a racial component to the incidence of twinning in the world population. Twins occur in decreasing numbers within the black, Caucasian, Hispanic, and Asian populations, respectively. And even within that demographic breakdown, the incidence of twinning among the Yoruba tribe of western Nigeria is a stunning forty-five per thousand live births. This represents a rate of twinning that is four times that of the overall population! When we measure the naturally occurring hormone levels present in Yoruba women, we find levels that are equal to those in women taking medication to hormonally stimulate their ovaries in order to produce multiple eggs. We have not yet seen a study that definitively explains the extraordinary fertility of Yoruba women, but speculation ranges from genetics to nutrition to environmental considerations.

• *Mother's Age and Obstetric History*

We also know that maternal age factors into the incidence of twinning. Mother Nature, with her droll sense of humor, visits twins upon mothers of increasing age and, as if that were not enough, the forty-year-old mom who already has children is more likely to conceive twins than her forty-year-old neighbor who has never had children. So far, the scientific community is at a loss to explain this. We know that in order to conceive fraternal twins, the mother must release more than one egg at a time. Yet we do not have data that strongly suggest that a woman releases more eggs per cycle as she gets older. This increased rate of twinning for older moms does seem to drop off after the early forties, showing Mother Nature's ability to temper her humor with a little common sense.

• Genetics

The role of genetics in twinning remains open to continued investigation. It is commonly accepted that there may be an inherited trait on the maternal side that contributes to an increase in twin births, though a mother who is a twin has no guarantee that she will give birth to twins. There are, however, no equally compelling data to suggest a similar influence from the father.

• Infertility Treatments

The final factor known to influence twinning is treatment for infertility. It is accurate to say that for as long as we've marveled at the workings of nature, we've made attempts to improve upon it. Today, in the United States, three out of every hundred pregnancies results in twins. Until recently, medical texts cited the numbers of twins occurring in live births as about one in eighty. The current phenomenal statistic owes a large debt to the medical miracle of ovarian stimulation.

The approach to a couple struggling with infertility involves an evaluation of the woman's anatomy, as well as an assessment of the husband's ability to produce viable sperm. If ovulation irregularities appear to be the limiting factor in a couple's failure to conceive, medication to stimulate the ovaries is then considered. These medicines typically stimulate multiple follicles to develop within the ovaries, which subsequently produce multiple eggs. The first-line medication for hormonal stimulation is associated with an incidence of multiple pregnancies that can be as high as 20 percent. The next possibility is the use of stronger hormonal medications called gonadotropins. The gonadotropins stimulate the ovaries more significantly, resulting in a multiple-birth rate of between 18 and 40 percent.

For the last twenty years, hormonal stimulation of the ovaries has been an extraordinarily effective method for increasing the incidence of twinning. But correcting the ovulatory problem may not be enough to ensure successful con-ception. One hopes the use of medication will supply an ample number of eggs, but a blocked fallopian tube may prevent the proper movement of the eggs from the ovary to the fallopian tube, where the sperm and eggs must meet for fertil-ization to take place. In that event, there are multiple techniques that may be called upon to achieve pregnancy:

- in vitro fertilization (IVF)
- gamete intra-fallopian transfer (GIFT)
- zygote intra-fallopian transfer (ZIFT)
- ovum transfer
- intracytoplasmic sperm injection (ICSI)

Simply stated, these procedures involve the harvesting of a woman's eggs for fertilization outside her body and may include donor sperm as well as donor eggs:

- *IVF*

  A woman's eggs are harvested and sperm is introduced. Fertilization occurs in the laboratory and the fertilized eggs are then placed in the uterus.

- *GIFT*

  During laparoscopy, the egg and sperm are separately placed in the fallopian tube to undergo fertilization.

- *ZIFT*

  The egg and sperm are introduced to each other in the lab and the fertilized eggs are then placed in the fallopian tube.

- *Ovum Transfer*

  Eggs are harvested from one donor woman, fertilized in the lab, and transferred via IVF into the uterus of a second woman who is attempting to become pregnant.

- *ICSI*

  This procedure is most commonly used to overcome male infertility problems. A single sperm is injected directly into an egg to enable fertilization.

None of these methods is as much fun as the traditional method of conception, but all are effective nonetheless. Egg and sperm join together and when fertilization occurs, the result is called a zygote. The zygotes, whether placed in the woman's uterus or in her fallopian tube, begin their valiant attempt at implantation. It is at this point in the process that a doctor will speak with the mother or the prospective parents about the possibility of multiple gestation, including the likelihood of higher-order multiples such as triplets, quadruplets, and beyond. Since the placement of multiple zygotes opens the portal to multiple pregnancies, it is very important for doctor and patient to thoroughly consider the implications of pregnancy with higher-order multiples. It would seem that with judicious understanding of the risks and benefits of implanting multiple zygotes, pregnancies with quadruplets and even higher-order multiples are happening with less frequency. A doctor will make it clear to a woman undergoing a treatment for assisted fertility that although it is unlikely that every zygote implanted in her uterus will become viable, should she choose, for example, to have four zygotes implanted, she may have as many as four zygotes proceed to viable pregnancy. The toll—physical, emotional, and financial—notwithstanding, this extraordinary technology must ultimately be matched by thoughtful and thorough collaboration between parents-to-be and their doctor.

While the parents of babies achieved through various fertility practices can attest to the miraculous nature of assisted conception, it is a remarkably straightforward and mechanical process. Ovaries are stimulated excessively, the resultant eggs are mixed with sperm, and because one egg might not turn into an embryo, doctors—with the blessings of hopeful would-be parents—use multiple embryos and hope for success. Fraternal twinning—two eggs fertilized by two sperm—is the norm for women who give birth to twins following fertility treatment. The average woman with no need of fertility enhancement will ovulate one egg during each menstrual cycle. In the event that she drops more than one and both are fertilized, she has a naturally occurring twin pregnancy: no family history of twins, no hormone stimulation, just the luck of the draw.

2

prenatal care

before the twins are a twinkle in your eye

While it is likely that many couples reading this book already know they are pregnant with twins, it is very important to discuss the importance of pre-conceptual counseling. If—as a result of fertility treatment, genetic predisposition, or just plain old-fashioned luck—you are one of the increasing number of couples who will become parents of twins, it is important that you become an advocate for your own prenatal health. Any couple contemplating pregnancy can take appropriate steps to prepare for it, long before they consult a health-care practitioner. The first thing to do is evaluate your life and the life of your partner for any risky behavior in which you might be participating.

DO YOU SMOKE, USE ANY RECREATIONAL DRUGS,
OR DRINK ALCOHOL?

It is almost inconceivable that a person living in the United States today would be unaware of the health risks associated with smoking. For a woman contemplating pregnancy, the stakes are about as high as they get.

- Tobacco is associated with decreased fertility and low birthrate.
- Smoking is also associated with a rate of miscarriage that is twice the rate of the general population.

- There is an increased degree of risk of placental problems, stillbirth, and low-birthweight babies among smokers.
- There is some evidence to suggest that the incidence of sudden infant death syndrome (SIDS) is higher in the homes of smoking families than nonsmoking families.
- There is evidence to support an increased risk of childhood respiratory problems, including an increased incidence of asthma, among the families of smokers.

The protocol here is very clear: Stop. Albert Einstein might very well have been right when he told us that God does not play dice with the universe. But Mother Nature is not above the occasional game of craps when it comes to your fetus's exposure to potentially harmful substances. There are always examples of someone who defies the odds. We all know of at least one hard-drinking, chain-smoking, ninety-nine-year-old granny who died peacefully in her sleep after winning a bundle at the track. But we also know that our hospitals and nursing homes are filled with prematurely aged men and women whose lives have been laid to waste by the ravages of smoking.

The good news is that there is substantial improvement in individual pregnancies when mothers stop smoking. There are many support programs for people who want help in putting an end to their addictive habits, and there is no greater gift you can give your unborn (even unconceived) babies than a commitment to be tobacco- and drug-free. Today we know that some of the harmful substances in secondhand smoke are present there in higher concentrations than they are in the smoke first inhaled by the smoker. A smoker in your household places everyone at substantial risk for allergies, asthma, emphysema, and lifelong respiratory illnesses. Clearly, smoking has an impact on the entire family, not just a pregnant woman and her unborn child. Before you even begin to worry about the harmful effects of tobacco on your babies, you and your partner need to make a healthy commitment to yourselves and each other. Here are some practical tips to help you put your smoking habit out to pasture:

- Ban smoking in your home.
  Throw away the ashtrays, and ask friends and families to please step outside and well away from the house if they need to have a smoke.

- Get rid of items that you associate with smoking.

   Sell your beloved lighter shaped like a pirate ship at a yard sale.

- Take a break from activities, and maybe even friends, that you associate with smoking.

   If your Friday-night poker buddies are tobacco fiends, try and round up a new smoke-free game.

- Choose smoke-free environments to socialize.

   Many cities have no-smoking laws in place in restaurants, bars, and even many workplaces.

- Limit your consumption of nicotine and alcohol.

   Both these substances are known to stimulate the desire for nicotine.

- Get moving!

   Activity is the enemy of tobacco use. Get out there and get some exercise, whether it is walking the dog, chasing the kids around, or playing tennis.

ONE IMPORTANT NOTE: Nicotine-replacement products are not to be used during pregnancy, because nicotine, whether or not it is inhaled, is toxic and potentially harmful to a fetus. The best time to stop smoking is before you become pregnant, when cessation products may be used under a doctor's care. If you or your partner is still smoking when you become pregnant, please try the steps outlined above and speak with your physician about other strategies to help you with your tobacco habit.

As far as alcohol is concerned, if you are used to the occasional social drink, or wine with dinner, anticipate giving it up for the duration of your prenatal prep time as well as your pregnancy. If alcohol is a serious problem for you, it falls into the tobacco and recreational drug category and you should seek whatever help you need in getting sober before you become pregnant. Alcohol use during pregnancy is associated with low birthweight, preterm delivery, and fetal alcohol syndrome, a severe condition associated with neurological and structural deficits.

WHAT, IF ANY, PRESCRIPTION OR OVER-THE-COUNTER DRUGS ARE YOU TAKING?

While pregnancy in and of itself is an extraordinary time in a woman's life, unfortunately it does not occur to the exclusion of many of life's other fairly standard medical conditions such as colds, indigestion, or the occasional headache. Some of these conditions will respond successfully to changes in your daily life as you try to take particularly good care of yourself during pregnancy—taking half an hour to lie down when you feel a headache coming on may just do the trick. But other times, appropriate medication is very help-ful. It is a good idea to have a discussion with your practitioner early on in your pregnancy about which medications are considered safe to take in the event of, say, a cold or a case of heartburn. *The use of any medication, even those that are obtained over-the-counter, should be discussed with your doctor, and the package di-rections should be carefully adhered to.* The following is a list of common condi-tions and the nonprescription medications and lifestyle changes that can be safely used for their treatment during pregnancy:

- Cold, mild fever, headache pain

    Acetaminophen, the active ingredient in Tylenol, is safe to use for re-ducing fever and for mild to moderate pain control. Where possible, take additional time to rest, and in the case of headache, you may want to lie down in a darkened room.

- Nasal congestion

    Saline nose drops are safe and effective in many cases of mild conges-tion. *Nasal sprays containing decongestants should not be used without con-sulting your doctor.* Your doctor may recommend Tylenol Sinus medication if needed.

- Sore throat

    Gargling with warm salt water two to three times daily and the use of throat lozenges such as those produced by Hall's, Sucrets, Cepacol, or Vick's can be used to provide relief from a scratchy throat. Chlorasep-tic throat spray is also acceptable.

- Cough

    Robitussin is considered safe for use during pregnancy, but *be sure to use the preparation that has no antihistamines or other additives.* Plenty of rest and fluids are also important. A camphor or mentholated chest rub ap-plied topically is safe as long as it is used according to package direc-tions and there is no indication that any of the other ingredients is to be avoided during pregnancy.

- Nausea and Vomiting

    Emetrol is considered safe and may be helpful in controlling nausea and vomiting. Some women find that wristbands that put pressure on the inner wrist limit the nausea associated with pregnancy. Up to

two grams of ginger per day, in ginger candy, ginger tea, or soda fla-
vored with real ginger, is safe for treating morning sickness. Speak
with your doctor about the use of vitamin B_6 in the treatment of
nausea.

• Constipation

Psyllium products such as Metamucil are very helpful in treating constipation. Milk of magnesia and Colace can also be used. A diet rich in
fiber and six to eight glasses of water daily are very practical aids to regularity during pregnancy.

• Diarrhea

Kaopectate is effective and safe to use during pregnancy.

• Heartburn or Indigestion

Antacids, such as Maalox, Mylanta, Tums, and Gaviscon, are considered safe for use during pregnancy. You may find that your digestive
system is more comfortable accommodating small meals every few
hours, as opposed to three larger meals each day. Limiting your intake
of fatty foods may help you to avoid digestive discomfort.

• First Aid

Topical antibiotic creams such as Neosporin or Bacitracin are safe to
use on minor skin abrasions during pregnancy. Witch hazel, applied
topically, is safe to use for minor skin irritation.

• Rashes and Other Skin Conditions

The effects of hydrocortisone skin creams during pregnancy have not
been widely studied. A mild over-the-counter hydrocortisone cream
used on a small area of the body for a brief period of time is considered
safe. Nevertheless, you should consult your doctor about the use of
these preparations for rashes or other dermatological concerns. Soothing oatmeal baths, perhaps several over the course of a day, may prove
comforting and are safe throughout your pregnancy.

• Hemorrhoids

Topical ointments such as Preparation-H and Anusol cream are safe
and may provide relief from this very common problem of pregnancy
and labor. Witch hazel pads applied topically may be helpful in safely
reducing inflammation. Many women find a warm sitz bath for ten
minutes several times daily to be very soothing.

There are medical conditions for which your doctor may choose to modify treatment when you consider becoming, or indeed become, pregnant. Some medications are known to be safe during pregnancy; some have not been studied comprehensively enough to assess their risk; some are judged to be appropriate when the need for the medication outweighs the potential risk to the fetus; and some, called teratogens, have the effect of possibly or most definitely producing birth defects or anomalies in growing embryos or fetuses. Teratogens are to be avoided during the pre-pregnancy planning time, as well as throughout your entire pregnancy.

The Food and Drug Administration (FDA) categorizes drugs (as seen below) by the degree of risk they pose to fetal development:

- A

    controlled studies in women indicate there is no demonstrated risk to a human fetus
- B

    cautions that while animal studies do not appear to show risk to the fetus, we do not yet have good human studies; if animal studies suggest some risk, human studies show no demonstrated risk
- C

    clearly indicates that the drug has had some effect in animal studies, but nothing definitive with humans; or there is no data available from animal or human studies
- D

    shows positive evidence of risk to humans, but it might be appropriate in certain situations considered to be life-threatening to the mother
- X

    should never under any circumstance be used by a pregnant or possibly pregnant woman because risk demonstrated in animal and human studies outweighs any benefits

The majority of drugs fall within the B or C classifications. The impact of most medicines and substances is greatest between days thirty-one and seventy-one of your pregnancy, which corresponds roughly to four-and-one-half to ten weeks.

Certainly, you should only use medicines that are essential for your health and always consult your practitioner before taking any drug if you are pregnant or planning a pregnancy. Your frank discussion of all medical concerns will enable you and your doctor to work together and weigh the risks and benefits of any treatment.

Let's look at several common categories of medicines. Some have greater risks than others for use during pregnancy; some are to be absolutely avoided for the term of the pregnancy and where possible during the pregnancy planning period. Be sure to speak with your doctor for a more comprehensive survey of drugs or substances that are teratogenic.

anticonvulsant agents

Lamotrigine (class C)
Valproic acid (class D)
Dilantin (class D)
Phenobarbital (class D)
Tegretol (class D)

These are all anticonvulsant drugs, prescribed for the treatment of seizures in diseases such as epilepsy. Women taking anticonvulsant drugs have approximately twice the risk of having babies with fetal defects as occurs in the general population. Most physicians agree that under certain circumstances the benefits of therapeutic use of these drugs outweigh the risks, because seizure activity itself can be dangerous for a pregnancy. Lamotrigine, a class C drug listed above, is a newer anticonvulscent agent and initial studies are showing no increased risk for its use during pregnancy.

Some women who have been seizure-free for at least two years may be able to stop taking their medicine and become pregnant. Such a step would require a thorough assessment by the patient's neurologist and should never be undertaken without medical supervision.

antihypertensive agents

Aldomet, an alpha-methyl-dopa drug (class C)
Labetolol, a beta blocker (class C)
Captopril, an angiotensin-converting enzyme inhibitor (class D)

Aldomet and Labetolol have been thoroughly studied in pregnancy and are the first line of therapy for chronic hypertension in a pregnant woman. There are certain antihypertensive agents that are known to be dangerous in pregnancy. As we all know, untreated hypertension can also be dangerous. It is vital that patients discuss with their doctor the appropriate medicines to control their blood pressure. Angiotensin-converting enzyme inhibitors (commonly referred to as "ace inhibitors") are to be avoided throughout an entire pregnancy because they can alter placental blood flow and development of the fetus. A woman using an ace inhibitor should consult her doctor prior to conception so that she can change to a more acceptable antihypertensive medicine.

blood-thinning agents

Coumadin (class X)
Heparin and Low-Molecular-Weight Heparin (class B)

Coumadin should not be taken if you are pregnant or may become pregnant. While Coumadin is important for treatment of certain conditions, it is highly associated with congenital birth defects. Both Heparin and Low-Molecular-Weight Heparin are likely to be better choices during pre-pregnancy and pregnancy. Your physician will work with you to develop an alternative treatment.

antidepressants

Fluoxetine (class C)
Sertraline (class C)
Fluvoxamine (class C)

When it comes to treating patients with mood disorders, most doctors agree that the preferred treatment throughout preconception planning time and pregnancy is a behavioral approach—lifestyle changes such as diet modification, exercise, adequate sleep, relaxation opportunities, and stress reduction are preferable to medication. Psychological intervention in the form of therapy has provided valuable support for many individuals.

However, if medication is necessary, it is still important to make a reasonable attempt to avoid it during the first trimester of pregnancy, when a baby's organ development is underway. The most commonly prescribed antidepressants for use during pregnancy are selected serotonin reuptake inhibitors (SSRI). The largest trials of SSRIs do not show any obvious structural teratogenic effects on fetal development; however, more recent studies seem to indicate some concerns about behavioral disturbances in children of women who used them during pregnancy. As is the case with all medication, use of an antidepressant must be assessed for its risk-to-benefit ratio: A patient, working with her prescribing doctor and therapist, needs to ascertain if this medication is necessary in order to maintain a normal lifestyle throughout her pregnancy. If so, these medicines can be used with caution. For more severe forms of depression, it is vital that a patient consult with her doctor about appropriate treatment.

antibiotics

Penicillin derivatives (class B)
Cephalosporin (class B)
Tetracycline (class D)
Ciprofloxacin (class C)
Streptomycin (class D)
Kanomycin (class D)

There are many safe and effective antibiotics for use during pregnancy; however, the three class D drugs and the one class C drug listed above are to be avoided: tetracycline, because of its association with abnormal skeletal and dental development, ciprofloxacin because it affects skeletal and cartilage development, streptomycin can be damaging to hearing, and kanomycin may cause kidney damage. Antibiotics such as the penicillin derivatives and cephalosporin are well studied and considered safe and effective for use in pregnancy.

retinoids

- Accutane (class X)
- Vitamin A—megadose of 25,000 units daily (class D)

Taken orally as a treatment for certain skin conditions, Accutane is highly associated with structural defects to the fetus. Dermatologists are likely to prescribe it for treatment of various skin conditions. It is one of a handful of drugs that is known to consistently cause birth defects. On average, if there were ten pregnant women in a room who had all consumed Accutane during the first trimester of their pregnancy, one of them would have a baby with a serious problem. Any woman who is considering becoming pregnant should avoid orally prescribed Accutane for at least six months prior to conception. When used topically, Retin-A (class B), a related drug, is not associated with any ill effects on fetal development. Oral vitamin A, when taken in doses for certain nutritional benefits, is associated with the same teratogenic risk as Accutane.

nonsteroidal anti-inflammatories

- Aspirin and ibuprofen
  The woman who takes an aspirin for a headache and discovers a week later that she is pregnant need not be concerned about any ill effects. We do not see evidence of risk to the fetus in cases where women used aspirin for pain relief a few times early in pregnancy. However, there is evidence of a condition called premature closure of the ductus arterio-

sus in babies exposed to aspirin and nonsteroidal anti-inflammatories in the third trimester of pregnancy. Use of these drugs can also alter uterine contractility, causing the uterus to relax—not a great idea when one is going through labor. Aspirin, in certain doses, can affect clotting and can contribute to excessive bleeding in mothers and babies at delivery. Yet there are certain conditions in which daily low-dose aspirin can be beneficial in pregnancy and is not associated with any ill effects on mother or baby.

Ibuprofen (Motrin, Naprosyn, Advil, etc.), a frequently used aspirin substitute, should be treated with the same caution as aspirin. If you have a headache, acetaminophen (Tylenol, etc.) appears to be safe in pregnancy, but always ask your practitioner before taking any drug during your pregnancy.

The best approach to understanding the use of all medication on your pregnancy is to bring it up as a topic of discussion with your practitioner during preconception planning. If you become pregnant without having had that opportunity, bring a list of all medications you have taken in the last four months to your first pregnancy appointment with your doctor.

doing what comes naturally: supplements and herbs

Of the many dictionary definitions of the adjective *natural*, the one we tend to think of when considering natural supplements is "present in, or produced by nature, rather than being artificial or created by people." The impulse to seek out what we might think of as "kinder, gentler" health remedies is understandable—particularly during pregnancy, when our kindling maternal instinct seeks to protect our unborn babies. But if we take a moment to consider this definition, we see that nothing in it implies that a natural product is necessarily a safe product—and the lack of regulatory policy surrounding the development, marketing, and sales of the multibillion-dollar natural supplements industry supports our concern. Certainly, there are products described as natural supplements that are safe, but oversight of these products by the FDA is limited to the following conditions:

- The FDA requires that manufacturers label the ingredients in their supplements.
- There are eight chemicals banned from use in supplements.

As long as a natural supplement meets these criteria, it can be sold until such time as it is proven dangerous to consumers. This is in marked contrast to drugs, which are overseen by the FDA and undergo rigorous testing to determine that they are safe and effective for the prevention, treatment, or cure of disease before they are marketed to consumers.

There are hundreds of herbs available for purchase throughout the United States today. You can readily buy capsules, tablets, oils, extracts, and teas in specialty shops, groceries, pharmacies, and on the Internet. These preparations—whether herbal, mineral, hormonal, or non-food—have simply not undergone the rigorous level of testing that would reassure us of their safety for pregnant or breastfeeding women. So how can we safely approach the use of these non-regulated supplements during pregnancy and while breastfeeding? The answer is to err on the side of caution: If you have any questions at all about whether a supplement is safe during pregnancy, speak with your doctor before using it. The March of Dimes (www.marchofdimes.com) has published a list of herbs that are contraindicated for use during pregnancy, which you may find a useful tool for discussing your concerns with your doctor.

complementary and alternative medicine

When we consider health care today, many of us recognize that there are medical opportunities that were barely given consideration when our mothers were pregnant with us, and were certainly not widely available. In 1998, the National Center for Complementary and Alternative Medicine (NCCAM) was founded by the United States Congress, from which it continues to derive its funding. It is one of the twenty-seven institutes and centers that make up the National Institutes of Health (NIH). This is noteworthy in that it sends a clear signal that there is an interest within the medical and scientific community in integrating *scientifically proven* complementary and alternative medical practices into conventional medicine.

Acupuncture is just such an alternative practice. A technique that originated in China more than two thousand years ago, it has been used there for centuries in the treatment of many medical conditions. The acupuncturist inserts very fine needles just beneath the skin on one or more of the two thousand acupuncture points that Chinese medicine traditionally ascribes to the human body. These needles are said to stimulate and balance energy (called *qi* and pronounced "chee"). In China, where the emphasis on acupuncture is as preventive medicine, it is thought to be useful in the treatment of a variety of medical conditions. Acupuncturists may also use pressure (acupressure), heat, or electromagnetic impulses to stimulate acupoints on the body. In the United States, the NIH has issued a consensus development statement on acupuncture, saying that ". . . evidence clearly shows that needle acupuncture is efficacious for providing relief from postoperative pain, chemotherapy-induced nausea and vomiting and, probably, nausea of pregnancy."

Most states have standards for acupuncture certification. While certification is not a guarantee of excellence, it does provide a degree of confidence that your practitioner has risen to a standard agreed upon in his or her profession. Acupuncture as an adjunct or complementary practice is increasingly available in traditional medical offices, and even some medical doctors are becoming trained in the practice. Ask your friends and family if they have had any experience with an acupuncturist in your area. Anticipate that your acupuncture practitioner will want to know about your medical history, including any medications you are taking at the time of treatment. Take a look in the Resource Guide at the back of this book for more information on acupuncture and the National Center for Complementary and Alternative Medicine.

WHAT IS THE EXTENT OF YOUR EXPOSURE TO
ENVIRONMENTAL HAZARDS SUCH AS COMMON HOUSEHOLD
CHEMICALS, RADIATION, OR HAZARDOUS CHEMICALS
IN YOUR WORK ENVIRONMENT?

Even the woman who has shunned cigarettes all her life may be vulnerable to less obvious environmental risks. If you read the labels on some very effective but noxious household cleaning products, you'll find that they carry warnings about toxicity and the importance of avoiding contact with skin, or of using the product in a well-ventilated area. Now is the time to really pay attention to those warnings. Careful use of pesticides (use the natural ones if you can) and fertilizers out in the garden is equally important. Basic precautions for the home gardener will go far when it comes to ensuring your health and the health of your babies: Wear gardening gloves, wash your hands as soon as you're done, be sure to use sunscreen, and wear a hat.

Since it is possible for a pregnancy to go undiagnosed until after a considerable amount of fetal development has occurred, it is very wise to limit exposure to toxins in the workplace well before you try to conceive. The occasional Sunday gardener need not curtail her hobby as long as she wears gloves while handling pesticides or fertilizers. But an agricultural worker, exposed daily to chemical pesticide spray, may want to rethink her working status.

Painting a room in your house is fine as long as there is adequate ventilation, but if your job entails daily exposure to paint, you might want to look for alternative employment. Prolonged exposure to lead-based paints, solvents, or any chemical fumes is unwise. Educate yourself about your work environment so you can make informed decisions about prenatal health.

A cross-continental airplane flight up to your twentieth week of pregnancy should be fine, but we are exposed to additional radiation from the sun while flying. The closer to the poles one flies, the greater the dose of radiation. Pilots, flight attendants, and women making very frequent long business trips should consult their local Federal Aviation Authority guidelines regarding risks attendant to particular routes and frequency of travel.

WHEN DID YOU LAST HAVE A COMPREHENSIVE PHYSICAL AND DENTAL EXAM?

A woman in good health is already advocating for her as-yet unconceived child. Prenatal considerations should include any significant radiological evaluations that need to be performed. Now is the time to have any dental work done that you think might otherwise require attention in the coming year. Even if you have no nagging suspicions about a tooth that is acting up, medical research indicates a possible link between periodontal disease—common in women of childbearing age—and preeclampsia and preterm labor. A thorough dental exam should be a top priority in your pre-pregnancy planning. And don't forget to schedule at least one checkup during your pregnancy.

If you are planning to become pregnant, consider getting your annual mammogram during your pre-conception planning time. There is always the possibility that an X-ray will be necessary during your pregnancy. Diagnostic X-ray doses are exceedingly low in most situations, and if there is a possible fracture of your ankle, the consequences of failing to have the X-ray are potentially devastating. Always tell the examining physician as well as the X-ray technician that you are pregnant, or that you may be pregnant, so you can effectively cover your pelvis and abdominal area with a lead shield.

WHAT FORM OF BIRTH CONTROL ARE YOU USING?

The decision to try for a baby can be as simple as tossing your diaphragm in the trash and lighting some candles, or it can require a little more planning. It is recommended that a woman using birth control pills allow her body to go through two or more regular menstrual cycles before attempting to become pregnant. The most dependable form of birth control to use during this waiting period is a condom. Another good method of birth control, the intrauterine device, is far safer now than it was twenty years ago. It does not appear to interrupt the reproductive cycle, so you can in theory have your IUD removed in the afternoon and conceive that very night! If condoms and spermicide have been your birth control method of choice, you do not need to enforce any waiting period before attempting to conceive.

But there are more subtle questions about your life that are equally deserving of thoughtful consideration. It is the rare couple that is able to take stock of their situation and proclaim, "This is the perfect time for us to start our family." And it is rarer still for that couple to march into the bedroom, firm in their resolve, and have the extraordinary good fortune to immediately conceive their baby (or babies, as the case may be). The decision to have children, whether your first or fourth, is often made as a sort of good-faith agreement between couples who wish to reaffirm their shared desire to move forward, together, into the next phase of their lives. There are no guarantees in this agreement and the only absolute is that there *is* no absolute. That said, it is probably wise to take some time to look at your relationship as a couple.

- If there are fertility problems, are you in synch about exploring your options?
- Have you thought about the implications of becoming parents as far as your careers and finances are concerned?

- Are you prepared to delay exotic travel plans or even modest vacations if need be? (See Appendix for *The American College of Obstetricians and Gynecologists Immunizations During Pregnancy* Table.)
- Are you living in a place that is suitable to raising a family?
- Have you read your health insurance policy and determined that you have adequate coverage?

After thinking about these things, it is time to see your practitioner for an evaluation of your medical history. This is the time to speak with your mother, sisters, or grandmothers about their obstetric and genetic histories. Any established inherited genetic disorders should be made known to your physician prior to pregnancy to determine your level of risk for passing on a problem to your child. Now is the time for your grandmother to tell you if she is aware of any history of twinning in the family. And most important, if it is possible, sit down with your mother and learn what you can about her reproductive history. It is particularly important for your practitioner to know if diethylstilbestrol was prescribed for your mother during her pregnancy. DES was prescribed in the 1950s for women who were thought to be at risk for miscarriage. Women born to DES mothers frequently have unusually shaped reproductive tracts, so their pregnancies can be a bit complicated.

Determine if anything in your family medical history puts you in a different risk category than you may have anticipated. Is it responsible to contemplate pregnancy, or are there risks associated with your own health that must be managed and carefully monitored? Far from discouraging you, your physician should be eager to work with you to control any preexisting conditions that might put you or your babies at risk:

- diabetes
- hypertension
- certain forms of arthritis
- anemia
- hypothyroidism/hyperthyroidism
- asthma
- systemic lupus erythematosus (SLE)

All of these conditions should be evaluated prenatally in order to develop the most effective regimen for their control during pregnancy. Any known infection is best treated before becoming pregnant so as to reduce concerns about antibiotic use. That would include sexually transmitted diseases as well as an infection of the sinus or urinary tract.

There are also recommended screening tests that can determine if a patient or her fetuses might be at risk for problems that could compromise an otherwise healthy pregnancy:

- Rubella is highly associated with birth defects and can be screened for easily by measuring the antibodies in a patient's bloodstream. Look into your own history of childhood illnesses. Remember that rubella can be devastating to your fetus. If it is found that you never have been exposed to the disease, you should be vaccinated to avoid the risk of contracting it during your pregnancy.
- The American College of Obstetricians and Gynecologists (ACOG) recommends screening all pregnant women for sexually transmitted diseases such as human immunodeficiency virus (HIV), gonorrhea, syphilis, and chlamydia.
- Group B streptococci (GBS) is a leading cause of illness and death among newborns in the United States. ACOG recommends universal GBS screening of women at thirty-five to thirty-seven weeks of pregnancy.
- Cystic fibrosis is a genetic disorder severely affecting the respiratory and digestive systems. ACOG recommends that screening be made available to both mother and father, as cystic fibrosis is passed on to a newborn only if both parents carry the gene.

There are additional screening tests that your doctor might recommend based on your particular family or medical history. The diseases they can detect include:

- Toxoplasmosis, an infection that occurs in humans as a result of eating food such as undercooked meat that contains the *toxoplasma gondii* organism, handling an infected cat, or exposure to the feces of an infected cat. Infection during pregnancy poses risk to the developing fetus.

- Cytomegalovirus, which while rarely serious to a healthy non-pregnant person can cause serious physical or mental damage or even death to a newborn.
- Racially associated health risks such as sickle cell anemia among the black population (and in rare cases, some Mediterranean populations); Tay-Sachs disease among Ashkenazi Jews; and thalassemia in people of southern Mediterranean or Asian descent. In each of these cases, the disease is caused by a recessive gene and can have a devastating effect on the fetus if both parents pass the gene on to their child.

Every woman contemplating pregnancy should have her history of obstetrical and gynecological surgery assessed. *Gravity* describes the number of pregnancies experienced and *parity* indicates the number of natural births or C-sections, the number of children delivered, and whether they were premature or full-term. Documenting a miscarriage, elective termination, or ectopic pregnancy is equally important in assembling a complete reproductive history. If this is not your first pregnancy, sharing any history of bleeding during pregnancy, as well as noting the size of your babies, will be beneficial in helping your practitioner assess any likely risks to you or your unborn children. Certainly these issues will come up in any initial visit to a practitioner once a woman knows that she is pregnant. But it is valuable to have that information on hand before pregnancy occurs.

eating healthfully for two or three: nutrition for while you're planning and when you're pregnant

A registered dietitian can be a supportive resource to you during your twin pregnancy. Often, obstetricians refer patients to registered dietitians. But patients themselves can ask for a referral, whether to answer a one-time question or for more comprehensive support throughout the course of their pregnancy. Netty Levine, MS, RD, and Marlene Clark, RD, are registered dietitians at Cedars-Sinai

Hospital in Los Angeles with many years of experience counseling pregnant women in matters of nutrition. Here, in our section on nutrition, they contribute several important discussions that we are calling "Levine and Clark on . . ."

Levine and Clark are coauthors with Paula Bernstein, Ph.D., MD, of Carrying a Little Extra—A Guide to Healthy Pregnancy for the Plus-Size Woman.

There is a great deal of information to support the time-honored tenet that you are indeed what you eat. Medical literature is filled with observational studies that link pregnancy outcome to maternal nutrition. Surely there is enough anecdotal evidence of that theory. Well-fed women have an uncanny proclivity toward making healthy babies with high birthweights. The classic studies in the medical literature are observational studies that record the birth weights of babies born to a specific segment of previously well-fed European women during the nutritionally deprived years of World War II. When the women were eating well, their babies were bigger and healthier at birth. During the war, when food was in short supply, the birthweights dropped, and after the war they rose again: The findings are very simple, and hard to refute.

It seems clear from our more recent and sophisticated research that while good nutrition is important for maternal health in the first trimester of pregnancy, it doesn't have a proportional impact on the weight of the babies at birth. This is great news to twin moms who may experience considerable nausea and/or vomiting during their first trimester. The fact that your appetite is compromised need not compromise the health of your babies. You'll have plenty of time after your symptoms disappear to regain a great appetite for healthful food.

Many mothers of twins are concerned about weight gain. They want to provide their babies with the best possible start, but they are not eager to gain more weight than is necessary. Keep in mind that once you are pregnant, a weight-loss diet is out of the question. If you are overweight and considering pregnancy, a healthful diet can go a long way toward helping you shed unwanted pounds. If you are overweight and discover you are pregnant with twins, your metabolism will go into high gear and the weight you gain can all go toward making healthy babies. Women who are underweight can get excellent guidance from their

LEVINE AND CLARK ON
A GENERAL NUTRITIONAL APPROACH
TO TWIN PREGNANCY

The first thing we tell any mom-to-be, and certainly this is the case for twin mothers, is that good prenatal nutrition is extremely important to you and your babies. You are going to need some extra calories in a twin pregnancy, but you don't have to eat double what you normally would. We usually recommend that twin moms gain from 4 to 6 pounds in the first trimester, and approximately 1.5 pounds per week for the rest of the pregnancy. These numbers are approximations, but the general weight gain should be between thirty-five and forty-five pounds. Naturally, this is going to vary from pregnancy to pregnancy, and each woman should be getting specific advice regarding weight gain from her own doctor.

What does this mean on a practical daily basis? A pregnant woman needs to eat about 300 extra calories per day during pregnancy, so in accordance with the American Dietetic Association Manual of Clinical Dietetics, we would recommend that a twin mom add 150 additional calories to that number. But we do not want our patients to obsess about calories: we simply make sure that they are getting their daily nutritional requirements. If a mom is either failing to gain adequately or is gaining too much, then a dietitian can do an in-depth analysis of her diet and suggest realistic adjustments.

One of the tools that may be vital to that process is a daily food diary, and that is an idea you may want to familiarize yourself with. If your doctor or dietitian asks you to maintain a food diary, it will be the guide not only to the food and beverages you consume, but also to your patterns of eating and drinking throughout the day—and especially if gestational diabetes should enter into your pregnancy, modifying your patterns of eating are going to be as useful to you as the foods and drinks themselves. You may find it a little difficult (or at least a little irritating) at first, but a food diary can be an incredibly helpful and enlightening tool.

practitioners on how to supplement their diets throughout pregnancy. Your doctor, or even your health insurance provider, may be able to direct you to a registered dietitian, who, like the two R.D.s whose comments appear in these pages, will be very knowledgeable about helping you to eat happily and healthfully throughout your pregnancy. These nutrition experts can also provide excellent information regarding any specific dietary needs that may be a part of your pregnancy.

Remember, it is never too late to start eating right. For any woman, pregnant or contemplating pregnancy, it is important to keep these basic concepts on the table at all times:

- The quality of your food is more important than the quantity. A healthy woman can certainly indulge every once in a while, but as a rule you'll want to avoid the empty calories of sugary snacks. Fill your home with fruits, vegetables, and other healthful snacks. If you are the only person in the house trying to eat healthfully, the temptation to indulge may prove too great. Get your husband and children on track with you.
- You are likely to feel more comfortable all the way through your pregnancy if you get used to eating three small meals a day along with snacks, instead of three large ones. (Our R.D.s offer some specific direction in this chapter.)
- Avoid the American dining tradition of eating progressively larger meals as the day goes on. Along with the bonus of an additional baby, mothers of twins are prone to additional gastrointestinal distress. You will eventually discover that going to bed with a very full tummy is not a good idea.
- Chronic constipation in pregnancy is associated with inadequate fiber and fluid intake. Daily servings of fresh vegetables, whole-grain products, fruit, and at least eight glasses of water daily are a requirement for every mother of twins. If you begin to get constipated, get in the habit of carrying around a bottle of water and drinking the equivalent of a glass of water each hour. Moms of twins need to be superhydrated during pregnancy.
- Proteins contain amino acids, which are fundamental to the creation of human cells. A diet low in protein has been associated with low birthweight in babies. A healthful diet makes efficient use of each of its

LEVINE AND CLARK
ON FAD DIETS

It is hard to imagine that there will ever be a time in this country that there will not be some kind of fad diet being heralded as the solution to everything from weight loss to eternal youth. But the reason these diets come and go is that at their worst, fad diets are dangerous to health. At the least, they are not a long-term realistic answer to a weight problem. The bottom line is that fad diets are about short-term weight loss, and weight loss of any kind is just not something you want to occur during your pregnancy. Yet fad dieting is a part of our culture, so we meet a number of clients who have been on severely carbohydrate-restricted diets prior to pregnancy. These women's reactions to food now that they are pregnant can be all over the map: some are very distraught at the idea of putting on weight, while for others, pregnancy has an oddly liberating effect, and they feel justified in eating everything they desire! In either case, once a woman begins to reintroduce carbohydrates into her diet, she may experience more weight gain than a woman who has been eating a balanced diet all along. Interestingly this occurs, at least in part, because the body, unused to the new influx of carbohydrates, causes the carbohydrates themselves to retain water, which can result in significant weight gain. For some women who have worked so hard to lose weight prior to pregnancy, that weight gain is very disturbing. But at the risk of repeating ourselves, pregnancy is not the time for a weight-loss diet. It is the time for healthy weight gain that is doing its job for you and your babies.

As dietitians, our job is to help moms to add in the healthy carbohydrates that will work best for them and their babies. This is an opportunity to make excellent use of a food diary to monitor food choices and quantities. By monitoring a food diary, we can help women to modify their food choices, in this case finding the carbohydrates that will be successful for them. We believe in "everything in moderation"—we're not about to deny a pregnant woman some ice cream on a summer afternoon, but she might want to choose the single-scoop cone over the giant hot fudge sundae.

sources. Fat is an inefficient source of calories, while protein is highly efficient.

• An increase in calcium consumption is absolutely essential to the skeletal and dental health of every mother-to-be. Nature has designed this miracle of pregnancy to make sure that your growing babies will receive the calcium they need from their mother's supply. If your calcium intake is inadequate, it will result in health hazards—including osteoporosis, which may not be reversible.

• Mood swings are associated with fluctuations in our levels of blood sugar. In case the empty calories of sugar are not enough reason to minimize it in your diet, the last thing a mom of twins needs is the sugar-related highs and lows associated with candy bars and too many cookies. Also keep in mind that sugar is associated with increased risk of gestational diabetes, and as a mother of twins that is already something you're watching out for.

• Complex carbohydrates—such as those found in whole grains, brown rice, and legumes—are rich sources of B vitamins, protein, and trace minerals. It's not the whole-wheat bread that adds unwanted calories; it's the thick pat of butter you put on top of it!

• Avoid foods that are highly processed or filled with additives whose names you can't pronounce. It is possible to eat a lot of food and still be malnourished. Too many empty calories will help you to put on weight but may leave you seriously deficient in the vitamins and minerals necessary for your twins' development.

• Listeriosis is an illness that can cause miscarriage as well as serious problems for a developing fetus. The following foods are at risk of carrying the listeria bacteria and should be avoided by pregnant women: unpasteurized milk or soft cheeses; cold luncheon meats or hot dogs that have not been thoroughly heated; and undercooked or raw animal foods such as refrigerated pâté, sushi, or refrigerated smoked seafood such as lox. Be sure to wash all fresh fruits and vegetables thoroughly before consumption.

• Unless your practitioner tells you otherwise, do not go on a salt-restricted diet. Your body needs salt to retain all the water needed for the increase in blood volume, as well as additional fluids required for your changing breast tissue and amniotic fluid. So while you should not add salt to your diet, don't restrict it either.

• • a fish tale • •

The Food and Drug Administration and the Environmental Protection Agency have advised women of childbearing age, as well as children, to limit their intake of swordfish, tilefish, shark, and king mackerel, all of which have been found to contain methyl-mercury, a naturally occurring element in the environment as well as a byproduct of industrial pollution. Mercury is known to pose a danger to a developing fetus.

These predatory fish, which are relatively large and long-lived, have ample opportunity to accumulate high levels of mercury as a result of consuming smaller fish containing trace levels of mercury themselves. The FDA recommends that pregnant or nursing women eat no more than twelve ounces per week of a variety of smaller, well-cooked fish.

Having discussed the need for a healthful, well-balanced diet, the following is a general guideline for how you might approach great nutrition for yourself and your babies. The recommended amounts should be consumed daily:

- Four to five servings of complex carbohydrates, simple carbohydrates, and starch.
  whole-grain breads; whole grains such as wheat, barley, oats, rice, corn, and millet; soy; whole-grain cereals; whole-grain pastas; potatoes; beans such as navy, red, black, lima, soy, and lentils; green peas
- Three to four servings of dairy products and other calcium-rich foods.
  low-fat or nonfat milk, yogurt, cottage cheese, and buttermilk; hard cheeses such as Swiss, cheddar, and Jarlsberg (*milk products fortified with vitamin D as well as eggs and fish, which are high in vitamin D, can be useful to ensure better calcium metabolism*); broccoli; spinach; greens; seafood; legumes
- Three to four servings of protein from meat or other sources.
  liver, dark poultry meat, cooked oysters, and sardines (which are also very high in iron); all the milk products listed above; eggs; poultry; tofu; fish; shellfish; meat; nuts

- Three servings of iron-rich green, leafy vegetables or yellow fruits. Iron is important for maintenance of hemoglobin. Low levels of iron are certainly common in pregnancy and can signal the onset of anemia. Symptoms of anemia include fatigue and irritability, and severe anemia has been associated with poor pregnancy outcome. These foods are also rich in vitamin A, beta carotene, vitamin E, folic acid, vitamin B_6, calcium, and trace minerals:

    spinach, kale, Swiss chard, mustard, beet or collard greens, broccoli, cantaloupe, carrots, apricots, mango, papaya, winter melons, pumpkin, dark lettuces

- Two to three servings of fruit. This provides vitamin C and all the sugar you are likely to need. If you are concerned about sugar, fruit juices can be cut with carbonated water (check labels for hidden sodium) or still water. Grapes and pineapples are great but are very high in sugar, so don't go overboard.

    citrus juice; fruits such as grapefruit, orange, honeydew melon, lemon, tangerine, and lime; berries such as strawberries, blackberries, and raspberries; tomatoes

- Substitute with these fruits and vegetables for sources that are very rich in vitamin A, potassium, and magnesium.

    cantaloupe, apricots, mangos, nectarines, peaches, carrots, pumpkins, sweet potatoes, spinach, squash, beets, bananas

Vitamin supplementation is uniformly embraced as a good idea for pregnant women. There has been a tremendous amount of discussion in the medical literature about the beneficial effects of folic acid in decreasing the risk to fetuses of certain neural tube defects such as spina bifida. It appears that folic acid supplementation is most important prior to pregnancy and in the early weeks postconception, when the central nervous system is developing. The recommended dose for women contemplating pregnancy is 0.4 milligrams per day. Women who have a personal history of neural tube defect, who have already given birth to a child with a neural tube defect, or who are taking anticonvulsant medicine are advised to increase their folic acid supplement to 4.0 milligrams per day.

Nutrient	Nonpregnant	Pregnant	Percent Increase	Dietary Sources
Energy (kcal)	2,200	2,500	+13.6	Proteins, carbohydrates, fats
Protein (g)	50	60	+20	Meat, fish, poultry, dairy
Calcium (mg)	800	1,200	+50	Dairy Products
Phosphorus (mg)	800	1,200	+50	Meats
Magnesium (mg)	280	320	+14.3	Seafood, legumes, grains
Iron (mg)	15	30	+100	Meats, eggs, grains
Zinc (mg)	12	15	+25	Meats, seafood, eggs
Iodine (µg)	150	175	+16.7	Iodized salt, seafood
Vitamin A (µg RE)	800	800	0	Dark green, yellow, or orange fruits and vegetables, liver
Vitamin D (IU)	200	400	+100	Fortified dairy products
Thiamin (mg)	1.1	1.5	+36.3	Enriched grains, pork
Riboflavin (mg)	1.3	1.6	+23	Meat, liver, enriched grains
Pyridoxine (mg)	1.6	2.2	+37.5	Meats, liver, enriched grains
Niacin (mg NE)	15	17	+13.3	Meats, nuts, legumes
Vitamin B_{12} (µg)	2.0	2.2	+10	Meats
Folic Acid (µg)	180	400	+122	Leafy vegetables, liver
Vitamin C (mg)	60	70	+16.7	Citrus fruits, tomatoes
Selenium (µg)	55	65	+18.2	

Recommended dietary allowances for pregnant and nonpregnant women

Adapted with permission from *Recommended Allowances: 10th Edition*. Copyright 1989 by the National Academy of Sciences. Courtesy of the Academy Press, Washington, D.C.

dr. agnew on folic acid supplementation

For many years folic acid deficiency has been associated with neural tube defect in infants, but now we have proof. The American College of Obstetrics and Gynecologists has reported on a definitive statistic that is probably one of the most remarkable public health matters that I am likely to experience in my lifetime as a physician: In the six years since folic acid supplementation was widely introduced to the diets of reproductive-age women, there has been a 20 percent decrease in the incidence of neural tube defects in babies born in the United States. Amazingly, this was accomplished at least in part by an FDA mandate that all breads and grains sold in the United States be fortified with folic acid. Nevertheless, we absolutely recommend that women *even thinking about getting pregnant* take a folic acid supplement of 0.4 milligrams per day, and that women who have had a child with a neural tube defect take 4.0 milligrams daily.

In addition to folic acid supplements, the woman who is pregnant with twins should have about 1,800 milligrams of calcium daily—and that may be hard to manage without a vitamin supplement. The other supplement that may be appropriate for a twin pregnancy is iron. The strain on the multiple mom to increase her blood supply makes her vulnerable to anemia. You may also need help getting your fifty milligrams of iron each day. Talk to your practitioner about your diet and any recommended vitamin and mineral supplements.

LEVINE AND CLARK ON A NUTRITIONAL APPROACH TO GESTATIONAL DIABETES

A diagnosis of gestational diabetes can be scary to a pregnant mom, but there is a great nutritional approach to this temporary condition. We try to see everyone who calls us with this diagnosis within twenty-four to forty-eight hours, because we know that they may simply stop eating and may even lose a pound or two, and that is not our goal. We're talking here about patients who are not on insulin or other diabetes medication. If a patient has a high fasting blood sugar on the three-hour glucose tolerance test, then she is likely to be placed on insulin, and that is outside the scope of our conversation here.

For those women who are going to manage their gestational diabetes nutritionally, we immediately tell them to cut out the sweets. Obviously that means the standard culprits: the cookies, donuts, and sugary soda. But it also means fruit juice and smoothies. This does not mean these women are going to eliminate fruit from their pregnancy diet, but they will take in those great fruit calories, vitamins, and fiber with the whole fruit, rather then starting the day with a big glass of orange juice.

The manner in which the body handles sugar improves as the day goes on, with glucose tolerance being at its worst in the morning. That means we recom-

(continued)

mend that women with gestational diabetes avoid cereal and milk for breakfast. The point is not to deprive the body of the carbohydrates and milk sugars that it needs, but to refrain from challenging your body to process those cereal carbs and milk sugar (lactose) in the morning, when it is least effective at doing so. Instead, breakfast will combine protein, starch, and fat: say a scrambled egg cooked in a little olive or canola oil, a slice of whole-grain toast with a bit of butter, and a cup of decaffeinated or herbal tea. If you are someone who loves that bowl of cereal, great! You can have a measured quantity of it as a snack later in the day. Our general approach is to suggest three meals and three snacks each day, spacing the meals about five hours apart, with a snack in between, and a final snack in the evening after dinner. When your body is experiencing a challenge at managing blood sugar, it will respond best to a regular schedule of eating, and work more effectively when it is digesting smaller meals. Sometimes we describe it to a patient as having breakfast number one and breakfast number two: instead of a two-egg omelet and two pieces of toast at one sitting, perhaps you have one egg with a piece of toast at 7 A.M., and a repeat performance at 10 A.M. We are not necessarily seeking to reduce the total calories you are managing each day, but tailoring consumption of those calories for your body to metabolize them most effectively.

At lunchtime your meal should include starch, protein, and vegetables, and you can add milk and fruit back in, though large quantities of either are discouraged. An example of a lunch might be a salad (filled with deeply colored vegetables like red or green pepper, tomato, and maybe even some raw snow peas) lightly dressed, with some turkey and perhaps half an apple cut into chunks; a slice or two of whole-grain bread, and four ounces of milk or some cheese. You can do essentially the same thing by placing your protein and vegetables on a sandwich, and having half to a whole sandwich for lunch and another half sandwich for an afternoon snack, with half an apple or orange at each sitting. Dinner is a variation on lunch, and after-dinner snacks might include an apple, banana, or a celery stick with a spoonful of peanut butter, or some popcorn with a piece of string cheese. A big part of the message here is the same as it is generally: your body needs sugar and carbohydrates, but when treating gestational diabetes, you want to be particularly careful to avoid the unhealthy options (the boxes, bags, and bins of sweets that tempt us throughout the center aisles of the grocery store) that are filled with empty calories and minimal nutrition.

ARE YOU OVERWEIGHT OR UNDERWEIGHT?
DO YOU HAVE A HISTORY OF OR DO YOU
CURRENTLY EXPERIENCE ANY EATING DISORDER?

As the conduit through which all nutrition will pass to her babies, a woman's body is the first line of defense when it comes to protecting and nurturing fetal well-being. Physical health, as well as informed attitudes about food and your own body, is all-important in the pre-pregnancy planning stage. For many women, the joy of pregnancy holds the added bonus of a little indulgence. For the woman expecting twins who is used to eating well and staying fit, an occasional brownie with a glass of milk may be just what the doctor ordered. But if you are one of the legion of women in this country waging a daily battle against the bulge, pregnancy presents a whole new challenge. Perhaps you have been on a weight-loss diet. It is not unusual for a woman to become pregnant inadvertently while she is dieting. Naturally, it's daunting for the woman who has literally worked her fanny off for a year to look at the prospect of regaining the weight she has struggled to lose. Which is not to say she isn't thrilled to be pregnant; she may very well be. But it is not unusual for a woman diagnosed with a multiple pregnancy to express concern about managing her weight. The first thing your practitioner is likely to tell you is that a weight-loss diet is not recommended during pregnancy. You certainly can choose nonfat milk over heavy cream in your tea or a lean cut of beef over those fatty ribs, but you must maintain adequate levels of caloric intake to nourish your growing babies.

There are specific concerns for the very young woman who may become pregnant with twins. Anyone who has ever observed the eating habits of teenagers left to their own nutritional devices will concur—there are reasonable concerns about the diets of teens. A poll of the teen population accounts for an impressive amount of pizza, French fries, and potato chips, but the incidence of eating disorders among young women is also alarmingly high.

The good news is that women and their physicians, therapists, and support groups report very positive news about their ability to manage healthy pregnancies while continuing to battle their dietary demons. Women struggling with dietary problems that range from a mild obsession with chocolate to life-threatening bulimia or anorexia can have healthy babies. But it is very important to be frank with yourself, your mate, and your health practitioner when it comes to handling food issues and your pregnancy. While all pregnancies share certain common characteristics, each one is also unique. It stands to reason that a woman who is significantly over- or underweight has her own set of specific concerns, ranging from genetics to her lifestyle to psychological factors that have influenced her weight. But whatever her issues may be, pregnancy often signals a kind of dedication that enables a woman to be very strong and make healthful choices that she perceives—and rightly so—to be necessary for herself and for her babies' health throughout pregnancy.

LEVINE AND CLARK ON
EATING DISORDERS AND STARTING PREGNANCY
OVERWEIGHT OR UNDERWEIGHT

It is interesting that a woman with an eating disorder, such as bulimia (in which a person binges on food and routinely purges herself of a meal before it can be fully digested), may refrain from unhealthy practices around food during pregnancy and nursing, but may then return to the habits of her eating disorder. We do not understand all the mechanisms involved with this condition, but we can recognize a woman's motivation to care for her child by eating well at least until her child is delivered and has had the opportunity to nurse. In the case of bulimia or anorexia nervosa, we often encounter women who are highly motivated to eat well and provide their babies with adequate nutrition. When women begin pregnancy severely underweight, sometimes the pregnancy has taken them by surprise because malnourishment has kept them from having regular periods. Such a woman needs to develop a program that first gets her closer to a healthy weight, and then helps her to gain the additional weight needed for the pregnancy. Most times women are willing and able to do this, but understandably, they need a lot of support from us, the rest of their medical team, and others close to them and the pregnancy. When a woman who is five foot four inches tall comes to us weighing ninety pounds, we would like to see her get closer to 120 pounds—the "desired body weight" for her height—before she adds the additional weight for her pregnancy. The truth is that once she begins to eat and retain her food, her body will respond and will put on weight. This is a great accomplishment for someone battling an eating disorder. We try to avoid too much talk about the specifics of weight gain and how many calories she needs to consume, because all that detail can do more harm than good. Eating the six small meals each day is a helpful technique for someone who is not used to eating very much. And we also suggest that women try to drink some of their calories: smoothies and milkshakes can be excellent high-caloric, nutritional alternatives for someone who is much more likely to have reached for diet soft drinks in the past.

When a woman begins her twin pregnancy at a weight that her doctor believes to be considerably higher than is ideal, we are going to suggest that her weight gain remain at the lower end of the range typically recommended for twin pregnancy. In other words, with the four-to-six-pound weight gain during the first trimester that we mentioned earlier, we are now going to adjust her suggested weight gain for the rest of the pregnancy from one-and-a-half pounds to one pound weekly: a total weight gain of about thirty-five pounds. But let's face it; sometimes a woman will come to us distraught at having already gained fifty pounds as she begins her final trimester. She may ask us how to lose weight or avoid gaining any more. Our response is that we are starting that day to look at all of her food issues, and we will work with her to lose the weight after pregnancy, but weight loss is not an option to consider until after the birth of her babies. And there are many issues that can cause a lot of weight gain: ravenous appetite, food cravings, a missing nutrient, too much time between meals. This is another time to utilize a food diary, making it as easy as possible to keep it accurate and up-to-date. Sometimes it is much easier for women to e-mail their diaries, rather than keeping a notebook. We try to respond frequently, because it is almost like a buddy system and we know it provides welcome support. The food diary sometimes opens up useful discussion. A woman may write down that she had "a bowl of pasta," and learn much to her surprise that when she measures the amount of pasta in that bowl, it is two or three times more than what she imagined she was eating. Women are so inspired by pregnancy to want to do

(continued)

well by their babies that they are really willing to try to improve their eating habits.

When it comes to any eating disorder, there is a lot of sensitivity required. Pregnancy tends to have varied effects on women and their issues with food: sometimes it is "Wow! I have permission to eat." Other times it is incredibly challenging to get enough good nutrition. The medical literature confirms what we see over and over—that the majority of patients with eating disorders will step up to the plate and make the decisions that support their baby's health. Afterwards, some will return to pre-pregnancy eating behaviors, but some will not. Regardless of the situation, the health of the babies is of utmost importance, and that is something that mothers-to-be are eager to embrace.

3

diagnosis: it's twins!

reasons to suspect that you might be carrying twins

Maybe you've been going through assisted reproductive technology and you know that you are likely to be blessed with a multiple pregnancy . . . or, you've done your home pregnancy test and you're pretty sure you're pregnant, but have not the faintest idea that it's twins . . . or, you've had a first appointment with your practitioner, who has confirmed that you are pregnant, and you've raced home to share the great news. No matter which scenario applies to you, at some point fairly early on in your pregnancy, you are going to have certain symptoms that are going to make you, or your practitioner, suspect that you are carrying twins.

Certainly, you and your doctor will be looking for any indications in your medical history that point to twins: family history, age, race, or the use of fertility drugs. But there are other indicators that may tip off your practitioner:

● *Rate of Weight Gain*
The rate at which a pregnant woman gains weight can be the first tip-off to a twin pregnancy. A twin pregnancy is likely to show additional weight as early as the first trimester due to increased blood volume and uterine size. But some-

times a woman and her practitioner do not discover the twin pregnancy until the second trimester, when considerable weight gain raises their suspicions.

The average weight gain (and of course these are approximate) in a singleton pregnancy is as follows:

- five to seven pounds from week one to week twelve
- ten to twelve pounds from week twelve to week twenty-six
- ten to fifteen pounds from week twenty-six until delivery at forty weeks

The average total weight gain tends to be in the realm of twenty-five to thirty-five pounds. In a twin pregnancy, weight gain is increased as follows:

- five to ten pounds from week one to week twelve
- ten to fifteen pounds from week twelve to week twenty-six
- fifteen to twenty pounds from week twenty-six until delivery

The average total weight gain tends to be in the realm of thirty-five to forty-five pounds.

Size of the Abdomen and Increased Itching on Its Surface

A uterus that seems exceedingly large based on the date of the last menstrual period is a very strong indicator of a multiple pregnancy. All women experience a sensation of itchiness as the skin of the abdomen stretches, but the feeling may occur earlier and be more pronounced for the twin mom.

A Feeling of Heaviness in the Pelvis or Vagina

Greater Tendency to Retain Water

The woman pregnant with twins will retain more water than her singleton counterpart. "A feeling of unexpected kinship with Lake Superior" was the way one surprised Michigan mother of twins put it. The unwitting mom of twins may develop swelling in her lower extremities and hands earlier than would normally be expected.

• *Varicose Veins*

There is a tendency for relaxation of the walls of the blood vessels during pregnancy, and this may be increased in the event of a twin pregnancy. Oh, boy . . . support hose!

• *Increased Fatigue*

This is sort of a dicey symptom, since fatigue is one of the early hallmarks of any pregnancy. But a woman who has been pregnant before and feels that her exhaustion in this pregnancy is excessive should mention it to her practitioner.

These indicators are pretty straightforward. But there is also a fair amount of discussion in the medical community about whether women carrying twins feel more movement in the early stages than singleton moms. Even when a twin pregnancy has been diagnosed, it is hard to say in the early stages exactly when a mom is feeling the babies move and if she can distinguish which baby is moving. Both babies can be active or quiet at the same time. But a mom's sense that there seem to be several muffled drum solos going on at once in there may be a reason to call for a diagnostic ultrasound. Finally, many very experienced obstetricians agree that it is exceedingly difficult to confidently identify two separate heartbeats, even with the use of sophisticated listening devices. Using a Doppler tone, which is a device that utilizes ultrasound technology, the earliest opportunity to definitely hear a heartbeat is between ten and twelve weeks. By the sixteenth week, the heart can be heard with a specially designed stethoscope.

at your diagnostic visit

The first thing that is likely to happen is that you will be asked to fill out an extensive medical profile, including details of your menstrual and obstetric history as well as what you may know about the reproductive history of your mother and sisters. Then you will undergo a thorough physical exam. In the case of a first pregnancy, this may be a woman's most thorough health evaluation since she began her reproductive years.

• *Measurement of Vital Statistics*

The exam inevitably begins with the recording of your height, weight, and blood pressure.

• *Evaluation of Your Skin*

Your practitioner will begin by looking at and touching your skin, noting its color, texture, and the presence of any varicosity due to high estrogen levels. (Pregnancy is an equal-opportunity condition, and it is possible for veins other than those in your legs to become swollen or dilated during pregnancy.) Your skin is a remarkable organ, offering insight into many facets of overall health. Very dry skin, for example, is indicative of hypothyroidism. Certain skin lesions on the skin can suggest the presence of infection. An increase in estrogen levels during pregnancy creates a distinct redness to the palm and heel of the hand. You may also develop a redness or an increased pigmentation on the bridge of your nose extending beneath your eyes, as though you have a light tan. This "mask of pregnancy" is another hormonal reaction that can be expected to fade after delivery of your babies.

• *Examination of the Neck*

This exam will include palpation of the neck to look for any thyroid enlargement or abnormal masses.

• *Breast Exam*

The breast exam will include observation of the skin, nipple, and areola, and palpation of the axilla (armpit) for any masses or nodularity.

• *Assessment of Your Lungs and Heart*

If this is your first visit, your practitioner has not yet had an opportunity to get to know you or your body. This is an opportunity to hear how your lungs sound. Later on, you may have complaints about shortness of breath, and this exam offers a sort of baseline assessment of your pulmonary function. It is also important to determine that the size, location, and rhythm of your heart is normal and to rule out the presence of any heart murmurs.

• Evaluation of the Abdomen and Kidneys

This will help to determine the size of your uterus as well as assess the size of your liver and spleen. Palpation of the kidneys is key to determining the presence of any kidney infection.

• Appraisement of Your Back

This will rule out or confirm the presence of scoliosis or any suggestion of arthritis of the back that would have an impact on how you might deliver your twins.

• Pelvic Exam

The pelvic exam will include observation of your external genitalia as well as viewing within the vagina to make sure the skin looks normal and is free of lesions. Then your practitioner will go on to palpate the uterus, checking for any enlargement of the ovaries, and go on to look at the cervix, making sure there are no areas of concern there.

• The Musculoskeletal System

The rest of the exam is largely related to the extremities—making sure the musculoskeletal system appears normal and checking for any limited range of motion or history of trauma. Finally, checking your reflexes will give your practitioner insight into your nervous system.

Having completed the physical exam, you'll move on to the laboratory tests that are performed in the beginning of a pregnancy:

• Human Chorionic Gonadotropin (HCG)

This is the pregnancy hormone, and it can be measured in the blood or the urine to determine if a woman is pregnant. It is the presence of this hormone that is reliably detected in home pregnancy tests, whereas the blood test can help to gauge how far the pregnancy has advanced. A greater-than-anticipated level of HCG in a blood sample is sometimes a practitioner's first clue that a twin pregnancy is likely.

• *Pap Smear*

This will check for any abnormal cell growth on the surface of the cervix.

• *Vaginal Cultures*

These tests are obtained in order to rule out the presence of gonorrhea, chlamydia, or vaginitis.

• *Routine Blood Tests*

This will include a VDRL, which is a serologic test for syphilis; the rubella titer, to determine if you are immune to rubella; a complete blood count (CBC), to check for normal levels of hemoglobin and to test for anemia; and assessment of your blood type and Rh in the event of any Rh incompatibility with your fetus. You will also be offered screening for HIV and hepatitis A and B.

early use of diagnostic ultrasound

Use of the ultrasound can be very enlightening during every stage of pregnancy. If you have one or more indications of a multiple pregnancy, your practitioner may call upon ultrasound technology for confirmation of the diagnosis.

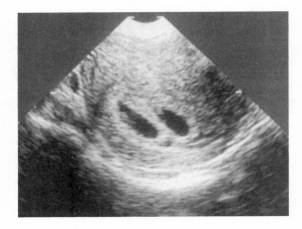

Early diagnostic ultrasound image: two sacs with small poles.

Many obstetricians argue that all pregnant women would benefit from the use of such routine ultrasound screening, but unfortunately many health insurance carriers object to the attendant costs. A recent article in the *American Journal of Obstetricians and Gynecologists* supports wider use of routine ultrasound, but this debate—like so many others in the arena of health care—is likely to rage on without consensus from health-care providers and insurance companies.

In an initial evaluation during the first trimester, the ultrasound can be invaluable in documenting the number of gestational sacs present, and then looking for the number and size of embryos that inhabit them. The ultrasound can also be helpful in the first attempts at determining the form of twinning your pregnancy has taken. If, for example, there appears to be just one gestational sac containing two embryos, that is an indication of the presence of monozygotic (identical) twinning.

The ultrasound is also helpful in determining how far along the patient is. Of course, there is always some margin of error in the dating capabilities of ultrasound. In the first trimester, when we try to measure the size of an embryo to predict its gestational age, the margin of error ranges from five to seven days in either direction. It is also very useful to use ultrasound to confirm the length of the cervix and the location of the placenta or placentas. That early diagnostic information helps to verify that the cervix is doing its job, the placenta is in a good position, and there is no evidence of bleeding within the uterus.

It is also possible to have an early diagnosis of twins and then, with progressive observation of the pregnancy, discover that one of the gestational sacs has failed to develop. This is a phenomenon known as vanishing twin syndrome. While some women may experience bleeding, cramping, or even some passage of tissue, frequently there are no signs of miscarriage, and the patient will go on to have an uncomplicated pregnancy and deliver a perfectly healthy singleton baby. Of course, miscarriage can be a matter of great emotional consequence to parents, even if it occurs in the earliest weeks of pregnancy. But it is sometimes helpful to consider that the failure of one of the twin embryos to thrive may be nature's way of averting serious difficulties further down the line. The parents who understandably grieve over the loss of one of their unborn twins may find some comfort in recognizing that the survival of the second embryo is an early indicator of the vitality of that baby.

The placenta delivers nutrients to the fetus and carries waste away.

the miraculous placenta

When we describe the development of the placenta, we are talking about a miraculous system of blood vessels that are derived either from fetal cells or from the maternal uterine wall. These two separate sources come together as an integral part of the network of the placenta. In fact, sometimes the two sources are so close together that there is little more than a few cells separating the blood supplies of the mother and each baby. The nutrients carried by the mother's blood are transported across that cell layer and diffuse their important load of nutrients, oxygen, calories, and fluid into the baby's blood. At the same time, the baby's blood needs to have waste products removed. The baby's waste products will be transported out of its bloodstream and into the mom's, to be disposed of as she would her own waste.

The development of this extraordinary organ, on temporary loan to every mother-to-be, will determine how well your twins are going to receive the nutrients that are so vital to their well-being. If, as is the case in some monozygotic twinning, twins share a placenta, there is additional attention paid to whether there is equal sharing of the goodies. And there are occasional circumstances in which there is some vascular communication between the two placentas, so your practitioner will want to track those twins very carefully.

are you seeing the right practitioner?

Okay. So you've got your diagnosis. And you've begun to make your transition from stunned to numb to overjoyed. First of all, you can be sure that one time on the roller-coaster ride of these emotions is not going to be enough. Most couples report at least several weeks of riding these feelings up and down: eyes wide open, eyes shut tight; hands clutching each other, hands thrown sky high just for the thrill of the ride. But as the reality sinks in, the prospect of twin birth is overwhelmingly met with a deep and abiding impression of having been favored with a miracle.

Now it is time to begin thinking about assembling the team that will help you to make this miracle become real. Perhaps you have gone through fertility treatments or have been seeing a practitioner since your prenatal preparation. If that is the case, you may have been developing a relationship for years. But many couples get their initial diagnosis from a home pregnancy test and find themselves in the position of needing to choose a health-care provider. Whether you have a practitioner in place or are just beginning your search, ask yourself the following questions:

- Is this person accessible?
- Is he or she receptive to my thoughts about my own health care?
- Are we able to communicate effectively and with respect, even if there is a difference of opinion?
- Has this practitioner handled many multiple births?
- Does this person clearly acknowledge that my time is equally valuable to his or hers?

If you can answer yes to these five questions, then you have found an excellent provider, and you and your twins are off to the best possible start. Ease of communication is the engine that will drive your whole pregnancy. The more time you spend as a couple talking out your own attitudes toward pregnancy and childbirth, and discussing your joint expectations of a practitioner, the better off you'll be when it comes time to interview candidates. It is important to trust your instincts. Behavioral scientists describe instinct as an unalterable tendency of an organism to make a complex and specific response to environmental stimuli without involving reason. Hey, if it has been good enough for the survival of the species, it is good enough for you to trust yourselves when it just feels right as you interview a potential member of your twin team. Conversely, someone may say all the right things in an interview, but if you walk away with an uneasy feeling about the long-term survival of the alliance, keep on looking. The realities of health insurance cost and availability, as well as geography, will play a big role in the process. The couple living in a large metropolitan area is going to have more options when it comes to choosing health care than the couple in a small town. But even an area with a limited number of doctors is likely to have access to the diagnostic capabilities available in urban medical centers. The more informed you are as a consumer of health care, the more effectively you will be able to advocate for your own pregnancy. And advocate you will!

If none of your friends or family members has experience with health-care practitioners in your community, start with a call or visit to the nursing staff in Labor and Delivery at your local hospital. Many obstetric nurses will have wonderfully informed opinions about providers in the area. Find out who they trust, who handles the greatest number of multiple pregnancies, and who delivered their babies. These are dedicated professionals who are under no obligation to promote anyone's practice. The people who specialize in this area of nursing are concerned only with your health and the health of your unborn babies.

Finally, as you consider all the factors that go into choosing your practitioner, you need to make inquiries into the kind of practice in which that person participates. The most common scenarios are as follows:

• The Group Practice

It is not unusual to find a practice comprised of four obstetricians who will divide their patients equally. This equates to your having a 25-percent chance of seeing any one of them for an appointment, an emergency, or the delivery of your babies. You can inquire about the possibility of seeing one of them on a consistent basis, but be very specific in your questioning and don't assume that you will be able to choose which member of the practice will be on hand to deliver your twins.

• Shared Office Space

You may find a four-person obstetric practice where the practitioners share office space as well as nursing and clerical help, but where each has a specific list of patients and, under most circumstances, you will see the same practitioner exclusively throughout your pregnancy. Again, it is important to ask about that practitioner's commitment to delivering your babies, but in this type of practice each tries to deliver his or her own patients except in the case of an emergency.

• *Private Practice*

As health care in our country continues to change, the number of private practices is diminishing. But you can still find practitioners who work without benefit of partners or office mates. If you have done your homework and know that this is the practitioner for you, you have the advantage of knowing that, barring an emergency, this will be your exclusive provider from your first visit through your labor and delivery. Of course, if unforeseen circumstances prevent your practitioner from being available to deliver your babies, you run the risk of being delivered by a physician with whom you have no prior relationship.

Your decision-making process will be informed to some to degree by your health insurance coverage. Read your policy carefully, and don't hesitate to call your insurance provider or to speak with your obstetric office about how to most effectively take advantage of its benefits.

It is also important to note that a multiple pregnancy is considered high risk and should (whenever possible) be treated by an obstetrician with a track record of attending to multiple births. Certainly, there are many highly skilled nurse-midwives in practice throughout the country, but they have been trained to attend to low-risk pregnancies and uncomplicated births. If you are interested in enlisting the support of a certified nurse-midwife, look for an obstetric practice that has a CNM on staff. You then have the best of both possible worlds: a member of the team with a natural approach to childbirth, and an obstetrician with a lot of experience handling multiple births.

The proliferation of fertility enhancement throughout the country has made twinning a much more frequent occurrence throughout the general population. As a result, even obstetricians with smaller practices are growing increasingly familiar with the particular needs of women delivering twins. If you live in a smaller town, be sure to ask about your obstetrician's experience with multiple pregnancies and find out whom he or she consults and what diagnostic resources will be available to you if something comes up that requires additional attention.

4 to 8 weeks

your developing twins

At four weeks, what shows up on an ultrasound are two little gestational sacs, or in some rare cases of monozygotic twinning, only one. The amniotic sac, the fluid, and the embryo reside within but are not visible at this time. Between four and eight weeks the brain, bladder, kidneys, liver, reproductive tracts, spine, heart, and extremities are all in development. Twins are developing at the same rate as singletons at this point. By the sixth week, we can see some evidence of a fetal pole or embryo on an ultrasound. The first time your twins are visible, they are about two to three millimeters long, less than the size of a grain of rice. By the seventh or eighth week, each is about the length of two grains of rice and cardiac activity is visible by ultrasound.

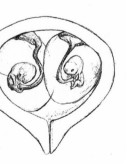

Twins' development at four to eight weeks.

your pregnant body

One of the first and most remarkable symptoms of pregnancy, whether singleton or multiple, is a change in appetite. Most women experience an increase in appetite

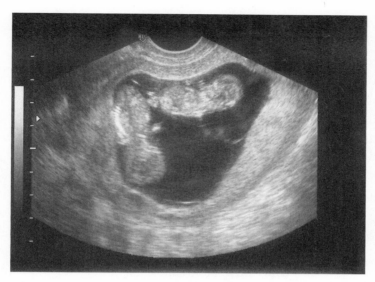

Ultrasound image of twins at four to eight weeks.

between the fourth and sixth weeks. This increase is perfectly normal and may continue throughout the pregnancy. Many women report appetite swings. For the most part, this is your body indicating its increased caloric needs. The woman carrying twins has about one-and-a-half times the caloric need of the singleton mom, and she should listen to what her body is telling her and eat accordingly.

You may have complained of feeling tired at times before pregnancy was a consideration, but a couple of nights of uninterrupted sleep or a weekend to take it easy put you back to normal. The fatigue associated with pregnancy is another thing entirely. You may just feel pooped—from the moment you haul yourself out of bed to the moment you hurl yourself back in. This is true of most pregnant women, and most of them are not carrying twins. It's a symptom of the body as factory—and you're manufacturing twice the product with no extra personnel. You are working to produce two, brand-new life-support systems with the ultimate goal of their being independent of you. But for now you're the only game in town, and as such you need to take extra-good care of yourself. Aim for extra sleep every night, and maybe you'll actually get it half the time. A good diet, consistent exercise, and managing stress will help, but be prepared to slow down. Traditionally, the fourth month of pregnancy begins a second-trimester respite from fatigue, but twin moms may not experience it as dramatically as their singleton pals.

You may also notice an increase or decrease in saliva formation during pregnancy. A dry mouth is most likely a sign of inadequate hydration. Pregnancy increases blood volume, as well as creating additional fluids in the breast, uterus, and virtually everywhere else in your body. Again, twin pregnancy calls for more hydration than singleton pregnancy, so you must be sure to drink water throughout the day. Increased saliva seems to be related to nausea and perhaps vomiting in the first trimester of pregnancy. The saliva production remains the same, but a woman with an irritated stomach will naturally refrain from swallowing as much as she otherwise would.

Almost all pregnant women report increased frequency of urination in the first trimester of pregnancy. The bladder is a little sac that fills and empties at a rate that corresponds to how large and how full it is. The enlarging uterus in the pelvis of a pregnant woman is adjacent to the bladder. When there is pressure from the uterus, the bladder can only fill to a certain size before it is compressed between the back of the uterus and the front of the pelvic bone, sending you the signal that you need to urinate. So, even in the early weeks of pregnancy, the uterus begins to take up extra space and the bladder does not have its usual capacity. If you have any burning sensation or pain associated with frequent urination, or if you notice any blood in your urine, you should alert your practitioner at once. Pain in the flank or lower back, or fever associated with any of these symptoms, is also reason enough to call your practitioner so that you can be screened for the presence of a urinary tract infection. An untreated UTI can quite quickly develop into a serious infection of the kidneys. Women with undiagnosed bladder infections are at increased risk of kidney infection during pregnancy. This may be because the urethra, while an adequate barrier

Your pregnant body at four to eight weeks.

to vaginal bacteria in nonpregnant women, seems to relax during pregnancy, allowing bacteria to find its way up toward the kidneys.

The pregnant woman with an undiagnosed, or asymptomatic, urinary tract infection needs to be treated as aggressively as the patient who has symptoms. This is one of the most important reasons for taking a urine sample at each of your obstetric office visits. Ampicillin (a penicillin derivative) is a frequently prescribed antibiotic for treatment of urinary tract infections during pregnancy. Macrodantin (a non-penicillin antibiotic) is also safe during pregnancy and is used for patients allergic to penicillin. The broader-spectrum antibiotics such as cephalosporin are also safely used during pregnancy. It is very important to complete your antibiotic prescription. Don't be tempted to stop when your symptoms subside. Ciprofloxacin (known as Cipro) and all floxin derivatives are to be scrupulously avoided during pregnancy, though they are frequently used to treat UTIs in the general adult population.

The time-honored practice of drinking lots of water is extremely helpful, because the increased volume of liquid helps to flush out bacteria. And yes—cranberry juice does help! It alters the pH or acidity of the urine, making it less hospitable to bacteria.

A UTI that develops into a kidney infection is a potentially serious illness that needs to be treated aggressively with intravenous antibiotics and occasionally requires hospitalization. The most common symptoms are fever with chills and lower back pain.

The well-documented nausea and vomiting known as morning sickness is a common occurrence in pregnancy and seldom leads to a seriously disturbed nutritional status for the mother-to-be. The feeling of morning sickness is secondary to several physiological changes that take place early in pregnancy. A pregnant woman produces increased levels of progesterone. This hormone has the effect of decreasing the muscle tone and motility (the ability to squeeze) of the stomach. During pregnancy, the volume of the stomach increases, further contributing to its diminished capacity to empty completely. So the stomach works overtime, but with limited success. And in case that is not enough good news, the "morning" part of this sickness can also be a bit misleading. Nausea or vomiting can happen at any point throughout the day. However, nausea tends to be worst when your stomach is empty, such as when you first wake up in the morning.

A heightened sense of smell is also common in pregnancy and unfortunately can contribute to a pregnant woman's complicated appetite. Many women find that frequent small meals are the best approach to combating morning sickness. Speak with your practitioner about the value of vitamin B_6 in combating nausea. The onset of morning sickness is usually between week four and week eight of pregnancy, and it may persist until week fourteen or sixteen, though in twin pregnancies it tends to go on longer. In rare cases, nausea and vomiting are so severe and extended as to pose a threat to the health of the mother and her babies. This condition, called hyperemesis gravidarum, is associated with weight loss, significant dehydration, and electrolyte imbalance. Your practitioner will take this very seriously and may call for hospitalization to ensure adequate intravenous fluids to restore water and electrolyte balance as well as sufficient caloric intake. Once fluid balance has been restored, steps will be taken to develop a healthful diet that the mother can tolerate, and her fluids will continue to be monitored throughout her pregnancy.

Adding to the panoply of gastrointestinal delights that occur in pregnancy are heartburn and indigestion. Again, these symptoms appear to be secondary to physiological changes. The sphincter (muscular ring), where the esophagus joins the stomach, is also affected by increased progesterone and is acting with less efficiency. So, as pressure is increased on the abdomen, some of the contents of the stomach—now mixed with digestive acids—tend to push back up into the esophagus; the presence of that acid causes heartburn.

A twin pregnancy causes relatively more heartburn, and does so earlier in the pregnancy, due to additional pressure from a larger uterus. Antacids are usually very effective in controlling the symptoms of heartburn. Some have the added benefit of containing calcium, which your body needs during pregnancy. And let gravity work for you in controlling heartburn. Don't lie down after eating; stay seated or, better still, take a little stroll.

The final affront in the triple crown of gastrointestinal threats is constipation. Just as the motility of the stomach is compromised, so is motility throughout your entire intestinal tract. Matter is moving more slowly through the colon, and your pregnant body, ever vigilant in its nurturing of its precious cargo, is more efficiently absorbing water from your stool. As a result, the stool will tend to become hard and difficult to eliminate. Your first weapon in this battle is obvious: drink more water! Next, increase your intake of fiber-rich foods such as vegetables, fruits, whole grains, and legumes. Keep your meals small and frequent and, unless your practitioner advises against it at this time, develop a safe, consistent exercise plan.

Moving on to your respiratory system, the first symptoms you are likely to notice are stuffiness or nosebleeds. Both these symptoms are very common in pregnancy and have a lot to do with the fact that every mucous membrane in your body is experiencing an increased supply of blood. This makes the mucous membranes in the nose become a bit swollen and secrete additional mucus. Many women self-diagnose colds or allergies during their pregnancies that are, in fact, the pregnancy-induced swelling of their mucous membranes. It is important to avoid nasal inhalers to alleviate these symptoms, as they can alter the function of the tissues lining your nose if used on a long-term basis. Steam inhalers are a safe and soothing alternative treatment. A bloody nose may be the result of increased blood supply to the tiny capillaries in the nasal passage. However, frequent bloody noses, yellowish discharge from the nose, or fever associated with either event should be brought to the attention of your practitioner.

It is not unusual for pregnant women to describe a sensation of breathlessness (called dyspnea in medical texts). It is a feeling that you cannot quite catch your breath, or that you seem to be breathing regularly and then feel the impulse to sigh deeply every so often. As many as 70 percent of pregnant women experience this in the first trimester of pregnancy, and it is most frequently attributed to a change in the capacity of the rib cage. The size of a pregnant woman's rib cage increases, so she moves more air in and out of her chest. It follows that you have to use more effort to completely fill your lungs. In a twin pregnancy the uterus takes up substantially more space during the second and third trimesters, so this symptom is more pronounced than in the singleton pregnancy. By the last weeks of a twin pregnancy, shortness of breath is further exacerbated by the simple mechanics of the large uterus pushing on the diaphragm. Certainly, this contributes to discomfort in the final weeks before delivery, and breathlessness accompanied by a cough or wheezing should be reported to your practitioner immediately.

It is perfectly normal for a pregnant woman to experience an increased heart rate and the sensation of feeling her pulse. This is due to the combined effects of increased blood volume and decreased blood pressure. Your blood volume will increase by 50 percent during your pregnancy, and many of the hormones of pregnancy have the effect of lowering your blood pressure. As a result, your heart has to increase its rate to maintain blood pressure.

Breast tenderness is frequently an early symptom of pregnancy. It is interesting to note that soreness or tenderness of the breasts seem to diminish in subsequent pregnancies. But if this is your first pregnancy, especially with twins, you are likely to experience considerable tenderness along with associated swelling, particularly in the first trimester. A woman's breasts may increase by as much as three cup sizes before she delivers. It is not unusual for pregnant women, especially if fair-skinned, to notice a new prominence to the veins in her breast. This too is normal and is attributable to increased blood volume. Your nipples and the areola (the pigmented area surrounding the nipples) may show increased pigmentation during pregnancy. These changes are completely normal as long as the rest of the breasts' skin coloration is also normal and the tenderness is uniform over the whole breast. However, if you should find a localized area of swelling, like a small nodule anywhere in the breast, bring that to the immediate attention of your practitioner. Some women report a leakage of clear fluid from the nipple during pregnancy. That is probably an early discharge and is no cause for alarm. If, however, there is ever blood or opaque liquid passed from the nipple, your practitioner will want to know about it.

It is very important to adequately support your breasts during pregnancy. Avoid underwire bras, and choose bras with substantial straps across your back as well as over your shoulders. You don't have to make a special trip to a maternity store to find bras that are designed to accommodate your breasts during pregnancy. Most department, and even discount, stores carry reasonably priced pregnancy bras, some of which can be converted to use as nursing bras when the time comes. Sports bras are terrific at holding your breasts in a firm but nonbinding way. But, as your pregnancy advances, you may find these bras too confining.

dr. agnew on listening to your body

"You should never ignore a substantial level of pain in the chest. If it is severe and unrelenting, you may have a hiatal hernia, a condition that occurs when the sphincter located at the base of the esophagus fails to function at all. Under this circumstance, your practitioner will want you to be evaluated by a gastroenterologist."

the checkup

discussing your pregnancy

Unless you are seeing a practitioner with whom you have a long-established relationship, you are still in the early stages of building your relationship. Don't make assumptions about what may or may not be an important factor in your pregnancy. Ask about anything that you think might be important:

- How frequently will your practitioner wish to see you throughout your pregnancy?
- What is the procedure for handling your telephone calls?
- Whom would you expect to see if your practitioner is unavailable?
- How soon can you expect a response to your telephone messages?
- Is there a protocol for distinguishing between questions that might need an answer between visits and a genuine obstetric emergency?
- What constitutes an emergency, and how would your practitioner handle it?
- Describe to your practitioner the nature of your employment, including stress, physical activity, and environmental factors that might be important to your pregnancy.
- Mention any travel plans you have and discuss your practitioner's attitudes toward travel during your pregnancy.
- What sort of exercise plan is appropriate for you?
- Discuss your diet, and ask your practitioner about vitamin supplements if you plan to take them.

the physical exam

Your physical exam will first entail evaluating your blood pressure and the rest of your vital signs. Your practitioner will be very interested in gauging your blood pressure throughout the course of your pregnancy, with special attention paid to women who appear to be at risk of hypertension, a condition we'll discuss in greater detail in a later chapter. There will be discussion as the exam progresses: Are you tired? Are any unusual things going on in your family or at work? You are on far more intimate terms with your own body than your practitioner is, so offer any insights you can about your symptoms and concerns.

The physical exam will go on to assess your heart, lungs, breasts, abdomen, extremities, and skin, and will include a complete pelvic exam. The pelvic will include palpation of the cervix, uterus, and ovaries, and also a Pap smear if it was not done at your diagnostic exam. Any vaginal cultures described in chapter three that were not taken at the time of your diagnosis will be taken now. You will be asked to give a urine sample to measure glucose and protein and to screen for any evidence of a urinary tract infection.

transitions

The undeniable excitement of knowing that you are pregnant with twins is tempered by some sobering realities, not the least of which is the possibility of miscarriage. In the general population of women of childbearing age, there are some who are identified as being at greater risk of miscarriage:

- women with multiple pregnancies
- women with a history of miscarriage
- women with uterine abnormalities such as double uterus (*uterus didelphys*), heart-shaped uterus (*uterus bicornuate*), or uterine septum

While no one wants to unnecessarily alarm you, your practitioner will most likely discuss the most common symptoms of miscarriage in one of your early office visits:

• *Bleeding*

Many women experience spotty bleeding during the first few months of pregnancy without any ill effect. However, it can be a symptom of miscarriage and should be taken seriously. Even a small amount of bleeding should be brought to the attention of your practitioner, particularly if it continues for several days. Bleeding at the level of your menstrual period—enough to warrant use of a sanitary napkin—warrants immediate attention.

• Cramping and Pain

The sensation of menstrual-type cramping or pain—whether mild or severe—may be associated with miscarriage.

• Fever

If you have a fever associated with any of the symptoms already listed, this should also be considered a possible sign of miscarriage. If you have chills or feel feverish, take your temperature.

• Passing of Grayish or Pink Tissue, or Blood Clots

The presence of these materials may mean you have begun to miscarry. If possible, try to save the matter for analysis, as it may be products of conception.

If you experience any of these symptoms, call your practitioner right away. If you reach an answering service, follow the instructions for how to proceed in the event of a medical emergency.

If you have these symptoms and are advised to come into the practitioner's office or to go to the hospital, this is what you can expect to happen:

- Your vital signs, including pulse and blood pressure, will be assessed.
- There will a physical examination of your uterus and an abdominal exam to check for any other abdominal mass.
- A pelvic exam will check for any evidence of tissue or blood clots.
- Your cervix will be evaluated to determine whether it is open and there appears to have been a miscarriage, or if the cervix is in fact closed.
- Your practitioner may schedule an ultrasound exam.

At this point, depending on the findings, there are several options to consider. Your practitioner may want to confirm rising hormone levels. If the ultrasound shows evidence of a blood clot in the uterus, that does not necessarily mean a miscarriage will ensue. But decreased activity and some degree of bed rest are likely to be advised. A follow-up ultrasound will be ordered to make sure that the blood clot is continuing to shrink. Some practitioners will recommend the use of a progesterone supplement to a patient who is threatening to miscarry. There is an ongoing dialogue in the obstetric community about this practice because of continued controversy about its effectiveness.

If the embryo or fetus is the right size for your stage of pregnancy and the bleeding is what doctors call "acute and finite"—meaning you don't continue to spot for months afterward—then you and your practitioner can be very optimistic about your pregnancy continuing. Miscarriage of a twin may put you at higher risk for preterm labor, but there are two very important factors to remember when you hear that news:

- Preterm labor can frequently be identified and managed with good results.
- The miscarriage of one fetus does not seem to have negative implications regarding the health or genetic integrity of the surviving fetus. In fact, there is evidence that its survival probably denotes a healthy fetus with a high likelihood of continued survival.

Many professionals in the obstetric community would agree that, given the opportunity to evaluate the pregnancy material from one hundred women who had miscarried, more than fifty of those tissue samples would be found to have some sort of defect—either a genetic or chromosomal abnormality, some structural problem, or an anomaly of the placenta. Few people find that an easy statistic to absorb. It makes sense that we would struggle with this eccentricity of nature. Why, in the grand scheme of things, would nature permit a pregnancy to require all this effort, and then not allow it to thrive? It seems oddly uneconomical for an evolutionary process that we think of as being so discrete and energy-efficient. Perhaps it is nature's way of nipping a problem in the bud. So even while you grieve over the loss of one life, you should be encouraged about the probability of carrying your second fetus successfully and delivering a healthy baby.

exercise for the mom-to-be

Exercise is beneficial to everyone. Our bodies function best when they are regularly exercised. Pregnancy need not be a time to avoid exercise, but neither is it the time begin a new sport. Learning a new sport can be challenging, even for skilled athletes. Your center of gravity is different when you're pregnant and you might injure yourself. If you are a swimmer, continue swimming. If you are involved in aerobics classes or dancing, look to tailor your program to your pregnancy. Women pregnant with multiples are at risk of preterm labor, so it is particularly important that you work with your doctor to develop your own individualized exercise program that remains medically supervised over the course of your pregnancy. The goal of your team—and that may include your practitioner and anyone guiding you in your fitness regimen—is to tailor your exercise to suit your medical and obstetric history.

The most important aspects of exercising responsibly during pregnancy are to avoid getting overheated and not to exercise with more intensity than is safe for you and your developing babies. This stands from the first week of pregnancy to a week before you deliver. Our bodies dissipate heat fairly well through sweating, but it is possible to exercise to the point that you increase your body temperature. Your twins want to be in a 98.6-degree environment, so overheating your body is not in the best interest of the developing embryo or fetus. It is also very important to allow yourself adequate time to warm up and cool down, so as to avoid any undue risk of musculoskeletal injuries. Be sure to stay adequately hydrated before, during, and after exercise. The American College of Obstetrics and Gynecologists also recommends exercising regularly (at least three times per week) over intermittent activity.

Your heart rate during exercise is very important and should determine the intensity of your workout. If, for example, you are a highly trained athlete, I'd recommend that you decrease your maximum heart rate during exercise by 30 percent. No matter what form of exercise you choose, you should limit your heart rate to 110 to 120 beats per minute while working out. If you do not have the means to monitor your heart rate while exercising, give yourself the "talk test" as you work out: Are you able to speak in a comfortable conversational tone while exercising? If so, great! If not, it is time to stop or slow down for a while.

The best exercises during pregnancy provide all the benefits of calorie use, increased blood supply to the skin, and increased heart rate but don't allow the body to overheat. That is why swimming is such a superb form of exercise for the pregnant woman. It's recommended that the length of time you swim be proportional to what you are accustomed to: If you swim a mile each day, you might want to decrease that by one-third. However, if you are used to swimming only a few laps each day, say for twenty minutes, it is safe to continue doing so.

The woman who is not used to exercise and determines that she wants to discover its benefits during her pregnancy has a wonderful opportunity to begin by taking daily walks. Walking for fifteen to twenty minutes each day is of benefit to both mother and babies. With guidance from your practitioner, you may want to develop a moderate fitness program that will be a consistent part of your life even after the twins are born.

When developing an exercise program, it is important to exercise to the point of benefit but minimize the likelihood of injury. The pregnancy hormone progesterone has the effect of relaxing ligaments across every joint in your body. The benefit in pregnancy is that this helps the pelvis to be less rigid, allowing the process of birth to move forward with less resistance. The negative aspect is that it can predispose you to spraining an ankle or knee. You are more likely to injure yourself participating in exercise that requires sudden changes in direction, with tennis being the classic example. Even the trained athlete is wise to avoid tennis during pregnancy.

Any high-impact sport, such as running, is to be avoided, particularly after the twentieth week. There are many other forms of exercise that will benefit your health and the health of your growing babies; for example, you can get a great cardio workout using a stationary bike, an elliptical trainer, or a stair climber. Swimming or low-impact aerobics will also benefit your heart without giving your joints a pounding. Any exercise that puts you at risk of abdominal trauma should be avoided. These activities include ice skating, roller skating, in-line skating, skiing and snowboarding, surfing, fencing, scuba diving, water skiing, and team contact sports such as basketball or soccer. It is also important to refine your exercise program if spinning has been part of your weekly regimen. Spinning is a high-intensity cardiovascular workout that may cause an extremely fast heart rate and significant dehydration. Even the experienced spinner should consider an alternative form of exercise during her twin pregnancy. Spinning, unlike swimming or low-impact aerobics, is not easily dialed down to a moderate level—the fun is in getting your heart and legs pumping really hard!

when is it time to stop exercising?

If you experience any of these symptoms, you should sit down. Do not hesitate to call your practitioner immediately.

- Headache
- Shortness of breath
- Lightheadedness
- Vaginal spotting or bleeding
- Chest pains
- Muscle weakness
- Sudden swelling in the ankles, hands, or face
- Obvious redness in the calf area

julie tupler, rn, on the importance of correctly exercising the abdominal muscles

Julie Tupler, a registered nurse, childbirth educator, and fitness expert, is the director of Maternal Fitness (maternalfitness.com). Tupler is also the author of Maternal Fitness *and* Lose Your Mummy Tummy.

I've worked with almost eighty twin moms. I always tell them that the two muscle groups that come most into play in the support of every pregnancy—the abdominals and the pelvic floor—are stretched out even more during a twin pregnancy, and they are the hardest to get back into shape if they have not been worked before and during pregnancy. Toning and strengthening these muscles is going to be an important advantage through every pregnancy, for labor and delivery, as well as when regaining post-pregnancy abdominal muscle fitness. But for mothers of twins, who are carrying the weight of two babies, these muscles are called upon to work even harder. I tell all pregnant women that the exercise they are doing should be functional—that is to say, it should be something that helps them during their labor. I'm not saying that you should ignore the pleasure and benefit to be derived from a daily walk or swim, but the abdominal work should absolutely be in the service of your back comfort during pregnancy and your ability to push more effectively in labor.

The second thing we always discuss is the importance of getting started early with exercise, because twin pregnancy places a woman at a somewhat higher risk of the possibility of bed rest, with exercise curtailed. So the more work you've done, the better shape you'll be in to deliver your babies. I like to talk with my clients about "muscle memory"—if these muscle groups have been worked during pregnancy it is easier to use them again after they've been stretched. Exercising mindfully and carefully is a gift you give to your babies and yourself, and you can count on the fact your recovery will be easier.

So let's talk a little bit about the abdominals:

- First there is the outermost muscle layer—the rectus abdominus. This is the six-pack we hear about all the time. This muscle is made up of two halves that are joined together in the middle by a piece of long fibrous tissue called the linea alba that may also be visible in people with very well-developed abdominal musculature.
- The next muscle layer is the internal and external obliques, which insert into the linea alba and serve to twist the torso and bend the upper body toward the legs.
- The innermost muscle of the abdomen is the transverse muscle, which also connects to the linea alba and wraps around the body like a corset.

The rectus abdominus is very important when it comes to helping your abdominals do the important work of supporting and holding your uterus in place as it grows heavier with each week of your pregnancy. You also know that the powerful hormones of pregnancy are surging through your body right now, and one of those hormones is called relaxin. Just as its name suggests, this hormone relaxes the tissue of the linea alba, making it prone to stretching sideways.

Now imagine the linea alba actually stretching sideways, and instead of the recti muscles doing the work they were designed to do—supporting your internal organs, including the uterus—the linea alba is now filling in for those muscles like a piece of overstretched saran wrap. A diastasis is a separation of the two halves of the rectus abdominus that sometimes occurs in pregnancy. So it makes sense that the work you do to tone and strengthen your abdominal muscles should be in support of limiting or lessening the occurrence of diastasis: We want to keep that separation as small as possible. I participated in a study undertaken by the program in physical therapy at Columbia University on the effect of exercise on diastasis. I was thrilled, but not surprised, when the results of that study concluded that the women who had participated in the Maternal Fitness program had a smaller diastasis than the control group of women who did not exercise during their pregnancy.

To test for diastasis, you lie on your back with your knees bent. (If you are uncomfortable on your back or experience any lightheadedness, roll on to your side and use pillows to prop up your upper body.) Place two fingers in your belly button pointing down and slowly lift your head. You may feel a gap between the two sides of your abdominal muscles. You can think of that gap either as a space between the two halves of the rectus abdominus or as the increasing width of the linea alba. In either event, that is a diastasis and you will want to design your exercise, and indeed the way you move around in your life, to avoid exacerbating this condition.

A diastasis in pregnancy is not the end of the world, and you can certainly discuss any concerns with your practitioner. But knowing that there is the potential for this problem may inspire you to get started with exercises either before you become pregnant or during the course of your pregnancy. And I like to take an approach that suggests it is not only during exercise, but also the way you move your pregnant body through your environment over the course of each day that may really help you to avoid back pain during and after pregnancy. Remember, for example, that if you are in bed and are in a back-lying position (let's say it is early in your pregnancy and there is no contraindication to lying on your back), avoid lifting your head and coming straight up. Instead, engage your abdominals, roll to the side without lifting your head, and use your arms to get yourself up to a sitting position. And do the same thing in reverse to lie back down. Just getting into the habit of using your abdominal muscles—not only during exercise, but really all the time—is going to best serve abdominal fitness throughout your pregnancy and beyond.

If the abdominal muscles are there to surround your growing babies in the uterus, the pelvic floor is the foundation that their temporary housing rests upon. As a mother of twins, the weight of carrying a second baby places additional strain on the muscles of the pelvic floor. You want to make the effort to exercise the pelvic floor so that it doesn't turn into a pelvic basement by the time your pregnancy is drawing to an end. This is accomplished by doing Kegel exercises, with which most pregnant women are quite familiar. The Kegels actually have a triple benefit:

Fitness expert Julie Tupler works with pregnant client Jane Rancusin.

- By strengthening the pelvic floor you improve the support needed for your internal organs, including the uterus.
- You are better able to suppress urine leakage when sneezing or coughing.
- The Kegels have been shown to condition the vaginal canal to better retain its narrow shape after vaginal birth (or births!), thereby providing improved sexual intimacy for you and your partner when intercourse following pregnancy is resumed.

Kegels are done by squeezing the muscles used to stop the flow of urine. I recommend twenty repetitions (each repetition is a ten-second hold or tightening of the muscle) five times each day. Kegels are best accomplished sitting, or with your legs up on a wall. Do not perform these exercises while urinating, because that can cause urinary tract infection.

making great exercise choices

Certainly, walking and swimming provide both conditioning and cardiovascular benefit. Low-impact aerobics and dancing are also fun and can be accomplished in the privacy of your home or out and about with friends in the gym or dance studio.

When it comes to a twin pregnancy, remember to speak with your doctor about your interest in using free weights as a part of your exercise program. In general, a pregnant woman who has never before used free weights should limit weights to a maximum of two to five pounds in her workout. I am in complete agreement with the recommendation from ACOG that multiple repetitions of light weights are safer than fewer repetitions with heavier weights. By the time you reach your second trimester, and absolutely on into your third, you should be doing any weightlifting from a seated, rather than standing, position. One of the classic weightlifting postures—the Valsalva maneuver—should be avoided throughout pregnancy. Look for a certified personal trainer who has experience working with pregnant women.

———————————————————————————————————

Finally, we ought to talk a little bit about yoga and Pilates, two exercise practices that have grown very popular in our culture.

yoga

More and more women are showing an interest in the benefits of prenatal yoga—and with good reason. At the heart of yoga practice is the breathing technique that helps you to focus and relax—two skills that many women find invaluable during labor. There are many benefits to practicing yoga prior to, during, and after pregnancy:

- Yoga helps pregnant women to improve their shifting sense of balance as the body's center of gravity alters throughout pregnancy.
- Yoga is an excellent way to remain or become more limber, as it tones and strengthens muscles without creating undue joint strain.
- Yoga improves blood circulation, and many women say that the stretching they learn to do in their yoga classes helps them through some of the daily aches and pains of pregnancy.
- In addition to being very useful as a relaxation technique during labor and delivery, yoga may also support a busy mom to more calmly respond to the challenges of life after her babies are born.

Be sure to discuss your intention to do yoga with your practitioner, who may know of instructors in your area who have experience with prenatal yoga. If you have not done yoga before, start out with a beginner's class and proceed slowly and carefully. Whether you are a beginner or have practiced yoga for some time, make sure your instructor is aware that you are pregnant with twins, and just how far along you are in your pregnancy. *Even if you are very experienced in the study of yoga, Bikram yoga, a style that is typically practiced in heated rooms where temperatures can easily be above one hundred degrees, is absolutely contraindicated during pregnancy, as it raises the body's core temperature beyond what is healthy for you and your babies.*

As is the case with all exercise during your pregnancy, let your body be your guide. If you are uncomfortable, or certainly if you find that a particular yoga pose is painful, adjust your routine to suit your pregnant body. Practice standing poses with support: Either place your heels next to a wall, or use a solidly balanced chair for support. Remember to avoid poses that require you to be on your back for any length of time, because the weight of your growing babies on the *vena cava*—the large vein that carries blood from your back and lower limbs to your heart—can interfere with the blood flow to your uterus. Remember not to place too much strain on any muscles (especially your abdominals), because the hormones of pregnancy that allow the uterus to expand are also working on your other muscle groups. Stay very well hydrated before, during, and after yoga: Your babies and your muscles will thank you for it.

pilates

Pilates was developed in the early 1900s by Joseph Pilates and was first utilized by dancers seeking a method that would provide muscle strength tempered by suppleness and flexibility. The movements of Pilates were initially designed to be done on a series of machines, but much of the work done in modern Pilates classes is accomplished on a mat under the guidance of an instructor. Pilates technique targets what is called core strength: the muscles that support the abdomen and the back. Under the tutelage of an experienced prenatal Pilates instructor, many of the exercises designed to be done on the back or the stomach can be effectively revised to be performed while lying on one's side.

As with all exercise, discuss your participation in Pilates with your doctor *before* you get underway with any instruction. It is vital when considering Pilates that you work with an instructor who is very knowledgeable about the particular concerns of the effects of exercise on your twin pregnancy. Because Pilates work focuses so effectively on the abdominal muscles, it is possible to overwork and exacerbate a diastasis (the separation of the abdominal muscles discussed earlier). *Some doctors, as well as some Pilates instructors, recommend that women pregnant with twins wait until after they have had their babies to get involved with Pilates training.* Of course, if you are very fit and already well versed in Pilates, and your doctor agrees that it is safe, you may be able to continue—with some modification to your workout—until you are further along in your pregnancy. Even with training, however, your growing belly is going to impact your sense of balance, and in the case of a twin pregnancy, work with a stabilization ball is not recommended until after your babies are born. The following tips should be useful as you consider Pilates as an option:

- If you've never studied Pilates before, get some individualized instruction.
- Work with an instructor who has experience training pregnant women.
- Remember to breathe regularly, and do not hold your breath.
- Move in a controlled fashion, and do not hyperextend any of your joints.
- Work with your instructor to modify your position in order to avoid lying on your back.

Even if Pilates turns out not to be the right exercise for you during pregnancy, you may want to consider it as a part of your post-partum exercise routine.

5

8 to 12 weeks

your developing twins

From eight to twelve weeks, the last month of the embryonic period, your twins still have a remarkable amount of development ongoing within the kidneys, intestines, and extremities. At eight weeks they are about four centimeters long, and by twelve weeks they will have more than doubled to be about nine centimeters long. Each weighs only about one gram at eight weeks but will have grown to twenty grams by the twelfth week. By the end of twelve remarkable weeks, the embryological structure is complete.

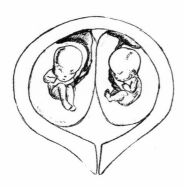

Twins' development at eight to twelve weeks.

your pregnant body

You may continue to notice changes in your appetite that make all those pickles-and-ice-cream jokes seem to make a little more sense. One of my patients pregnant with twins, who had been experiencing acute morning sickness since her pregnancy began, woke up one morning during her twelfth week and announced to her husband that she felt

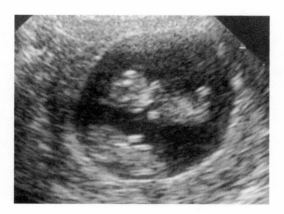

Ultrasound image of twins at eight to twelve weeks.

great, but was starving for a nice, big bowl of spinach and a glass of root beer! Just like that, weeks of nausea had become a thing of the past and she had entered the wonderful world of food cravings. Food cravings are probably your body's intuitive attempt to obtain some substance in which it is deficient. It is a good bet that a woman craving spinach is hungry for the iron it will supply. As for the root beer, maybe it was the sugar, or maybe she just liked root beer.

Mild anemia is not uncommon during any pregnancy. The woman pregnant with twins is certainly at increased risk of anemia, since her blood volume is way up while her red-cell production is down. Don't be surprised if, along with the spinach, you find yourself ordering up a steak or some other iron-rich food.

Change in sexual desire is a variable response to pregnancy. More women than not report a decrease in libido during the first trimester, which may be a secondary response to nausea, breast discomfort, and the increased pressure on the bladder at this time. But once the first trimester passes, that may all change. If you were to survey one hundred women it would be reasonable to find a third for whom desire is increased, a third for whom it has diminished, and a third with no noticeable change. Many practitioners report great concern from their patients' husbands about causing their wives discomfort or "hurting the babies" during sex. Men should be reassured that sex is perfectly safe during a twin or any pregnancy. Time of day may play a role in a woman's desire, and there may be a need for increased lubrication because of the tendency for pregnant women

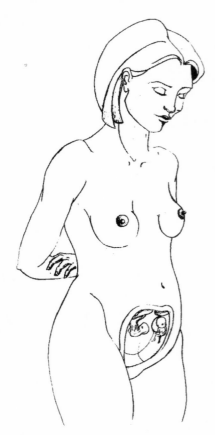

Your pregnant body at eight to twelve weeks

to be somewhat dehydrated. Sexual activity should be guided by both partners' comfort. This is a time to really communicate and get creative.

Changes to the complexion during pregnancy can be very obvious. The glow of pregnancy is a very real phenomenon. This time, that increase in blood volume has a lovely cosmetic payoff. Additional blood pumped nearer the surface of the skin creates a real look of radiance. Pay attention to caring for your skin. Pregnant women are more sensitive to sunburn, so do apply a moisturizing sunscreen to your face each morning, and use common sense along with a sunscreen when exposed to the sun at the beach or pool, or during any outdoor recreation. This increased blood flow to the skin is likely to make you particularly sensitive to skin products, so go with what has worked for you in the past. This is not the time to try a new line of skin-care products or makeup.

All pregnant women have an increase in their blood volume during pregnancy, and some swelling of the gums is a natural consequence of this. Bleeding gums, particularly after a trip to the dentist for a cleaning, should not alarm you. Be extra gentle when brushing and flossing your teeth.

Stretch marks are a natural and sometimes unavoidable consequence of skin that is doing its job to capacity. They are simply the telltale evidence of the collagen in your skin separating as your uterus expands or as your breasts enlarge. Good lifelong nutrition may be a factor in limiting a tendency toward stretch marks. We also know that the more pigment in your skin, the less obvious your stretch marks will be. It is best to develop an accepting philosophy toward stretch marks because while they will fade, sometimes becoming barely noticeable after pregnancy, no amount of oil, vitamin-E cream, massage, or exotic lotion is going to make them disappear.

symptoms that may be ongoing

breast tenderness
breathlessness
constipation
fatigue
frequent urination
increase or decrease in saliva
increased heart rate
leakage from nipples
morning sickness
nasal stuffiness

the checkup

discussing your pregnancy

If you have any questions that you forgot to ask at your last checkup, or that have come up in the interim, now is the perfect time to bring them up with your practitioner. Your successful participation in this partnership depends upon your being well informed every step of the way. We are used to hearing a twin pregnancy described as "high risk," but much of the time twin pregnancies are more about a high level of alertness and involvement. Practitioners nationwide concur that consistent participation from husbands who join their wives at most, if not all, office visits seems to have a wonderfully bonding effect on couples that are about to become the parents of twins. A twin pregnancy can be a very humbling experience to the husband or wife who is a take-charge kind of person. Suddenly, there are two tiny beings whose needs take precedence over pretty much everything else, and the couple who thought they had it all figured out may find themselves back at square one.

This is the time to review with your practitioner your family's genetic history, include inherited disorders such as:

- hemophilia
- muscular dystrophy
- cystic fibrosis
- sickle-cell anemia
- Tay-Sachs/Gaucher's disease
- Huntington's chorea
- thalassemia
- other devastating genetic illnesses

These are inheritable disorders that you might choose to investigate if they are known to be a part of your family history. In the absence of any history, they are unlikely to affect your twins or any other pregnancy you may have in the future. There is one very important question expectant parents must ask themselves before screening for genetic defects in their twins: Is this information that they care to know about their pregnancy? It is important to recognize that the question is not only about whether or not you would terminate the pregnancy based on the results. Some couples are certain from the outset that termination of a pregnancy is not an option they are willing to consider. Nevertheless, they may feel that screening information will help them to be better prepared psychologically, mentally, and practically for the birth of their babies. Others make the considered decision that screening information is nothing that they will find useful in preparing for the birth of their children. Couples, and indeed individuals within each couple, have very personal responses to results that indicate the likelihood of a genetic disorder. This is a very private decision and is not to be made by your practitioner, health insurance company, or anyone else but you.

the physical exam

- assessment of weight gain
- check blood pressure, pulse, and respiratory rate
- check heart and lungs
- breast exam
- external palpation of the uterus

- measure height of uterus
- check for fetal heartbeats
- urine screens for blood, sugar, and bacteria
- ultrasound assessment

At this checkup, you may be offered a screening test, sometimes called a nuchal fold scan, that uses ultrasound to measure the length of each of your developing babies, as well as the thickness of the skin fold at the base of each baby's neck. This test, which is performed at approximately eleven to thirteen weeks' gestation, can help your health-care provider to assess each of your babies' risk for Down syndrome as well as trisomy 18, a very severe chromosomal abnormality that is likely to result in miscarriage or very limited life expectancy for a newborn. The nuchal fold measurement, along with the baby's gestational age and the mother's weight and age, are entered into a formula that is calculated to determine the statistical risk of a chromosomal problem. An additional diagnostic test for Down syndrome that measures the presence of two proteins in the mother's bloodstream—pregnancy-associated plasma protein-A (PAPP-A) and estriol—may also be offered at this time. The combination of these tests seems to provide the most efficient and accurate diagnostic opportunity. It is important to remember that these screening tests are not meant to offer a definitive diagnosis. But they are painless and nonintrusive, provide no risk to mother or babies, and can help a mother and her doctor decide if additional, more definitive diagnostic testing, such as chorionic villus sampling (CVS) at ten to twelve weeks or amniocentesis at fifteen to eighteen weeks, may be appropriate.

dr. agnew on the nuchal fold scan

"The nuchal fold scan is thought to be approximately 90 percent sensitive, which means that nine times out of ten, the scan is able to make an accurate assessment as to whether additional testing is recommended. It does not mean that a chromosomal anomaly is present in each of those cases. When I describe the nuchal fold scan to patients I try to make it very clear that it is not a substitute for chorionic villus sampling (CVS), or an amniocentesis. Instead, it is a very useful tool to help us figure out who might be a candidate for those more definitive screening tests. Sometimes the decision is very straightforward: we know that family history, past pregnancy history, and maternal age are factors in assessing risk for chromosomal abnormality. But let's consider the thirty-year-old patient who is pregnant for the first time, and has no family history. A thirty-year-old woman is not typically offered amniocentesis, yet we know there is a very limited risk that even at her relatively young maternal age, she could have a baby with Down syndrome. By having this noninvasive screening, we are able to assess her risk, and discuss moving on to more definitive testing if the results indicate a possible problem."

If you and your doctor feel it is warranted, an appointment for chorionic villus sampling (CVS) can be arranged at this checkup. It is used to detect fetal genetic abnormalities including chromosome disorders such as Down syndrome or trisomy 18, and single-gene defects such as sickle cell anemia. This diagnostic test is offered earlier than amniocentesis, which we'll discuss in a later chapter. It is accomplished by inserting a catheter through the cervix (or rarely, through the abdominal wall) and into the placenta between the lining of the uterus and the chorion (which is destined to become the fetal side of the placenta).

A sample of the villi, the tiny projections lining the chorion, is retrieved and are cultured at the laboratory; this sample is considered a reliable source in evaluating the chromosomes of the fetus. The test is repeated for each fetus. In the case of a single placenta, you cannot assume the results are accurate for both fetuses. If there are separate gestational sacs, amniocentesis can be performed on both sacs at a later date to provide more definitive results. The procedure is frequently done in the tenth to twelfth week of pregnancy, and the results are usually available in less than seven days. The risk of miscarriage from CVS is thought to be about one in one hundred, whereas the risk of miscarriage from amniocentesis appears to be between one in two hundred to three hundred.

transitions

don't be a heroine

One of the first things you will need to think about is decreasing your expectations of yourself. Forget about your coworker who came into the office until the day her water broke, took two months off (but continued to work at home), and returned to post third-quarter sales that were higher than anyone else's. That is not going to be you. Get in the habit of delegating more and more physical activity to other people who really will be eager to help. Your fatigue from being pregnant with twins may very well be twice that of the singleton mom, especially in the first and last trimesters of your pregnancy. There is a certain simple logic to a twin pregnancy: You're going to have two babies. It follows that you're going to need to eat more, rest more, gain more weight, and spend more money. But with proper care, and a medical team you're confident in, you shouldn't really have to worry more. Your practitioner has most likely "been there, done that" when it comes to guiding couples through multiple pregnancies. Take advantage of all that wonderful experience. Be sure to talk with your practitioner about the term "high risk." Yes, it is true that multiple pregnancy has a greater risk of developing complications, but overall, women pregnant with twins deliver healthy, beautiful babies. They may deliver a few weeks earlier than their singleton pals, but the odds are in their favor that they will be fine. Ask questions; communicate with your practitioner.

The impact of ultrasound technology on twin pregnancy is considerable. You will have the extraordinary opportunity to look at two little people and watch their two little hearts beat as you carry them until their delivery. That relatively new privilege of actually seeing the babies seems to have the effect of making the notion of twin birth very real and very vital. Many twin moms who have struggled with symptoms of preterm labor say that the opportunity to see the irrefutable evidence of two babies gave them the strength they needed to move ever closer to a term delivery.

It is not too early for you and your partner to start talking to each other about practical matters:

- Can you cut down on your workload or stop working if necessary?
- What are the financial implications of cutting back on your work time?
- Before one of you drops your insurance coverage to cut down on expenses, are you really sure that is a wise idea?
- Is there someone in your extended family who would be just the right person to help out for the first few months?

You'll generate your own list once you start talking, but even though your babies are just a little bulge in your belly right now, twin pregnancy has a way of catching people by surprise. Start planning early!

making it work for the whole family

If you were to speak with teachers of elementary-school children about what factors outside the classroom seem to have an impact on their students' attitudes and behavior in the classroom, the impending birth and the appearance of a sibling would be right up there in the top five. We will discuss this at some length in the second half of the book, but it warrants some attention well before your twins are born.

The way you discuss the impending birth of your twins will have much to do with the age of your children. For the toddler, an announcement that there are going to be two new babies—especially before there is any visual evidence of their arrival—is likely to be confusing. To tell a two-year-old in January that the babies will come when it is summertime, or when it is hot outside, or when he gets to go in the pool, is not meaningful. Two-year-olds will not understand "next month" or "next year." They are just beginning to comprehend "Snack time is right after *Sesame Street*." What they *will* understand is that the mommy who was taking them to the park every afternoon, playing chase, and tumbling around on the living room floor is not as available for those activities. You can tell them you just know you'll feel more energetic after your first trimester ends, but we all know that won't mean a thing to a pouting two-year-old. This is the time to call upon the resources you've developed or to begin to look for people to help out. The mothers in your play group may be happy to scoop up your daughter for an outing while you get off your feet for a couple of hours. Your usual family outing to the park on Saturday can be just the father and kids while you sleep in. The fact that you can manage to drag yourself out to a birthday party or that you usually make Thanksgiving dinner for twenty-five doesn't mean you should be doing it when your body is working so hard to accommodate your rapidly developing twins.

Your children from ages four through nine are going to be more tuned in to changes in your body and are better equipped to begin to deal with the time element involved in your pregnancy. They, too, would benefit by having some extra support as far as managing their play and recreational time. But if you are just not up to taking your seven-year-old Rollerblading and don't have someone to pitch in, look for a less physically taxing alternative. How would your child like to make his own Play-Doh, or help you make dinner, or illustrate a book for Grandma's birthday? Your own sense of guilt at not performing up to speed can be your worst enemy. As you ponder the impact these two new babies will have on the lives of your other children, you are particularly vulnerable. Many mothers say they feel pressured to work doubly hard to make certain their other children don't feel displaced by the birth of the twins. The management of your time and limited energy are important reality checks, and can set the standard for how you choose to cope with many of the difficult decisions that will arise after your twins are born.

Once children hit the double digits, their social lives can be vitally important to them. They are more likely to be concerned with your availability as a chauffeur than your skill at in-line skating. But don't be fooled by a seemingly laissez-faire attitude about the impending births. Your teenagers also have a range of issues to deal with. One mom of twins said of her fourteen-year-old son, "He was so mortified by the very obvious evidence that my husband and I were 'doing it' that the double consequence of our actions assumed a secondary role. He was actually very relieved, and became super active as a big brother, after the twins were born." Encourage your older children to talk to you about what they may be thinking. Putting aside the bluster and independence that are completely appropriate to the teenage years, your children still need to know that you continue to see them as being vital participants in the life of the family. Their needs may have changed, but you are as much their parents as you've always been.

Roundtable Talk

PRESENT AT THE DISCUSSION ARE:
Dr. Connie Agnew
Jill Ganon
Tom & Sarah
Nick & Laura
Joan & David
Robert & Grace
Kate & Matt

TOPICS FOR DISCUSSION ARE:
Choosing a Doctor
Dad's Reaction

JILL: Let's talk about choosing your doctors.

LAURA: I was moving from Pasadena over to the West Side and asked my gyne-cologist to recommend somebody. I wasn't pregnant; in fact I was just mar-ried, but I got pregnant pretty soon. So it turned out that for my very first visit with this new doctor, I was pregnant. He asked me to come back in ten days so he could tell me how far along I was. He did a second ultra-sound and said, "It looks like there's two in there." I said, "Two what?" It's a good thing I was lying down. I think you really need to start researching right away what questions to ask. When you are pregnant with twins they ask you to do a lot of tests, and it doesn't matter if you're twenty-five or fifty. And you need to do a lot of reading and generate questions, because if you're informed, you have more of a say in your own care.

JOAN: Our first big decision came when I had to choose a different obstetrician [OB] because the doctor I'd always seen for checkups had just decided not to deliver babies anymore. And I also had some preexisting medical condi-tions that we knew would make my pregnancy and delivery high risk. So we had to find a doctor who was affiliated with a hospital that had the right level of intensive care unit for the babies. We ended up going with a doctor who came highly recommended for his capabilities in dealing with high risk. That was at Cedars Sinai in Los Angeles, a definite commute from our home in Ventura County. But our local hospital would not have been able to deal with potential complications either in my pregnancy or the babies' birth.

DR. AGNEW: You were fortunate to have that opportunity, because in many rural or suburban areas it might not be an option. When I have patients who are moving to a new area, I usually tell them to call the Labor/Delivery Unit of the local hospital and ask the nurses who they use. That seems to work out well. Generally, if there was a twin pregnancy and everything seemed to be going well from the obstetrician's point of view, everyone might sort of cross their fingers and hope their local hospital could handle things . . . and usually, nature does it just right and things are fine. Twins do have a tendency to come early, but under lots of circumstances it is not early enough to cause a significant problem. Sometimes if the OB has a concern, she'll call in a consultant or maybe send the patient to an urban center for a diagnostic ultrasound. Here in Los Angeles we have the luxury of being close to many Level III nurseries. But the truth is that, while you hope it isn't necessary, many smaller hospitals have excellent emergency medical air transport.

TOM: Our situation as regards choosing a pediatrician was kind of crazy since Sarah gave birth [to triplets, one of whom did not survive] at one hospital and when it was time to really decide about a doctor for the babies, we found that the doctor we wanted had no affiliation there. By the time we committed to him, it felt a little crazy because he had a very different approach than what we'd grown used to even in those first weeks. We started to have second thoughts because we were pretty green and felt concerned that no two doctors seemed to have the same approach. Our kids were born at twenty-eight weeks and were in the hospital for several months. There were a lot of complications. We felt very much at the mercy of whatever we were told. Pretty soon, we realized that the truth was that there were frequently several ways to achieve the same result and just because two doctors don't have the same approach, doesn't mean that one of them is wrong. But it wasn't easy.

JILL: I have a question for the dads. Can you talk a little about your reaction to the news that you were having twins?

NICK: Laura called me at work. I work in television and I was in a screening room with a number of colleagues. I was stunned. I said, "I have twins." Everybody thought I was talking about some idea for a sitcom or something. But as it sunk in I got really excited.

TOM: When I found out we were pregnant with three, Sarah says my face just drained of all color. We had an idea that it was possible. . . . Five weeks after confirmation of the pregnancy we had an ultrasound and there they were—three heartbeats. It was just incredible. I tried to imagine how you'd love three babies. It seemed so overwhelming. After we lost one I still loved him and it seems odd that I ever thought there was a question.

SARAH: But I was thrilled right away. I knew I wanted all three. I really didn't even want to consider having a reduction [a procedure to reduce the number of fetuses], so we decided to take our chances.

MATT: I thought it was great, especially with Kate being a twin. We had kind of put off having children, and now we were having two. I figured, you're already getting up in the middle of the night anyway. . . . And now we are at a time in our lives when we can afford it. We both knew we wanted to work and that good help would be very expensive . . . Okay, incredibly overpriced.

DAVID: I found out by walking into the doctor's consultation room and Joan was just sort of sitting there. The doctor walked in after me and said, "Have you told him?" I knew she was pregnant, so what else was there to know? I was shocked, because for so long we were not going to have children, and suddenly we were having twins. Neither of us had twins in the family. At our first ultrasound they showed up as little, black dots and the doctor said,

"One of these may disappear, but it looks like you have twins now." My shock wore off and I got really excited and didn't want that second dot to disappear. After they were born, I'd walk around the hospital and I felt kind of sorry for the couples with only one baby.

NICK: I think our reaction mirrors that. But then there are those times that you wish you could give all your attention to one of them. But I kind of figure they'll balance things out and they will have a lot of things that singletons won't experience. I think they'll be really good at sharing.

6

12 to 16 weeks

your developing twins

At twelve weeks, each embryo is now considered a fetus. The average weight for the fetus at twelve weeks is about twenty grams. By the beginning of the thirteenth week, each of your twins resembles the familiar tadpole image we have grown accustomed to seeing. Their embryological structural development is pretty much complete. They don't appear to have any obvious organization of movement, but seen through an ultrasound, they will show reflexive motions and move around in the amniotic sac. Between twelve and sixteen weeks, the size of each fetus grows from 20 grams to 120 grams, and they will reach a length of about four inches. At sixteen weeks we can observe water in the stomach, as well as urine in the bladder. This indicates that the fetus is swallowing and the kidneys are beginning to operate. Gastrointestinal function has begun. The production of urine by the fetus contributes to the amniotic fluid, and the fetus—no longer a passive passenger—is beginning to assert some control over its environment.

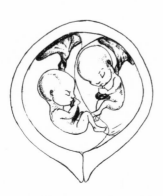

Twins' development at twelve to sixteen weeks

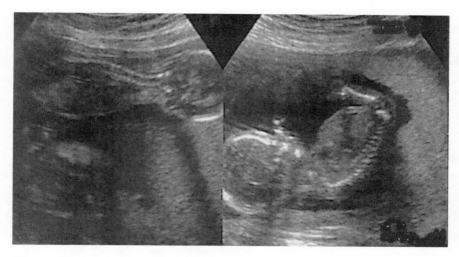

Ultrasound images of twins twelve to sixteen weeks.

your pregnant body

In the majority of pregnancies, nausea has dissipated completely and the pregnant mom is enjoying a hearty appetite. It is not unusual for moms of twins to describe their appetites as "ravenous," and that is fine. Follow the dietary rules that you and your practitioner have discussed, and enjoy knowing that you are providing for your growing babies. You may continue to crave certain foods, and that, too, is fine. But discuss extreme cravings with your practitioner, who might wish to prescribe particular vitamin or mineral supplements as needed.

Vaginal discharge that is white and creamy in texture is very common and is usually a function of estrogen production. Any discharge that is a color other than white, or is associated with any symptom such as itching or burning, should be brought to the immediate attention of your practitioner.

It is not too much of a stretch to imagine that a pregnant woman's need to urinate frequently during the night is another example of Mother Nature's droll humor—putting you in training for your new arrivals. But the end of your first trimester may provide a decrease in your frequency of urination. You still may not sleep through the night, but you won't need to stop several times on the hour-long drive to your in-laws' house.

In addition to waking less, there may be other sleep changes. Some women report increased dreaming, and more vividness to their dreams. Restlessness is the predictable result of a woman who is learning to find comfortable positions for her changing body.

There is an increased likelihood of constipation. Adequate exercise and hydration, along with fiber in the diet, are very important now. Your practitioner may recommend a fiber supplement. At least one bowel movement a day is optimum.

Some women report an increase in headaches. There are several types of headaches, and if you experience severe and/or frequent pain you need to report it to your doctor. It is probably wise to discuss headaches of every type with your practitioner since you should not be taking even an over-the-counter pain reliever without his or her advice and specific consent. As is always the case with regard to using medication in pregnancy, it is vital to your health and the health of your baby that you only use medication—whether it is over-the-counter or by prescription—that is truly necessary to treat your medical condition. We tend to be very busy, and have all grown so accustomed to reaching into the medicine cabinet to treat our ailments that we forget there may be nonmedical remedies available as a first line of defense. Remember, your body is working very hard in the service of your developing babies; if ever there is a time that you deserve a bit of pampering, this is it! A relaxing bath, a soothing compress over your eyes, or a nap in a darkened room may help with headache symptoms.

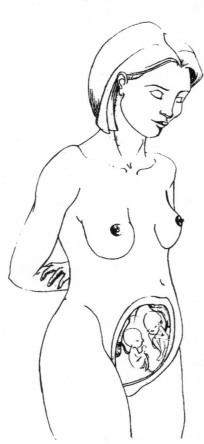

Your pregnant body at twelve to sixteen weeks.

The first medical response to headache should be acetaminophen, commonly known by the brand name Tylenol. But make sure it is just the basic Tylenol product and not one of the remedies with additional ingredients used for colds or allergies.

Migraine headaches are particularly debilitating, and there is speculation that they may be related to hormone production. Some women consistently have migraine headaches at a particular point in their menstrual cycle. There has also been speculation that a rapid decrease in caffeine consumption—a lifestyle choice made by many women upon discovering that they are pregnant—may bring on these painful headaches. If migraines have been an issue in your life, weaning yourself from caffeine in your preconception months could prove helpful.

A migraine headache is caused by a spasming blood vessel within the brain. It can be preceded by a condition called an aura for thirty to sixty minutes. The aura may be as mild as a slight change in vision, or it can be associated with nausea, vomiting, and neuromuscular problems such as numbness on one side of the face, tingling, or loss of sensation. Some migraine sufferers report either expressive or receptive aphasia, meaning they are unable to either articulate or comprehend what they wish to say or what is being said to them. The migraine pain itself can be localized to one side of the head or it can spread across the skull.

Among women who have had migraines prior to pregnancy, a third have them less frequently while pregnant, a third have no change, and a third have an increased incidence of migraines. If you have been diagnosed and have some insight into what may cause your migraines, such as stress, overwork, or a reaction to a particular food, be vigilant about caring for yourself. There are several medications that are very effective and safe for use during pregnancy. Fioricet is a non-narcotic barbiturate sedative that your doctor might prescribe to treat migraines. While the prescription drug sumatriptan, or Imitrex, is very effective in treating migraines in the general population, it is absolutely not recommended for use during pregnancy—*particularly in the first trimester, which is the most critical time for embryologic development*—as we do not yet have enough literature on its use in pregnancy.

pull that trigger

People often think that their migraines are triggered by an allergic reaction to a food or a substance in the environment. But a trigger is not an allergy; it is more like a heightened sensitivity to something you eat, come into contact with in the physical world, or even experience emotionally. And *your* migraine trigger(s) might not cause so much as a tinge of pain in a fellow migraine sufferer. So what are these triggers? When we look at the data, it covers such a broad spectrum that we're likely to ask, *what isn't a trigger?* The key is in determining which of the many possible sensitivities may cause or exacerbate your migraine symptoms. This process of elimination may not be easy, but if you do find out what is contributing to your migraine pain, it is well worth the effort. The following lists are by no means comprehensive but include all the usual suspects:

ENVIRONMENTAL TRIGGERS
air pollution
chemical fumes
fluorescent lighting
glaring lights
secondhand smoke

FOOD TRIGGERS
alcohol
aspartame
caffeine
chocolate
dairy products
fatty foods
MSG (monosodium glutamate)
nuts
sodium nitrite in deli meats
sour cream
yogurt

HORMONAL TRIGGERS
menstruation
oral contraceptives
ovulation

LIFESTYLE TRIGGERS
irregular sleep patterns
physical exertion

sudden intense exercise or physical exertion (sexual activity)
skipped meals

PSYCHOLOGICAL TRIGGERS
anxiety
depression
stress

By this point in your pregnancy, your usual waistline is something to commit to memory as your abdomen expands quite dramatically. This period of expansion comes early to the mom of twins. Loose, comfortable clothing will be your fashion statement for the duration of your pregnancy. Borrow your husband's shirts and maybe even his sweatpants for casual wear. The goofy, tentlike maternity clothes worn by our mothers have been relegated to museums and memory. Manufacturers of maternity wear are designing lovely, tailored, flattering clothing for every imaginable occasion. The price range in women's apparel is reflected in maternity clothes: You can spend a week's salary or find great outfits that are very sensibly priced. Keep in mind that as the mom of multiples, your waist is going to expand much more rapidly than that of the singleton mommy. Before you spend a fortune on a dress for your cousin's wedding, call friends and relatives to see what they might have in the closet.

It may also be time to let Victoria tell her secrets to somebody else for a while. Maternity bras are very important to the twin mom. Though your breast tenderness may have subsided, you're already likely to have noticed a significant increase in breast size. Now is the time to buy the bras that will see you through your pregnancy; wide straps around shoulders and back are very important. Some maternity bras are even usable as nursing bras after the twins are born. You may need to invest in new hosiery as well. Whether or not you are showing any sign of varicose veins in your legs, support hose can be very helpful in keeping up your energy, for walking or for any exercise program.

Swelling of your feet over the course of a day is natural at this point in your pregnancy. The increase of weight in your abdomen has the effect of increasing the curve of your spine. High heels exacerbate that curve, and the result is not good for the long-term health of your back. Fortunately, between the popularity of athletic shoes and increased awareness of women's health issues on the part of shoe manufacturers, it is possible to buy great-looking, nonbinding, low-heeled shoes with adequate support.

symptoms that may be ongoing:

increase or decrease in saliva

food cravings

constipation

breathlessness

change in sexual desire

change in appetite

breast tenderness

heartburn

sensitivity to sun

nasal stuffiness

bleeding gums

anemia

increased heart rate

leakage from nipples

glow of pregnancy

fatigue

stretch marks

the checkup

discussing your pregnancy

Any unusual symptoms should be discussed at this time. Weight gain in a twin pregnancy may really take off at this point. If you have concerns about weight—whether you're gaining too much or too little—bring them up with your practitioner. It is important to remember that it is never appropriate to attempt to lose weight during your pregnancy. Many practitioners encourage their patients carrying twins to pay extra attention to their exercise at this point in the pregnancy. Having your abdominal muscles in good shape throughout your pregnancy will go a long way toward regaining your waistline after the twins are born. If you are not used to exercising regularly, discuss it now and work with your practitioner to develop some moderate exercise goals.

Mood swings consistent with PMS are not unusual at this point. A woman pregnant with triplets told her practitioner that her mood seemed to change according to what aisle of the supermarket she was in. A walk down the baby-needs aisle had her in tears, just looking at the pictures of babies on the diaper boxes. By the time she got to the pasta, she was overcome with resentment that she had to cook dinner for her in-laws that night.

Dads are also likely to have questions at checkups. Any questions are better asked than wondered about.

the physical exam

- assessment of weight gain
- check blood pressure, pulse, and respiratory rate
- check heart and lungs
- breast exam
- external palpation of the uterus
- measure height of fundus
- check for fetal heartbeats
- urine screens for blood, sugar, and bacteria
- ultrasound assessment

Along with your standard physical exam, you may have an ultrasound assessment of the babies at this time. A blood test for hemoglobin may also be performed if there is a suspicion of anemia.

At this checkup, your practitioner may suggest doing the triple marker test, a screening test that tells us if a baby is at risk of chromosomal abnormality. It can be done as early as fifteen weeks (one week before amniocentesis is likely to be considered) and poses no danger to your babies, as it only requires a mother's blood sample. The test has limitations as far as its reliability and is not a substitute for amniocentesis. But it is an inexpensive and noninvasive way to take a first look at women (those who have no family history of genetic abnormalities and/or are under thirty-five) who would not otherwise undergo genetic evaluation. The triple marker measures certain proteins in the mother's blood:

- human chorionic gonadotropin (HCG)
- estriol
- alpha-fetoprotein (AFP)

Elevated levels of AFP may indicate an increased risk for neural tube defects such as anencephaly or spina bifida. We know what normal values are for singleton, twin, or even triplet pregnancies, and many times the elevated triple marker is a practitioner's first sign of a multiple pregnancy that is perfectly healthy. A lower-than-anticipated AFP can alert a practitioner to increased risk for chromosomal defects such as Down syndrome. An initial high reading can be a false positive, or it may be telling you that you are further along in your pregnancy than you thought you were. There is also a quad marker test—an expanded form of the triple marker—that adds a marker to the screening by examining the mother's blood for the presence of a protein called inhibin. It is thought that the addition of this fourth protein facilitates even greater accuracy in the detection of potential Down syndrome. Research into ever-more-exacting biochemical markers is ongoing, and we will continue to see new screening protocols designed to identify patients who may be at increased risk for carrying a fetus with chromosomal disorders. Don't hesitate to speak with your practitioner about a follow-up session with a genetic counselor to help you understand how to assess the results you have in hand and how to proceed with additional testing if appropriate.

transitions

spreading the good news

There is a moment in the life of each couple with a twin pregnancy when they receive their diagnosis for the first time. Whether it comes as a complete surprise or is the confirmed result of fertility treatments, the time will come when your practitioner tells you that you are carrying twins, or maybe even more. It is a moment you are not likely to forget, whether Mom and Dad hear it together or Mom brings the news home to share with an unsuspecting father-to-be. These moments frequently become part of the family lore, to be told again and again to delighted twins, their siblings, and happy grandparents. But it is important to consider carefully when to take that precious information and share it for the first time with anyone outside your exclusive circle of two.

For couples who have experienced the sorrow of miscarrying one or both of their unborn twins, this can be a hard-learned lesson—especially for couples who have endured months, or sometimes years, of in-vitro fertilization! The confirmation of a pregnancy seems like a victory of overwhelming proportions. These couples may feel almost guilty about not sharing the thrilling news with parents, siblings, or close friends who have supported them in their struggle with infertility. But those who have faced the loss of one or both of those embryos to miscarriage will tell you that making that call to tell Grandma to stop knitting, or telling a best friend that you won't be having your babies at the same time, has been terribly difficult. The pain of the loss is unavoidable. The need to relive it and even feel obliged to comfort your loved ones is compelling. There is something to be said for playing it close to the chest when it comes to spreading the word of your joyous event. Wait until at least your twelfth week to share your news. Most practitioners agree that in a twin pregnancy that's more than twelve weeks along, that has two normally growing embryos with normal heart activity, the likelihood of either one miscarrying is less than 5 percent. Remember that the mom of twins will most likely begin to show early—so you can begin to spread the fantastic news just as the world is beginning to suspect you might have something to share!

Roundtable Talk

PRESENT AT THE DISCUSSION ARE:
> Dr. Connie Agnew
> Jill Ganon
> Tom & Sarah
> Nick & Laura
> Joan & David
> Robert & Grace
> Kate & Matt

TOPICS FOR DISCUSSION ARE:
> Parents' Ages
> Traveling with the Twins

JILL: Was your age a significant factor in your decision to get pregnant?

JOAN: It was a real issue for us. I'll be forty in July. I was thirty-nine when the boys were born and I really feel that my energy level, or the lack of it sometimes, has been a factor in handling the twins. And just maintaining your overall health as you get older. It is almost more important than when I was in my twenties. It's not as if we'd been trying for a long time. It was a fairly recent decision, and we'd decided that if I didn't get pregnant the old-fashioned way, we would not take any other measures. We'd been married for twelve years and I'd been a career woman for a long time. Now, as we look at our friends, they either have older kids or no kids at all. It has not been easy to develop a support system.

LAURA: I was twenty-five when the babies were born. We're lucky in that my mom is our primary baby-sitter right now and she is very understanding even when we have to go out on short notice.

NICK: But it took a little educating. At first, everyone would want to come and see the babies and do this or that. . . . But they saw that with two babies, we both always had a baby in our arms and it was impossible to accomplish anything unless they were both sleeping.

TOM: I'm glad we waited, actually. Because I feel like I know more about myself. I wouldn't want to be twenty years old, raising twins, and not even know who I am.

JOAN: Even though the energy isn't there, I hope I have more wisdom and I think I do. I think I'm more patient with just letting them be kids than I would have been when I was younger. If I'd have had children earlier, I'd have been a little more pushy. Now I can let them learn at their own pace. I might have had more energy when I was younger, but I think I'd have been worn out from my own frustration.

NICK: Laura was twenty-five when our boys were born, but she is great. People say to us, "I don't know how you do it with twins," but I wonder how people with triplets survive.

JILL: Dare I ask you about traveling with the twins?

MATT: I fly a lot for my business, and I used to think when people brought babies on planes about when it would be my turn. We had to make a trip with the whole family and treated ourselves to first-class seats. So here we come into first class with all these people who have paid for premium seating and our guys are yelling at each other. . . . It was funny. I thought, this is it . . . this is my revenge. Right after that a couple boarded with triplets! [laughter] Our kids were six months old and they pretty much slept the whole time, and so did the triplets.

KATE: The biggest challenge is finding enough room. You really learn to pack light. My carry-on was the diaper bag. Red-eye flights are good because the babies will hopefully sleep. We each held a baby and switched off every once in a while.

MATT: You learn to book aisle seating. We were finally all seated in a row and they made us move because there are only three oxygen masks. It was ridiculous. Everyone around us offering us seats so we could sit together . . .

JOAN: We discovered the same thing. This was on the trip from hell. A series of canceled flights. Our boys were screaming . . . it was a two-hour flight.

DAVID: When we got back, the airline lost one of the car seats. Here we are at 2 A.M. . . . and we couldn't go anywhere because we didn't have a car seat. Luckily the airline loaned us this dilapidated seat. I'm sure it was unsafe—but it was a car seat. Eventually they found ours.

7

16 to 20 weeks

your developing twins

From week sixteen to week twenty, your twins grow from sixteen to twenty-five centimeters. At twenty weeks, each of your passengers is a little, seven-and-a-half-inch person. There is an increase in movement, and it is usually in this magical month that the mother begins to feel that movement. Now each fetus is almost solely responsible for producing its own amniotic fluid. Prior to this point, the placenta had been doing most of the job. Ultrasound can now clearly detect the membrane between the two babies. It is very thin, but very resilient, as the babies can be observed kicking each other through the membrane with great regularity. It seems logical to conclude that they have knowledge of each other at this time. They cannot yet see or hear, but each fetus has the very typical appearance of a tiny baby. By eighteen weeks, their movements appear very deliberate and far more coordinated. They seem to yawn, and then move their little hands after yawning just the way they will as newborns. With much of the development complete, now is the time that everything re-

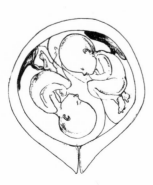

Twins' development at sixteen to twenty weeks.

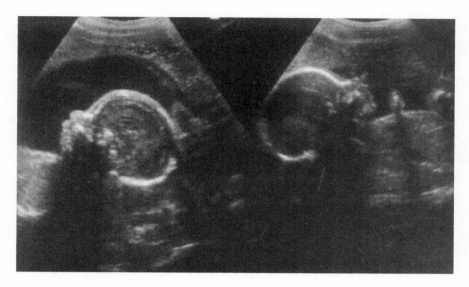

Ultrasound images of twins at sixteen to twenty weeks (the babies' heads are visible in profile).

ally needs to grow. The one structure that will continue its development throughout the pregnancy is the brain. It is this continuing development of the brain that makes it so important for the mother to avoid harmful substances throughout the second and third trimesters of pregnancy.

your pregnant body

There is no longer any doubt in the mind of anyone who looks at you: You are definitely pregnant. The singleton mom might be able to squeeze into her loosest jeans, but you have absolutely made the move to your husband's closet and maternity clothes. Your uterus is substantially larger to accommodate your extra passenger. The singleton mom feels the top of her uterus right at the level of her belly button, but the top of your uterus is at least two or three inches higher, because you have that additional amniotic swimming pool to account for.

Congratulations! You have entered the honeymoon period of pregnancy. Nausea and vomiting are a thing of the past, your appetite is probably great, and you are likely to have more energy than you've felt in months. This is at least in part because your uterus is no longer expanding downward toward your bladder, so you are sleeping a lot better.

The only new symptom likely to be troubling you is round ligament pain. It feels like a sharp pain in a very precise location on one side of your abdomen or the other, typically midway between the hip and navel. It may be brought on by movement or just appear out of the blue. This pain is caused by the stretching of the uterus and the ligaments that support it. It usually resolves within a matter of minutes and requires no additional attention. However, any recurring abdominal pain should be brought to the attention of your practitioner. Unfortunately, pregnant women are not immune from appendicitis or kidney stones, so always play it safe.

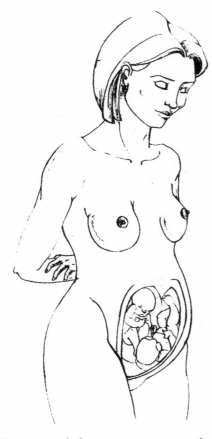

Your pregnant body at sixteen to twenty weeks.

symptoms that may be ongoing:

fatigue

sensitivity to sun

constipation

breathlessness

change in sexual desire

hearty appetite

sleep changes

heartburn

swelling feet

vaginal discharge

spine curving in response
  to heavier abdomen

nasal stuffiness

bleeding gums

anemia

increased heart rate

leakage from nipples

glow of pregnancy

abdomen larger

headaches

stretch marks

decrease in urination

the checkup

discussing your pregnancy

As always, discuss any new symptoms that you've noticed. This is the time to talk about the results of any screening tests that you have had to date. You will be discussing your ultrasound examination, and your practitioner will describe the amniocentesis if it is going to take place at this visit.

dr. agnew on "the little white lie"

"It is not unrealistic to suggest that at the halfway point in your pregnancy, you look to be about six months along. If you get tired of explaining this to friendly strangers in the supermarket, or even other women in your doctor's waiting room, tell them you are six months pregnant! There is no harm in a little white lie if it can save you a conversation you would rather not have for the third time in one day."

the physical exam

- assessment of weight gain
- check blood pressure, pulse, and respiratory rate
- check heart and lungs
- breast exam
- external palpation of the uterus
- measure height of fundus
- check for fetal heartbeats
- urine screens for blood, sugar, and bacteria
- ultrasound assessment

Your practitioner may perform a pelvic exam at this visit. This is an important time to make sure that the size of your uterus is increasing as it should. If you have a history of premature delivery, it is important to assess the length, size, and dilation of your cervix. This can be very important in determining if you are at risk for premature delivery of your twins.

The ultrasound exam that takes place at twenty weeks is probably the most important and visually extraordinary ultrasound of your entire pregnancy. This is the time that the anatomy of the babies can best be established. Each fetus is suspended in a relatively large amount of fluid. The twins are not overlapping each other, as they will be in later weeks. Your practitioner will locate each placenta, making sure there is sufficient amniotic fluid available to each baby. The ultrasound image offers a tremendous amount of information about the structural integrity of each twin. Since it shows the length of the cervix, it can also help to predict prematurity.

You will already have discussed many of the implications of genetic evaluation and had time to think about how you wish to approach it. It is very important to keep in mind that nature has a remarkable record of success when it comes to pregnancy. So how do we assess when, in the absence of family history, genetic evaluation should be used? If we consider Down syndrome, we know that it occurs with increasing frequency as mothers get older. A twenty-year-old woman has a one-in-two-thousand chance that her pregnancy will be complicated by a chromosomal abnormality. At thirty-five, the incidence is one in two hundred. By the time a woman is forty, there is a one-in-forty chance, and that increases to one in twelve for the forty-five-year-old mother-to-be. Clearly the odds increase as a woman ages. But what do those numbers actually mean? Let's consider the thirty-five-year-old with the one-in-two hundred chance: That means out of one hundred women, she has a one-half percent chance of her baby having the chromosomal abnormality that would cause Down syndrome. So the odds are 99.5 percent in her favor for a healthy baby. (See appendix C, "Midtrimester Risk for Chromosome Abnormalities.")

Genetic amniocentesis is typically performed between sixteen and twenty weeks on patients for whom it is recommended due to their age (thirty-five or older), family history, or an abnormal serum screening. The procedure is guided by an ultrasound image that locates each fetus and placenta before a thin, hollow needle is inserted through the abdomen and uterus and amniotic fluid is withdrawn from the sac. The fetal cells floating in that fluid are cultured, and chromosomal results are available within ten to fourteen days.

The risk of miscarriage from amniocentesis is less than one-half percent. Reactions to the procedure can include mild, menstrual-like cramping, and in some cases there may be a little vaginal bleeding or leaking of amniotic fluid. Report all symptoms to your practitioner.

dr. agnew on risk to twins
as a result of amniocentesis

"Patients with twins should be reassured that the incidence of miscarriage has nothing to do with the number of times a needle is placed into the gestational sac; therefore there is no increased rate of miscarriage for a multiple amniocentesis procedure."

dr. agnew on structural defects
unique to twins

"In a twin pregnancy that occupies only one gestational sac (this is the rarest form of monozygotic or identical twinning), the babies have a higher-than-average risk of birth defect. These defects can range from mild to very serious.

Twins (whether they are identical or fraternal) who occupy separate sacs are at no higher risk than any singleton birth. Twins in separate gestational sacs can be at risk of a lack of concordance, or an uneven distribution of nutrition from the placenta. The structural evaluation at twenty weeks is a vital tool in making sure the babies are tracking normally as regards their size. Most of these twins are fraternal, and though one may take after the 6'4" father and the other one, the 5'2" mother, that genetic aspect of growth has not yet entered the picture and both kids should be around the same size. When I estimate the weight of the twins, I look for them to be within 20 percent of each other's weight."

transitions

now you're (at least) halfway there

As you cross the threshold of the first half of your pregnancy, the undeniable physical implications grow very real. Singleton parents have the luxury of time on their side, but the likelihood of a somewhat early delivery is high for you. You will find it reassuring to discuss your various birthing options with your practitioner earlier than might be necessary for the couple expecting one baby. You'll want to discuss each of the scenarios that might apply to your birth. Find out about the labor and delivery capabilities in the facility you and your practitioner anticipate will be the likely place for the birth of your babies. What if your practitioner anticipates complications? Is there a different facility that would better suit your needs? Is it possible to arrange for you to deliver there? What is the protocol if your obstetrician is not available to attend your birth? Can you arrange to meet the OB who would be attending?

This is a good time to look into prepared childbirth classes. Certainly it is not prudent for the couple expecting twins to wait for the twenty-fourth week that is frequently recommended to parents expecting a singleton birth. The number of classes in a complete program can range from four to ten or more. Try to schedule to start around the twentieth week, just in case you need to be on bed rest some weeks before you deliver.

If you find a great program, these classes are terrific for moms, dads, and anyone who is acting as a birth coach. Even mothers who have already had babies will benefit. There is always more to learn, and these classes can provide their own little support groups for pregnant couples. If you have the opportunity to attend a class that provides a lot of information to parents of multiples, so much the better. There are several basic questions to ask a potential childbirth educator that may help you to refine your search for the class that is right for you and your partner:

- Are you certified by a national organization, and if so, which one?
- Can you tell me about your training in childbirth education?
- What, if any, experience do you have with multiple pregnancy?
- Can you describe your approach to pain relief and pain relief medication?

Once you have an overarching idea of a childbirth educator's approach, you are better equipped to zero in on the class that is right for you. Whether it uses Bradley, Lamaze, or some other method, these classes have three basic premises:

• *Educate the Family*

An understanding of the basic anatomy of mother and babies is a very important part of becoming comfortable with pregnancy, the mechanics of labor, and the process of delivery, whether it is vaginal or by cesarean section.

• *Offer Useful Techniques for Relaxing and Focusing*

Relaxation techniques help a laboring woman to focus her efforts on the birthing process. Establishing a pattern of calm, direct breathing is an effective way to manage pain and have a positive impact on muscular control. The techniques learned in this class carry through to stressful situations throughout life and can provide insight into lifelong stress management.

• *Foster the Relationship Between Mother and Birth Coach*

Whether the birth coach is your mate, another family member, or a close friend, you are entering into an agreement to share one of the most significant experiences either of you is likely to have. The remarkable spirit of cooperation and tolerance that develops can reveal to both partners aspects of themselves and each other that they had never before recognized. The process itself helps to decrease anxiety about the impending birth.

It can be helpful to speak with friends about the classes they have attended, but remember, they may not have needed the skills of a teacher who has had experience with twins. Make a call to the local twins club for references, or call Labor and Delivery at your hospital and ask for recommendations on childbirth preparation classes. Make sure the teacher is somewhat comfortable talking about aspects of twin birth and will not find your questions a diversion from what he or she is used to teaching. If you don't find a class that has other multiple-birth parents enrolled, you may still want to take the class and save some of your questions for your practitioner or the nurses at Labor and Delivery who are specially trained to handle twin births.

If you find that two weeks into your ten-week class you are placed on bed rest, inquire about private instructors who may be available to come to your home. Many hospitals have videos that offer excellent instruction in labor, childbirth, and newborn care as well. (See the Resource Guide at the back of this book for several options in childbirth education.)

dr. agnew on airplane travel
during pregnancy

"As far as flying during pregnancy is concerned, I think it is wise to stay off airplanes after twenty weeks. There are several concerns about airplane travel. It can be stressful due to business or time constraints. The best-laid plans can go awry and you can find yourself needing to haul around heavy luggage. Don't do it! Leave plenty of extra time for connecting flights and be certain that there is someone to handle your bags from beginning to end—that includes lugging them out of the trunk! Take bottled water with you, and once you're on the flight, be sure to drink plenty of it. There is no question that one gets dehydrated on a plane, most likely due to the air filtration system. On long flights, get up and walk around at least every two hours to enhance the circulation in your lower extremities. It is also a good idea to carry a copy of your medical records with you. Chances are good that you won't need them, but for the woman who has a medical emergency away from home, those records will be invaluable. Try to get the name of a practitioner wherever it is that you'll be. Just because you can't see your own doctor doesn't mean you should wait if you have any symptoms that worry you.

It is not unusual for my patients to come to me with concerns about radiation exposure during airline flights. The American College of Obstetricians and Gynecologists has stated, '. . . physicians can assure pregnant women who are concerned about radiation risks during flight that during casual travel under *normal* solar conditions the radiation risk to the fetus is negligible.' Since abnormal solar conditions called *solar particle events* can increase radiation, the U.S. Federal Aviation Administration has introduced an alert system that redirects flights to altitudes that are not impacted by unusual solar activity. As a result, radiation exposure to pregnant women is successfully restricted. For frequent fliers interested in calculating their per-trip radiation dose, software is available from the FAA. (See the Resource Guide at the back of this book under Travel.) The bottom line is that I tell my patients, especially those with multiple pregnancies, that after twenty weeks I don't like them to be more than sixty miles from home."

Roundtable Talk

PRESENT AT THE DISCUSSION ARE:

Dr. Connie Agnew

Dr. Alan Klein

Jill Ganon

Tom & Sarah

Joan & David

Robert & Grace

Kate

TOPICS FOR DISCUSSION ARE:

The Impact on the Family of Having Twins

Selective Reduction

DR. KLEIN: We haven't yet really touched on things like how and what and when you tell your extended family about your pregnancy, or relating to the babies after they are born. Many people have preconceived ideas about family. For women, these ideas may start as early as puberty. I don't really know how or when men start to really feel the import of the babies' births.

DAVID: I didn't do much visualizing about family life until it was upon me.

JOAN: When I look back on it, I think I always had a sense that children were an option for me. When we got married we talked about it but it was very noncommittal for both of us. Sort of maybe, maybe not . . . We were married for twelve years before the babies were born. And on a very personal note, my father was ill for nine years after cardiac arrest . . . very brain damaged. This was right before we married and for several years after. It was like caring for a very needy child. After he died I was not capable of caring for anyone else for some time. But after the earthquake [the Northridge, California, quake of 1994] I began to feel that life was short. I had very demanding work that I enjoyed. I'd gotten my master's degree, but something was missing. So I sort of started a time of transition.

DAVID: I didn't feel any transition time. It was sort of, wham . . . I'm the father of twins. And Joan's pregnancy was pretty rough on both of us. I don't feel like I did a lot of thinking . . .

ROBERT: We tried for a long time to get pregnant. So we were very, very excited about the babies.

GRACE: We had a miscarriage a year and a half before the babies were born. We were using fertility drugs, but it took us three and a half years to get pregnant again.

ROBERT: We were very cautious about telling people. It was very intense. First our amnio came back saying they were girls, and then we saw penises on the ultrasound. It was terrifying, but it turned out after another amnio that it was fine . . . that we had boys. We were bursting with excitement, but we kept quiet because the hardest thing we'd ever done was telling everybody after the miscarriage.

DR. AGNEW: It must have been that your blood cells were present in overwhelming numbers in the amniotic fluid and when they were cultured, you got a false reading of females.

ROBERT: I think that's probably what did happen, and at the time our doctor did his best to calm us, but he was very thorough about explaining all the possibilities.

GRACE: He was wonderful. He answered all our questions patiently and completely. Robert always asks for the worst-case scenario, and our doctor was used to it. He couldn't have done more. Through every stage, we were just terrified. Happy, but very nervous. Robert was with me every step of the way. At every appointment . . . he had his list of questions. We'd jot things down whenever we thought of it.

ROBERT: We felt constant fear mixed with excitement. We were kind of superstitious and had a sense that multiple pregnancy carried its own set of risks. We really talked about our marriage. We did not want to lose what we had.

So we kind of said, "This is what we'll do and this is how we'll handle things." But what looks good on paper is a lot of work to stick to in reality.

JOAN: I didn't say anything at work until I was starting to show. When I started to tell people I began to feel more excited. I had a great relationship with my OB, and that really helped.

KATE: I don't know if Matt would agree with this [Matt missed this discussion], but we were married for twelve years before the babies and I think Matt wanted children way before I was ready. I was kind of selfish. I liked my life the way it was. I didn't want to get fat and dumpy and the whole bit . . . but it reached a point where you realize you have all this stuff. A great job, lots of freedom, and so what? It's boring. So Matt was very gung ho when we found out it was twins. And being a twin, I really wanted twins and really wanted boys and sure enough . . . two boys. And Matt also had long lists of questions.

TOM: I always wanted kids, but I never dreamed about twins. We were married seven years before the babies were born, though we'd started trying right away.

SARAH: I knew there was a problem, so we started fertility counseling. We tried for years and years, but we gave up and decided to adopt. But we ended up trying one other fertility clinic and were pregnant within a month. I am very superstitious, so we didn't tell anyone until I was over three months. I was terrified we'd lose them because they were multiples.

TOM: And we were encouraged to consider reduction because we had three.

JILL: What exactly is a reduction?

DR. AGNEW: Selective reduction is used to decrease a pregnancy number. Usually the circumstances are such that a patient has a multiple-order pregnancy and wants to reduce risk in that pregnancy. In an age where there are magnificent advances in infertility, multiples in the orders of three, four, and five are more common than they used to be. If, after counseling about the risks of prematurity, a patient desires to decrease that risk, it is thought that if one stops the heart of a fetus, depending on the stage, the remaining fetuses will be less prone to prematurity and other problems. It is clearly something that should be the patients' decision.

DR. KLEIN: There may also be an element of personal ethics here in what a physician is or is not comfortable doing.

JILL: Might a reduction go from four to two?

DR. AGNEW: No, usually a reduction is done to accomplish either a twin or triplet pregnancy. And that is a gray area, because the data shows the risk of a triplet compared to a twin pregnancy is not much greater. But sometimes the reduction is not about risk of prematurity; it is simply that the patient does not want twins. Maybe she has five kids at home. Certainly, the expanded size and other side effects of a higher-multiple pregnancy put the mother at greater risk than twin pregnancy.

TOM: What's done is done. We made the decision not to have a reduction and didn't second-guess it. Though from what we saw on the screen, we thought the third one might vanish on its own. It was smaller. Intellectually at least, we know we did what we thought was right. It does come up between us, but less and less. We did it for the two who are still with us. Sometimes words aren't necessary. It's going to sound crazy, but sometimes when I'm holding one or the other of the babies I see them sort of looking over my shoulder and I swear that the spirit of their brother is around.

DR. KLEIN: Do you still discuss your decision?

TOM: Even though we lost our boy, even with all the pain, there is something very spiritual about it. We feel that though he was only with us for eleven days, we have all gained by having him.

8

20 to 24 weeks

your developing twins

By the twentieth week, each baby weighs at least one pound, and by the twenty-fourth week they'll weigh up to a pound-and-a-half and be approximately one foot long. Your twins are continuing to grow, and there is now a little bit of fat under their skin. They are developing the soft, furry growth of hair (lanugo) over their skin that we tend to see still covering the bodies of twins (and singletons) born prematurely. Your twins are also starting to be covered with a cheesy substance called the vernix caseosa coating, which appears to be produced by the cells of the skin and helps them maintain properly balanced levels of hydration. Now they are in constant contact, kicking and jostling each other for space. Amazingly, the membrane that separates them continues to exhibit great elasticity. Every joint in their little bodies is now flexed. The chin is on the chest, the elbows are tucked at the sides, and the babies' hands are frequently up at their face—like boxers with their guard up. The hips are flexed, bringing the knees up to the chest. Their feet, with ankles crossed, are frequently tucked up under their little rears.

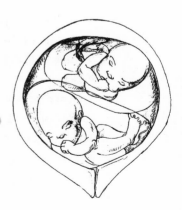

Twins' development at twenty to twenty-four weeks.

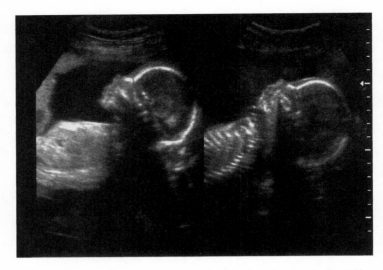

Ultrasound images of twins at twenty weeks. Heads and torsos clearly visible.

This is the classic fetal position. During their periods of wakeful activity (which won't always coincide), their extremities will extend and move around, and then they will resume their fetal positions.

your pregnant body

You should be feeling your twins moving every day. Whether you can tell which baby is which is hard to say. Don't be overly concerned if you feel movement on only one side, because it could be that both sets of legs are stretching out in that direction.

It isn't unusual for pregnancy to cause edema, which is an excessive accumulation of fluid in the connective tissue of your body. This fluid retention, which is exacerbated during twin pregnancy, sometimes results in carpal tunnel syndrome. This is a tingling or numbness in part of the palm and fingers caused by excessive compression of the ulnar, and sometimes the median, nerve within the wrist. Symptoms almost always retreat after delivery. The first course of action is to reduce the underlying edema, through rest and, paradoxically, by drinking lots of water. You can also purchase carpal tunnel wrist guards at any pharmacy, which will provide some relief. In order to decrease swelling in the hands and wrists, try to find a sleep position in which your hands are higher than your heart.

You are more and more likely to notice that you feel warmer than everyone else in the room. Your resting metabolic rate is increased during pregnancy and as a result, you may feel overheated. This is not a fever; it is just the sensation that you want to take off your sweater when everyone else is putting theirs on. If you are perspiring excessively, be sure to drink lots of water to replace the fluids you are losing.

Anyone who has ever been awakened from a sound sleep by a sudden cramping in the calf knows it can be terribly painful. Anyone, man or woman, can experience leg cramps, but the woman pregnant with twins is once again at increased risk. Your two little passengers are very greedy when it comes to getting the minerals that they need for sound nutrition. You may be suffering from a shortage of calcium. You and your practitioner should assess your diet and vitamin supplements to see if there are appropriate changes to be made.

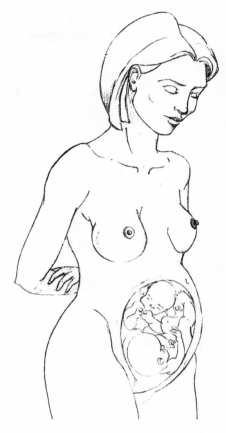

Your pregnant body at twenty to twenty-four weeks.

Treat the cramp by straightening your leg and flexing your ankle to position your foot at a right angle to your leg. You are likely to have awakened your sleeping husband by jerking to attention from the pain. Enlist his help in very gently stroking the long muscle of the calf. You may need to walk the cramp off for the first hour or two of the next day.

symptoms that may be ongoing:

nasal stuffiness

bleeding gums

sensitivity to sun

constipation

anemia

leakage from nipples

glow of pregnancy

abdomen larger

honeymoon of pregnancy

heartburn

swelling feet

stretch marks

spine curving in response to
heavier abdomen

change in sexual desire

hearty appetite

sleep changes

uterus expanding

fatigue

headaches

round ligament pain

vaginal discharge

decrease in urination

the checkup

discussing your pregnancy

Along with discussing any new symptoms you may be experiencing, take the time to review your nutrition and describe your exercise program. Your practitioner may want to see some element of your workout to make sure that it is indeed safe for you to be doing. Make sure you describe any changes to your lifestyle: Are you starting a new job? Have you decided to stop working? Maybe you are moving out of your apartment and into a house. Discuss how much activity is right for you at this time. It is vital that you get enough rest now. You may be feeling great and tending to overdo the physical aspects of your life. Any test results that have not yet been reviewed should be discussed now. Talk at length about the movement of your babies and the areas in which you feel them move. Any unusual change in the patterns of the twins' sleep and wakefulness should be described and discussed. At this time, your practitioner will also review the results of any tests you have not yet discussed.

the physical exam

- assessment of weight gain
- check blood pressure, pulse, and respiratory rate
- check heart and lungs

- breast exam
- external palpation of the uterus
- measure height of fundus
- check for fetal heartbeats
- urine screens for blood, sugar, and bacteria
- ultrasound assessment

Additional elements of the physical examination will depend on whether or not you have any symptoms that require further assessment. Particular attention will be paid to any edema or swelling that is present in your extremities. The results of the ultrasound of the twentieth week will be discussed at this time.

transitions

preterm labor and early delivery

The definition of preterm labor is delivery before thirty-seven weeks' gestation. So theoretically, many twins are delivered preterm. The majority of twins are delivered at thirty-six weeks or more and do just fine. And though many twins who deliver between thirty-four and thirty-six weeks are a little immature, after several days or weeks in the neonatal intensive care unit (NICU) they mature sufficiently to go home without any lasting deleterious effects of their early arrival. We'll discuss early delivery in much greater detail in the pediatric second section of this book. But it is an undeniable fact that twin births occur early with greater frequency than singletons. And since early birth is preceded by preterm labor, it follows that couples preparing for the birth of twins should familiarize themselves with its risk factors:

- *Obstetric History*
If you have had preterm labor in the past, your risk of having it again is high.

- *Multiple Gestation*
The fact that you are carrying more than one baby puts you in a higher risk category.

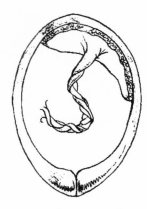

LEFT: *fundal placenta (the most common placement for placental implantation)*

CENTER: *placenta previa (the edge of the placenta covers the cervix)*

RIGHT: *central placenta previa (the bulk of the placenta completely covers the cervix)*

- *Early Symptoms of Preterm Labor*
Any early symptoms will mean that your practitioner will watch you very closely.

- *Incompetent Cervix*
This is a term that the medical community should banish! It means a cervix that is structurally different than most. Or it can be a cervix that is weakened as a result of a surgical procedure.

- *Vaginal Infections*

- *Placenta Previa*
A scenario in which the placenta completely covers the cervix.

- *Placental Abruption*
The placenta separates from the wall of the uterus, causing bleeding.

- *Polyhydramnios or Oligohydramnios*
The presence of too much (*poly*) or too little (*oligo*) amniotic fluid. (*See the discussion of twin-to-twin transfusion syndrome that follows.*)

• *Poor Growth of Either Fetus*

A structural malformation or failure to thrive is associated with preterm labor.

• *Medical Conditions of the Mother*

These can include hypertension, lupus SLE, or longstanding diabetes (as opposed to gestational or mild diabetes).

• *Inadequate Nutrition of the Mother*

• *Exposure to Alcohol, Cigarettes, or Recreational Drugs*

Twin-to-Twin-Transfusion Syndrome

Twin-to-twin transfusion syndrome (TTTS) is a rare condition affecting monochorionic/diamnionic identical twins. Their shared placenta contains some abnormal blood vessels that cause disproportionate blood flow from one of the babies to the other. One twin (the donor) fails to receive enough of the placental blood supply and becomes dehydrated and anemic, while the other twin (the recipient) receives too much fluid and blood supply and experiences an overload to its cardiovascular system. The result is an imbalanced distribution of red blood cells and a difference in size between the babies. These placental abnormalities may take place early in pregnancy, or may not manifest until later on.

Because this is a progressive condition, the earlier the onset of TTTS, the more serious are its implications for the health of the babies. Yet regardless of when in the pregnancy this syndrome occurs, the earlier a diagnosis is made, the better equipped parents and their medical team will be to make follow-up decisions. Before the use of routine ultrasound, there was no way to identify the discrepancy of blood flow associated with TTTS, and at least 90 percent of affected pregnancies resulted in an overwhelmingly poor outcome for both babies. Today, ultrasound is helping us to make an earlier diagnosis, the better to consider treatment options and optimize the babies' outcomes. Ultrasound is able to reveal extra amniotic fluid (polyhydramnios) in one sac and low amniotic fluid

(continued)

(oligohydramnios) in the other—the first warning signs of TTTS. The earliest that a diagnosis is likely to be made is during an ultrasound examination performed between sixteen and twenty weeks' gestation. However, the characteristic discrepancy in blood flow may not present itself until later on.

This is an undeniably serious condition for both the donor and recipient baby, but therapies have been developed that attempt to balance the blood supply to the twins. These treatments include serial amniocentesis, laser therapy, and umbilical cord occlusion. Consultation with a perinatologist will help parents to understand the risks attendant to the various treatments and procedures that may be appropriate to their particular situation. (See the Resource Guide at the back of this book for additional information about TTTS.)

Having identified the things that may contribute to preterm labor, how can you tell if you're experiencing it? The medical texts tell us that preterm labor is the progressive change of cervical effacement and dilation. But these are the symptoms you are likely to recognize:

- a sense of pelvic fullness
- recurrent contractions
- vaginal discharge
- bleeding
- ruptured membranes (you'll feel a rush or a trickle of fluid from your vagina)
- cramping

The fact that you are experiencing symptoms of preterm labor does not necessarily mean you are about to have your babies. First of all, call your practitioner no matter what time of day or night it is if you are concerned that you are experiencing signs of early labor. Next, you will be evaluated as to your general health. A physical exam will be done, and uterine contraction and fetal heart rate monitoring (the non-stress test) will also be evaluated.

At this point, it is likely that your doctor will recommend that you be screened for the presence of fetal fibronectin (fFN). Fetal fibronectin is a protein that serves to help the fetal sac attach to the lining of the uterus. It acts as a sort of naturally occuring glue that is present in the cervical/vaginal secretions of a pregnant woman through approximately the twenty-second week of pregnancy. In a pregnancy that is not threatening a preterm birth, fFN will not be detectible again until the last few weeks before the onset of labor. But the presence of fFN from about the twenty-third to thirty-fourth week of gestation is a strong predictor of preterm labor. A cotton swab will be used to collect a sample of the cervical/vaginal secretions (it's a lot like having your Pap smear done), and results will be available in one to two days. One of the best things about this screening test is that a negative result (fFN is not present) is an excellent and reassuring predictor that you will not go into labor within the next two weeks. A positive result does not necessarily mean your babies are going to be born early, but it certainly establishes the need for additional careful evaluation of your condition. The fetal fibronectin screen is an excellent tool in our efforts to evaluate and manage preterm labor.

An ultrasound evaluation at this time is another reliable indicator of your risk of preterm labor. If your practitioner suggests an ultrasound, it will be evaluated to determine the growth and well-being of the fetuses, as well as to measure the length of your cervix. When measuring the length and appearance of the upper cervical canal, your doctor may use either the term *beaking* or *funneling* to describe whether it appears to be opening too early. When looking at an ultrasound, a V-shape (it looks like a beak) in the upper part of the endocervical canal shows us that the cervix has begun to open. If you think of the cervix as a sort of cylinder, or a turtleneck sweater, the upper part has to open in order to allow the baby's head to emerge. Funneling is a similar occurrence, but it takes place in the lower uterine segment as it opens up and widens, allowing the presenting part of the baby to be lower in the pelvis and closer to the endocervical canal. If your cervical exam is suspicious, your doctor may prescribe decreased activity or even hospitalization for bed rest and evaluation.

If your doctor is concerned, a urine sample will either rule out or confirm the presence of a urinary tract infection. A vaginal culture will be assessed for the presence of bacteria associated with preterm labor. After treating any underlying medical problems, the first line of treatment is usually to administer fluids. Women who are dehydrated have significantly more contractions and are at higher risk of preterm labor. As you receive intravenous (IV) fluid, your medical team will observe how your contraction pattern responds to rehydration. If, after several hours, there is no dilation of the cervix and contractions decrease or stop, you may be sent home, though you might be admitted to the hospital just to err on the side of caution.

If you've gone home, your activity level is likely to be drastically reduced by your practitioner. This may be the first time you hear the term "bed rest." And it means exactly that: remaining horizontal. No cleaning out the closet, no hauling out the boxes of pictures to organize, no rolling a ball on the floor with your toddler. If you are directed to take bed rest, you will get instructions on how it is to be accomplished and you will probably be highly motivated to follow those instructions to the letter.

If symptoms recur, the IV fluids, monitoring, and observation begin once more. If the cervix shows progressive change and the contraction pattern remains high despite hydration and bed rest, you are going to be admitted to the hospital. There are several medications, called tocolytic drugs, that may be used:

- Magnesium sulfate delivered intravenously is considered safe during pregnancy and has the effect of relaxing the uterine muscle, thereby decreasing contractions. Unfortunately, it relaxes your other muscles as well, leaving you feeling rather tired and limp. There is also a sensation of flushing and overheatedness. If this treatment is successful, some practitioners follow up with a form of oral magnesium.

- Terbutaline can also be used to decrease the frequency of uterine contractions. It has the effect of making a patient jittery, and some women experience nausea. Regardless of its peculiarly fidgety effect, it can be used for several hours or several weeks as needed. This drug is contraindicated for a patient with heart problems.

- Indomethacin, administered orally, is one of the non-steroidal anti-inflammatory drugs (NSAIDs) that has been proven helpful in decreasing uterine activity to try to delay the onset of labor for approximately forty-eight hours. There are some concerns regarding side effects to the fetus; however, it appears that when used for no more than forty-eight hours, indomethacin is safe and is useful in decreasing the frequency of uterine contractions.

- Nifedipine is a calcium channel blocker, typically used to treat high blood pressure and heart disease. By blocking the passage of calcium into tissue, it helps to relax the uterine muscles. Its principle side effect is a decrease in blood pressure, so it may not be appropriate for every patient.

- If preterm birth is threatening, a steroid called betamethasone is likely to be administered. This has the effect of enhancing the babies' pulmonary maturity. It stimulates the fetal lungs to start producing the proteins that are critical to lung operation after birth. The use of betamethasone has had a monumentally positive impact on the outcome of babies born too soon. (We'll discuss this later in the book as we examine fetal development.)

What is the prognosis for stopping preterm labor in the mother of twins? Our success is directly proportional to how dilated the mother's cervix is when attempts to stop labor are made:

- The patient who is easily treated in less than twenty-four hours has a better than 50 percent chance of achieving a respite of up to several weeks.
- The woman whose cervix is more than three centimeters dilated, no matter the gestational age, has about a 20 percent chance of holding off delivery for up to forty-eight hours.
- The woman whose membranes rupture early stands a 90 percent chance of delivering within the week.

dr. agnew on symptoms of preterm labor

"While the interventions we've described here can be very helpful in enabling us to prolong labor for a period of time, we have no exceptionally effective treatment to stop preterm labor. The truth is that our most successful means of delaying preterm labor is to identify patients who are at risk, and advise them to make the changes in their lifestyle and activity level that will delay the onset of labor itself. You already know that preterm labor in a prior pregnancy, and/or the fact that you are carrying twins, increases your risk of delivering your babies early. I cannot stress enough how vital it is for you to work closely with your doctor and communicate any symptoms—even if they seem trivial to you at the time—that might herald the onset of preterm labor in the future. Having a healthy, successful twin pregnancy is a team effort and you are definitely the leader of the team."

dr. agnew on taking bed rest seriously

"To the casual reader, the idea of bed rest might sound great. . . . Write a few letters, plow through the teetering pile of books next to your bed, watch a bunch of movies. But it is actually very hard. Most of us are highly functioning individuals, used to accomplishing a lot each day. And bed rest can go on for anywhere from several days to several months. So recognize that you are making a huge investment in your babies. Every day you gain is another day they might not have to be in the neonatal intensive care unit at your hospital."

your very public pregnancy

There is something remarkable about the way people respond to obviously pregnant women: They want to touch them—and frequently they do! Whether an unassuming young woman in the grocery store or a high-powered executive at a board meeting, people seem to see an invisible "please touch" sign on the protruding belly of a pregnant woman. Complete strangers are liable to come up to you and put their hands right on your abdomen. It is a fascinating aspect of our culture. Think about how we tend to walk up to children, even those we don't know, and touch their faces or stroke their hair. It is as though the pregnant belly has broken through the usually inviolate barrier of personal space we all carry with us. Somehow, because you are carrying a child—or in your case, two children—inside you, it is suddenly okay to touch you, too.

Women express a whole range of reactions to this phenomenon—everything from amusement to anger to distaste. It is perfectly appropriate to affect whatever attitude best works for you at this time. If you wish to insulate yourself from unwanted attention, a well-timed remark can do wonders. If another person's fascination with your condition does not feel like a burden, then by all means, let that person experience the thrill of touching your belly—and maybe even getting to feel the babies move.

Unfortunately, this interest in your pregnancy, particularly a twin pregnancy, can bring every weird tale of pregnancy, childbirth, and misinformation out of the woodwork. It is difficult to comprehend why someone would feel the need to burden you with the usually exaggerated and frequently inaccurate saga of her hairdresser's sister's niece who endured some horrifying ordeal giving birth to her babies (twenty years ago). Again, this is the time to excuse yourself, thank her for her interest, and go home to your loving husband and a good comedy on the VCR.

dr. agnew on good intentions gone bad

"I usually tell my patients not to share the details of their pregnancy with casual acquaintances. It just seems to create problems when you mention that you are having this diagnostic test or that genetic screening. . . . I don't know why it happens, but people tell pregnant women scary things. I can't tell you how many times I've heard, 'My secretary told me they had to do her test eight times!' And I say, 'Not in my office.' I constantly reassure women who have been unnecessarily frightened with inaccurate information. Why is it that people don't share stories about nice, easy births? And strange and potentially bad advice is another problem. The one thing I tell all my patients is to remember that however misguided people's information may be, their intentions are usually good. So just try to be patient, listen to what they say, but take it with a grain of salt."

Roundtable Talk

PRESENT AT THE DISCUSSION ARE:
Dr. Connie Agnew
Dr. Alan Klein
Jill Ganon
Tom & Sarah
Joan & David
Robert & Grace
Kate & Matt
Laura & Nick

TOPIC FOR DISCUSSION IS:
Twins Clubs

JILL: Have any of you found it helpful to get involved with a twins club?

LAURA: We came into this knowing nothing. I read everything I could find
about babies in general. But I was the baby of my family and I just didn't
know about handling babies. I thought the twins club was great. The one I
belong to has about ninety members, and there is a once-a-month support
meeting. I was twelve weeks pregnant when I went to my first meeting and
I think it's especially helpful to pregnant women. It is really nice to talk to
women who have been through a twin pregnancy . . . hearing about all
their different experiences.

MATT: Neither Kate nor I have ever been to a twins meeting. My concerns
were more general . . . here's a baby and I don't know what to do with
it. Twin . . . single . . . it didn't matter. This little guy is looking at me
and he wants something and I don't have any idea what it is. We relied
on my brother and his wife for information. Kate's sister and her
husband have two kids, so we had a lot of "part-time doctors" to tell
us what to do.

JOAN: Ours isn't really a couples sort of group. It is more mom's night out or
something. Sometimes there are meetings that are sort of getting together
and doing crafts or something and they lose me there. . . . Actually, when I
first went I didn't feel as welcomed as I'd hoped. I still looked pregnant, my
boys were very young, and I was pretty overwhelmed. It would have meant
a lot for someone to talk to me . . . ask how old my twins were . . . something like that. So I actually stayed away for a couple of months. But then I
thought, no, I need support from people who are also dealing with twins.
So, now I go most of the time and I have bonded with some women in
that group. And sometimes there are good speakers on particular issues.

SARAH: I'm involved with three different twins groups. In the first one I just
didn't really feel like I belonged. So I joined another one at my temple. The

groups are small . . . maybe six families at a time. Most of the people I hook up with have small babies that were born at a pound or two. They are going through the same things we've gone through.

LAURA: Where we live, the original twins club started in 1955, so those moms have kids who might have kids themselves. It is more like a social club. They don't have that immediate need of, "my twins were just born—help me!" So the younger women split off. Originally it was moms with kids under six, but they finally became the twins club they are now and it is great. Most of the kids are between two and four and there is the sense that they have just been where you are.

SARAH: I'm also a member of The Most [Mothers of Super Twins]. So I'm in contact with people all over the United States who have been in my situation . . . have had triplets and lost a baby the same way. I feel like I've made friends all over the country. I stay connected through Internet, letters, pictures. . . . I feel very involved.

TOM: It's great. People pose a lot of questions. I pose my share of questions, too. But it can seem to end up on a little more negative note. When it's informative it can be great. But to be frank with you, by the end of a meeting I'm worn out. It really helps for someone like myself to keep it on a more positive note because the information is wonderful—it's really valuable.

DR. KLEIN: I'm sure that as parents of twins, and Tom and Sarah having had triplets, you feel you are in a unique situation that singleton parents don't relate to. Certainly the twin-specific things like feeding two babies at the same time won't interest them. But parents with one baby can also get a lot out of support groups.

LAURA: I think it's a great resource. You find out that you're not alone and that there are common difficulties and common joys. You meet with people who have "been there, done that" and they offer great perspective. . . . The speakers are really good and there are other resources. I found out about the "Mothers & Twins Notebook" newsletter. There are lots of interesting research studies, articles about development, and other resources. You can find out about cribs, car seats, and things like that. And that helps because you really have to economize with twins. I would tell people never to give up on twins clubs. Continue to go to meetings and take from it what you need.

9

24 to 28 weeks

your developing twins

It is at the magic gestational point of twenty-four weeks that your twins enter the stage of viability. By twenty-eight weeks, with the extraordinary advances that have been made in caring for preterm babies, they have a miraculous 90-percent rate of survival. Your twins are going to double their weight in these four weeks. By twenty-eight weeks, they may be fifteen inches long and will weigh as much as three pounds. The babies are starting to accumulate a more substantial layer of fat and get more pigment in their skin. The hair continues to grow and their facial features grow ever more distinct. It is during this time that your babies' eyelids will become unfused and we can observe them opening and closing their eyes, though the lack of light makes it very unlikely that they are seeing anything. Ultrasound observation shows that their little eyes move just like yours during rapid eye movement (REM) sleep, the stage of sleep associated with dreaming. We know that their brain waves register the four stages of sleep. Your twins are already very individual, with their own cycles of sleep and wakefulness. It

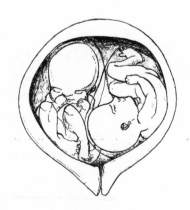

Twins' development at twenty-four to twenty-eight weeks.

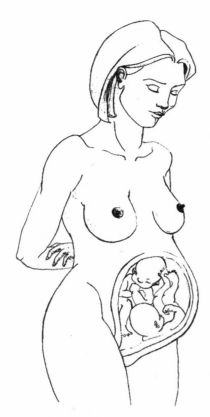

Your pregnant body at twenty-four to twenty-eight weeks.

is fun to speculate that the baby who is more active in utero will turn out to be the more physically active child, but there is not a lot of great observational data on intrauterine/extrauterine behavior. During this month, they begin to respond to sound. Up until now, they may have responded to some vibration in music, for example, but after the twenty-sixth week we believe they are hearing, as we can use sound to wake them. Now is the time to put on the Mozart.

your pregnant body

By twenty-eight weeks, you are likely to feel that the honeymoon is over. You are feeling pretty heavy, and the weight of your pregnancy is starting to really affect your back and your legs. As one mother of twins put it, "The hits just keep on coming." The pressure of your growing uterus can cause backaches. In some cases, the pain or pressure may be relieved when the babies shift position.

As the babies move down into your pelvis, you'll experience pelvic pressure and may also feel increased pressure on your rectum. And your old friend frequent urination is back to stay for the duration of your pregnancy. While you no doubt enjoyed the brief respite, as the twins move a little lower in your pelvis they are back to crowding the bladder.

The frequency of the babies' movement should be about the same, but the intensity of their movement may be perceived differently. Your twins are a little more confined in there, so they can't quite wind up and sock you like they used to.

Women carrying twins can expect to experience a lot more Braxton-Hicks contractions than singleton moms. A Braxton-Hicks contraction is a contraction of the muscle of the uterus. It feels like a menstrual cramp but is usually not painful. The sensation is a tightening in the uterus that some women have described as the baby "balling up." If you feel your belly at this time, it is not pliable or soft but feels hard, like a basketball.

You may notice that a change in position triggers Braxton-Hicks contractions. Many women experience Braxton-Hicks contractions after sex. That is a typical response to orgasm and is perfectly normal, as long as it doesn't continue in a pattern (see the sidebar "Dr. Agnew on Braxton-Hicks Contractions").

This is also a time to be particularly aware of any changes in vaginal discharge. You have probably become accustomed to more white discharge then you experienced pre-pregnancy. Any change in that discharge, especially if it grows more abundant and is associated with mild itching or burning, should be reported to your practitioner. There is a great deal of research to suggest that preterm labor is associated with an ascending infection from the vagina. These infections are are easily diagnosed and treated. The three bacterial infections most commonly associated with increased risk of preterm labor are:

- bacterial vaginosis or Gardnerella vaginalis
- trichomonas vaginalis
- group B beta streptococcus

dr. agnew on braxton-hicks contractions

"The thing that distinguishes Braxton-Hicks contractions from early labor contractions is that there is no pattern to them. A woman may have three in one hour and then have none for four hours. Braxton-Hicks contractions are perfectly normal and the woman pregnant with twins can have as many as three of them in an hour. But if you have four Braxton-Hicks contractions in an hour's time, you need to call your doctor. Pain is not an indicator here. Even if the contractions are pain-free, four in one hour is the magic number."

symptoms that may be ongoing:

nasal stuffiness	sensitivity to sun
bleeding gums	constipation
anemia	increased heart rate
change in sexual desire	leakage from nipples

change in appetite	glow of pregnancy
leg cramps	increase in fetal movement
fatigue	heartburn
overheating	stretch marks
carpal tunnel syndrome	edema

the checkup

discussing your pregnancy

At this point, the frequency of your office visits is likely to be increased from every four weeks to every two weeks. Your practitioner is likely to want to discuss scaling way back on your physical activity. The first thing to look at is your energy level. If you are overly tired, or the growth of the babies is less than what your practitioner wants to see, get ready to drastically modify your workout, give up your evening walk, or stop work if it entails being on your feet. It is time to start delegating, big time. Remember the friends who kept asking if they could do anything? The answer is now an emphatic, "Yes, thank you!" You can keep your brain going at top performance speed, but it is time to invest some energy into taking it easy. And be assured, it sounds a lot easier than it is. In an uncomplicated twin pregnancy, sex can continue to the degree a woman's changing body and a couple's imagination permits. You'll likely be advised that bleeding or contractions following intercourse are serious warning signs of preterm labor. If you've already been admitted to the hospital because of preterm labor, your practitioner is not likely to be enthusiastic about your resuming your sex life until after the babies are born.

the physical exam

- assessment of weight gain
- check blood pressure, pulse, and respiratory rate
- check heart and lungs
- breast exam
- external palpation of the uterus
- measure height of fundus

- check for fetal heartbeats
- urine screens for blood, sugar, and bacteria
- ultrasound assessment

You will be screened for group B streptococcus. If it is present, your delivery team can treat you when labor begins in order to prevent infection of the babies. This checkup may or may not call for a pelvic exam. Even if you are feeling great, your practitioner may want to gauge just where you are as far as the length and feel of your cervix at twenty-four weeks. Then, if you start to develop symptoms of preterm labor, there is a baseline established. If you have any signs of preterm labor, your practitioner may place you on a uterine contraction monitor at this checkup.

transitions

gestational diabetes

If a pregnant woman is going to develop gestational diabetes, it will most likely be identified in the second trimester of pregnancy. The rate is increased with multiples. It occurs when a woman's body fails to properly metabolize fluctuations in blood sugar. Due to the influence of pregnancy hormones, a situation of "insulin resistance" may ensue. Fortunately, it is a condition that frequently responds very well to a carefully monitored diet, though in some cases insulin is also needed. Gestational diabetes will abate after the babies are delivered, but there is a likelihood that it will recur in subsequent pregnancies, particularly if there is a genetic tendency toward diabetes in the family. If you do develop gestational diabetes, your best hedge against developing diabetes in the years to come, or in subsequent pregnancies, is to maintain a healthy weight through exercise and excellent nutrition.

• *Who is most likely to get gestational diabetes?*
Any woman who is pregnant is at risk. Known risk factors include:

- multiple gestation
- obesity

- previous history of gestational diabetes
- previous infant weighing nine pounds or more
- previous unexplained fetal death
- previous infant with congenital anomaly
- one or more family members with diabetes
- mother is over age twenty-five

how is gestational diabetes diagnosed?

Every pregnant woman not already known to have diabetes should have a glucose challenge test between the twenty-fourth and twenty-sixth weeks of pregnancy. A urine test for glucose is inadequate to test for gestational diabetes, so you'll be asked to drink a solution containing fifty grams of glucose (and you thought Coca-Cola was sweet!). One hour later your blood will be tested for its glucose level. A level of 140 ng/dl or less is considered normal. If the level is higher than that, it does not conclusively mean you have diabetes, but you will need a glucose tolerance test. This involves a three-day, specially designed diet that includes a lot of sugar and carbohydrates. Then, after having had no breakfast the day of the test, blood is drawn. You then consume one hundred grams of a very sweet drink and follow up with three more blood tests after one, two, and three hours. The results of these four blood tests will indicate whether a patient has developed gestational diabetes.

● *Are there symptoms that you should be aware of?*
Inordinate thirst and frequent and excessive urination are classic symptoms of this condition and should be brought to your practitioner's immediate attention. You may show elevated glucose in your standard urine test, which would prompt your practitioner to administer the glucose challenge test.

● *Will your babies be affected?*
Identification of the condition, followed by close monitoring and careful treatment, will minimize risk to your babies. Timing is on your side here. Gestational diabetes is not associated with increased risk for birth defects. However,

diabetes that was diagnosed prior to pregnancy is. Your twins will not be born with diabetes, though children born into a family with a history of diabetes are at risk for developing the condition later in life. There is, however, a likelihood of high birthweight due to the babies having been "overfed" on their mom's glucose. Your medical team will monitor you and the babies closely to determine if increased size will be a factor in deciding how your babies should be delivered.

Low blood glucose in either baby can occur as a result of that baby's increased production of insulin in response to its mother's high blood glucose. This can have the effect of excessive insulin production after birth. Again, your medical team will need to be alert to prolonged low blood glucose in the newborn twins and take appropriate steps to control it.

• *Is a weight-loss diet an appropriate response to a diagnosis of gestational diabetes?*

Weight loss is never recommended during pregnancy, but we have identified gestational diabetes as putting a woman at risk of developing diabetes within five to ten years of her pregnancy, particularly if she is overweight. Weight control, exercise, and a carefully developed diet are very important in helping a woman to postpone or completely avoid diabetes in future pregnancies, as well as throughout her life.

• *Does gestational diabetes affect labor and delivery?*

Happily, many women with gestational diabetes are able to carry their babies to term and begin labor naturally. If you have been able to treat your condition during pregnancy without the use of insulin, you will not need to take insulin during labor or delivery.

Gestational diabetes is not necessarily a mandate to perform a cesarean delivery but, if your doctor feels one or both of the babies is too large to labor through the birth canal for a vaginal delivery, a C-section may be appropriate. If you are diagnosed with gestational diabetes, it is important to discuss each of the possible birthing scenarios with your doctor in order to minimize your stress over the unknown.

treating gestational diabetes

The goal of treatment is to maintain blood glucose levels equal to those of a pregnant woman without this condition. Careful attention to diet may keep blood sugar levels in the normal range, effectively managing the problem without resorting to insulin injections. Your doctor may enlist the help of an experienced nutrition specialist who will no doubt pay careful attention to your caloric intake, have you avoid foods that increase blood sugar, and emphasize the use of foods that enhance the body's ability to sustain normal blood sugar levels. Your blood glucose will be carefully managed through the use of meal plans and, where possible, a moderate schedule of regular exercise. An accurate food journal will help you and your medical team to assess your progress. The following nutritional guidelines are recommended:

- Avoid going longer than four to five hours without eating. Eat three meals and three snacks each day.
- Choose water over fruit juices, as juice contains high levels of naturally occurring sugar.
- Fruit-sweetened foods, as well as dried fruits, are to be avoided.
- For breakfast, choose high-fiber, whole-grain cereals or bread with no more than half a cup of milk. Avoid most commercial breakfast cereals.
- Eat a high-protein breakfast that includes eggs, hard cheese, cottage cheese, or lean meats.

Sweets, such as cakes, candies, pastries, pies, and frozen desserts, are obviously high in sugar and should be avoided. But it is important to read labels on all foods and condiments. If sugar, corn syrup, corn sweeteners, honey, molasses, dextrose, fructose, or glucose is one of the first four ingredients, that item should be off your meal plan. The following foods may contain hidden sugars, so be scrupulous in your label reading:

- jams and jellies
- ketchup
- spaghetti sauce

- teriyaki sauce
- honey mustard
- canned fruits

- granola
- baked beans
- nondairy creamer

Remember, weight loss is not an appropriate response to a diagnosis of gestational diabetes. If you are overweight, it is absolutely advisable to control your weight gain by limiting your intake of fats such as oil, butter, margarine, and mayonnaise. Select nonfat or low-fat dairy products and lean meats, skinless poultry, and broiled or poached fish.

dr. agnew on helping to manage gestational diabetes with exercise

"Our bodies are wonderfully responsive to exercise—even moderate exercise done on a consistent basis. Most women who are diagnosed with gestational diabetes during pregnancy are not insulin-deficient, they're insulin-resistant—their cells are not able to utilize the insulin they have. Exercise helps the insulin hormone to grab the sugar molecules in our blood and bind them to a cell so they are no longer floating around in the blood and causing blood sugar levels to be unhealthily high.

A diagnosis of gestational diabetes between weeks twenty-four and twenty-eight of your otherwise uneventful twin pregnancy is not a signal for you to begin a strenuous cardiovascular regimen. But assuming your doctor gives you the go-ahead, a thirty-minute walk at a moderate pace or a comfortable half-hour swim each day will go a long way in helping you to manage your blood sugar."

Roundtable Talk

PRESENT AT THE DISCUSSION ARE:
Dr. Alan Klein
Tom
David
Robert
Matt

TOPICS FOR DISCUSSION ARE:
Fathers on Fathering
Would You Have Another Baby?

DR. KLEIN: Do you all love being dads?

ROBERT: People ask what is fatherhood like, and I say I don't know yet; I know more what mothering is like. My kids aren't old enough for me to be a father . . . or my idea of a father. You know . . . I can't throw a football to them yet. I am more like a second mother. Because of my idea of what a father should be as opposed to a mother, I tend to handle the one that is easier to handle and my wife will deal with the difficulty, whatever it is. I get the one that is doing more, is looking around more. . . . It is sort of more having a relationship and not just nurturing.

MATT: I travel a lot and now I'll do anything to get out of going. Generally speaking, it's not that I didn't love spending time with my wife, but if there was a meeting that had to happen I was there and I just didn't think about it. Now . . . if it can possibly be done without my being there, that is what I'll do. I just want to get home and see the guys.

TOM: I've really worked to be ready to be a father. If you don't know who you are, how can you instill values in a child? I had to look at myself. I'd like to talk to someone who was just thrust into fatherhood to see how they cope.

MATT: I was always more ready to have children than my wife was. And what is really amazing to me was how she has changed. I don't think she could imagine life without the boys.

DR. KLEIN: How have your twins affected your couple relationship?

ROBERT: We try, but it is very hard. In the back of my mind I wasn't sure if she wanted them as much as I did. We talked about how it would affect our relationship. But you don't really know until they are born.

MATT: We were married eleven years before the babies, so we'd gotten a lot out of our systems. Travel and freedom is not a loss. I think it is more traumatic to people who haven't been married so long. I'd rather talk about the babies than discuss our work.

DAVID: Our relationship is totally different, but I think it is better now. We're closer. It was like we were living parallel lives. I had my life and she had hers. Having the boys brought us together.

TOM: After you have your kids there is no such thing as "no shop talk." Our kids are us. Everything we imagined about child-rearing went right out the window as soon as the kids were born. Certain things that I'd always thought were important have changed; career goals and such. It is interesting, since the kids were born, that she is Jewish and I am Christian and we never really examined that together, but now with all the problems our babies have had, we pray together and some spiritual element has drawn us closer. And I remember that before the kids were born we always said we'd never fight in front of our children. Well, that went right out the window. It is new territory. We are not the same people we were.

DR. KLEIN: Do you think it is different having twins than if you'd had a singleton?

ROBERT: I remember before people knew we were expecting twins they said, "Get your sleep now before the baby is born." Now, when it is some ridiculous hour and we are each holding a baby, we think one would have been so easy. You can take turns. Just feed it, burp, and throw it in the crib . . . no big deal.

TOM: It is kind of abstract because these are the first babies for all of us.

MATT: I don't think it would have been that different.

TOM: There are so many factors for us. What if we'd had all three and what if they had all been healthy? I mean, we had three. Two survived but were in the hospital for three months. I remember they told us at the ICU to try and relax and maybe even go away for a weekend. That seemed irresponsible . . . impossible to me.

DR. KLEIN: How about more kids?

ROBERT: I'd love to have more but I'd like them to be twins. It is the only way I know to be a parent. . . . There is so much work at this stage of the game and it all feels worth it for the five minutes of peaceful time with the babies. . . . And the quiet times get longer and the intensity of the work diminishes. I feel like I could do it again. We'd both love it.

DAVID: We were not home a week, when Joan said to me, "You know, I could maybe do this again." You have to understand that she did not have a well day throughout her entire pregnancy. She'd gone through delivering one vaginally and one by C-section. . . . She could barely get up to go to the bathroom. I was astonished.

TOM: If we stop here, that's fine; but if we had more that would be great, too. Either way.

10

28 to 32 Weeks

your developing twins

Your babies will weigh four pounds each by the end of their thirty-second week. Twins are still tracking along quite similarly to singletons at this point. They are thirty-five to forty centimeters in length, and mom is likely to be very familiar with their patterns of movement. They are putting on a lot of fat now. There is continued growth, and the vernix and lanugo are still present. It is during this month that the size of the body begins to grow a little larger in relation to the size of the head, which up until now had been disproportionately large. The organs are operational with the exception of the lungs.

your pregnant body

You will probably notice a somewhat more reliable pattern in the babies' activity now. And it will surely be more difficult to determine who is who. You may notice a new type of movement from the babies that could be described as repetitive or jerky. Your babies may have the hiccups. This is quite normal and will come and go.

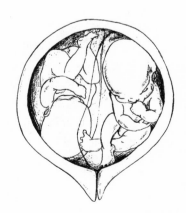

Twins' development at twenty-eight to thirty-two weeks.

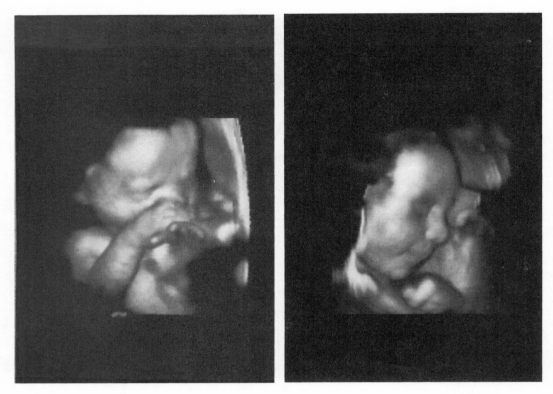

3-D images of two different babies at twenty-eight to twenty-nine weeks. 3-D images are beautiful, but twins are so crowded by the time they reach this size, that it is difficult to obtain effective images.

Fatigue grows ever more pronounced and it is important to listen to what your body is telling you and take naps, or at least get off your feet at regular intervals throughout the day. Try to be conscientious about putting your feet up to minimize swelling in your lower extremities.

Breathlessness may be more pronounced and has to do with your diaphragm accommodating a very large uterus at this point. It is harder to take a deep breath because your diaphragm can't expand downward as effectively as it should. Sitting upright may be your most comfortable position.

You may have difficulty sleeping and will have to struggle to find a comfortable position in bed. By now, you may have filled your bed with pillows, and you may want to buy a full body-size pillow to get you through the night.

You may have more conspicuous backache. Pay attention to any new or unusual pain or aching in your back—it could be a sign of preterm labor. Alert your practitioner if you have any questions. For backache that is not associated with labor, try a nice, warm bath. There is nothing wrong with taking the strain off your abdomen and lower back by sitting in the tub for a long, soothing soak. Several baths a day are not unusual for a woman seeking relief from a constantly aching back. But stay out of the Jacuzzi, which is too hot for you and your babies at this point.

An increase in hemorrhoids is likely to be noticed if you spend long periods of time standing or even sitting upright. Continue to maintain a healthful diet and drink lots of water to alleviate any constipation that could be contributing to hemorrhoids. You may find relief in applying cold packs that are shaped like sanitary napkins to soothe the rectal area. Taking a sitz bath for fifteen or twenty minutes a few times a day is likely to make you more comfortable.

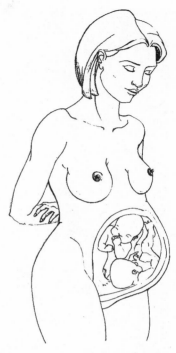

Your pregnant body at twenty-eight to thirty-two weeks.

symptoms that may be ongoing:

nasal stuffiness

bleeding gums

anemia

change in sexual desire

change in appetite

leg cramps

fatigue

overheating

carpal tunnel syndrome

sensitivity to sun

constipation

increased heart rate

leakage from nipples

glow of pregnancy

increase in fetal movement

heartburn

stretch marks

edema

the checkup

discussing your pregnancy

You may have some questions at this time about the positions of your babies and their implications as far as your delivery. This is the time to discuss a frequency in Braxton-Hicks contractions, if you're experiencing them. If you are not on bed rest, your practitioner will want an accurate accounting of how you spend your day in order to assess any need for additional rest. The practitioner may recommend Kegal exercises, which help to firm the pelvic muscles, if you are experiencing any stress incontinence as a result of pressure on your bladder from your increasingly large uterus. If your childbirth preparation classes have raised any unanswered questions, you may find it helpful to bring them up. As always, it is important to discuss any new symptom at your checkup.

dr. agnew on preeclampsia

"During weeks twenty-eight to thirty-two of your pregnancy, you can expect your practitioner to discuss the warning signs of preeclampsia. Preeclampsia affects nearly 25 percent of all pregnancies, and is more common in first pregnancies, multiple pregnancies, and patients with prior hypertension. This uniquely human pregnancy disorder is characterized by hypertension (elevated blood pressure), edema (swelling of the face, hands, and feet), and proteinuria (the presence of protein in your urine). The symptoms to be aware of are:

- changes in your visual field, such as blurriness or dark spots
- headaches
- abdominal pain
- increased swelling of the face, hands, or feet

When preeclampsia is diagnosed prior to term, some prolongation of the pregnancy is possible. For mild forms, bed rest (accompanied by frequent monitoring of the mother's blood pressure and biophysical profiles of both fetuses) is the mainstay of treatment. I really want to stress that bed rest means exactly that! While it may seem like the perfect time to organize your closet or assemble the crib you've bought for the nursery, your job is to plant yourself in that bed and follow your practitioner's instructions to the letter. If you have young children at home, you may be placed in the hospital in order to take every precaution that you'll stay off your feet. This is something that only you (with more than a little help from your friends and family) can do for your babies, and the benefits are very significant. In more severe cases, early delivery may be necessary.

the physical exam

- assessment of weight gain
- check blood pressure, pulse, and respiratory rate
- check heart and lungs
- breast exam
- external palpation of the uterus
- measure height of fundus
- check for fetal heartbeats
- urine screens for blood, sugar, and bacteria
- ultrasound assessment

Your physical exam may include a pelvic examination to determine if there has been any dilation of the cervix. The ultrasound will confirm fetal well-being and make sure that the level of amniotic fluid is normal for both babies. This exam may also include a biophysical profile, which uses the following components to assess fetal well-being:

- the volume of amniotic fluid
- fetal breathing
- the non-stress test
- the rate of fetal movement
- fetal tone

transitions

banked blood—will you need it?

It is very rare that a woman will require any banked blood after vaginal or cesarean delivery, though the risk is a little higher for mothers of twins. The uterus may be so stretched from its need to accommodate two babies, their placentas, and amniotic fluid that it takes a little longer to contract. The mother of twins will continue to lose blood until contraction of the uterus is completed.

Our concerns about contaminated blood products have had the effect of making our blood-banking systems very sophisticated in their abilities to screen blood, but many mothers still prefer to make an autologous donation of their own blood so that it can be at the hospital waiting for them if it is needed. This may not be possible if you are severely anemic, but you can discuss it with your practitioner and with the local blood bank. You can never accept your husband's blood, because mixing it with yours could create complications during future pregnancies.

storing or donating umbilical cord blood

As we discuss whether or not a mother will decide to bank her own blood prior to delivery of her twins, another question arises: whether to store (for potential personal use) or donate (for public use) your twins' umbilical cord blood. We've heard a great deal in recent years about stem cell research. Storing cord blood for future harvesting and transplantation of stem cells is an option that more and more parents are going to consider as this relatively new technology becomes more common throughout the United States. Let's take a moment to answer several basic questions in this discussion.

WHAT IS CORD BLOOD?
It is the blood that remains in the umbilical cord and placenta after your babies are born.

WHAT ARE STEM CELLS?

Stem cells, which are found in cord blood, are the primitive precursor cells from which all cells originate. They hold great promise in the fight against certain diseases because of their capacity to regenerate into other types of cells.

IS THERE A RISK TO COLLECTING CORD BLOOD?

No. Whether your births are vaginal or cesarean, a member of the medical team will collect the appropriate amount of cord blood after the umbilical cord is clamped.

FOR HOW LONG ARE THE UMBILICAL STEM CELLS
OF USE FOR TRANSPLANTATION?

The most successful transplants using human umbilical-cord stem cells are freshly stored samples. Some studies have shown a good response in cord blood use up to ten years after initial storage, but study into the shelf life of umbilical-cord stem cells is ongoing and we do not yet have conclusive results as to their effectiveness in complete marrow reconstitution after prolonged storage.

The scientific and medical communities are excited about our capacity to harvest and store cord blood for future use in combating very serious diseases, and with good reason. Often these are genetic diseases of the blood, such as bone marrow–related anemia or chemotherapy-resistant cancers. Doctors describe the use of cord blood as a "clinically acceptable alternative to bone marrow transplantation (BMT)." This is indeed an extraordinary step forward. In the past, a patient who required a bone marrow transplant had to have a donor who was a human leukocyte antigen (HLA) match. And that meant that the most likely compatible donor would be a sibling, where there is estimated to be a one-in-four chance of suitability. If there was no match among siblings, the chances of a match with any other family member were doubtful at best. The next step would be to search for an unrelated donor through a source such as the National Marrow Donor Program (NMDP). Those searches have limited success—and even where an unrelated HLA match is made, there remains the very high likelihood of a serious condition called graft-versus-host disease (GVHD) developing, in which cells from the donor bone-marrow graft attack the patient and can result in death.

Remarkably, researchers have discovered that cord blood not only is an acceptable alternative to bone marrow transplantation, but it offers several additional benefits:

- There is decreased severity of GVHD.
- There is an increase in transplants among ethnic minorities and people of mixed ethnicity for whom finding a suitable bone-marrow match is a greater challenge.
- Cord blood transplants are less costly than bone morrow transplants.

So what does this mean to you as parents? Certainly, there is a great deal of optimism in the medical community that the use of umbilical cord blood is offering new life to patients who had limited options prior to this technology. But we must also face the ethical challenges that develop in the wake of modern medicine. In the past, the collection and storage of blood and blood products in the United States has been overseen by hospitals. Today, in addition to the possibility of *donating* umbilical cord blood to a cord blood bank available for public use, you may have the option of storing your babies' cord blood with a commercial blood-banking business for your family's personal potential use. Commercial blood-banking ventures are cropping up in cities throughout the United States, but they are by no means available everywhere. And the costs of harvesting, processing, and storage are considerable—judging by reports from several private banks as we write this book, costs for storing both your babies' cord blood today could reach almost six thousand dollars by the time your twins are twenty-one years old. This makes private storage out of the reach of many, if not most, American families.

Of course, we all want to do the very best we can by our children, so let's consider the chances of your family's need for stored cord blood. The data covers quite a range—anywhere from one in 1,000 to one in 200,000. But the overwhelming likelihood is that you have less than a one-in-10,000 chance of utilizing cord blood stem cells for either of your unborn twins. If you are reading this book as you are pregnant with twins, it is probably a time of great joy and hopefulness and not one when you should be overwhelmed by fearfulness. We think the following statement issued by the American College of Obstetricians and Gynecologists speaks to the spirit and intent you bring to your twin pregnancy: "Commercial cord blood banks should not represent the service they sell as 'doing everything possible' to ensure the health of children. Parents and grandparents should not be made to feel guilty if they are not eager or able to invest in these considerable sums in such a highly speculative venture."

When a genetic condition that might be helped by a cord blood transplant runs in a family, or is present in a family member at the time of a baby's birth, cord blood storage might be very appropriate. Conditions such as sickle cell anemia, leukemia, aplastic anemia, or other genetic or metabolic disorders fall within this category. But for the vast majority of families, the chances of needing cord blood are extremely limited.

The philanthropic donation of cord blood, at no cost to the donating family, is also a possibility. When considering donating cord blood, parents may wish to remember that since certain genetic traits are associated with particular races or ethnicities, the broader the range of donors, the richer our national cord blood–banking opportunities will be. The records of donors to cord blood banks are kept confidential, and there is no information exchanged between donor and receiver that identifies one to the other. There are not that many cord blood banks in the United States, but there are more cord blood–collecting hospitals, and there might be one in your area. In the event that your twins' cord blood is stored for donation or personal use, whether fraternal or identical, both babies' samples will be carefully identified and individually stored.

Because the questions surrounding cord blood storage are complex and emotional, it is an issue that is best discussed prior to delivery. Bring it up with your practitioner around the time you might discuss banking your own blood prior to delivery—some time between your twenty-eighth and thirty-second week, as suggested in this chapter. (See the Resource Guide in the back of this book for additional information regarding umbilical cord blood storage.)

Roundtable Talk

PRESENT AT THE DISCUSSION ARE:
Dr. Connie Agnew
Jill Ganon
Tom & Sarah

Nick & Laura
Joan & David
Robert & Grace
Kate & Matt

TOPIC FOR DISCUSSION IS:
Some Pregnancy and Birth Experiences

LAURA: All through the pregnancy we were concerned with what to expect at any given point. I would really advise you to think about things early. We were just starting to look for a pediatrician when I was put on bed rest. So there I was, totally restricted—no driving, no going to interview doctors—when the twins were born on the first day of my thirty-fourth week.

ROBERT: The day the babies were born, after calling to tell family about the birth, I had to call three pediatricians to cancel our interviews. Our babies were born the thirty-fourth week, too. We asked our obstetrician who he took his kids to. We figured if it was good enough for him, it would probably be good enough for us. But I would say that as far as the obstetrician is concerned, find out what the backup plan is, because when the primary isn't there, you can suddenly find yourself in the hands of someone you don't know at all.

JOAN: The doctor I had been seeing for checkups and things had just decided to stop delivering babies. I had some preexisting conditions that made me high risk apart from the twin aspect. We needed to think about the hospital the doctor was affiliated with—making sure it had the right level of NICU in case there were problems with the babies. We live outside Los Angeles, but we chose our doctor here [in Los Angeles] because we didn't know if a local doctor and hospital could handle potential complications. I think it is really important to feel confident in your information. I'm a nurse, and I would say that one thing that disturbed me was that in a lot of the books I read during pregnancy, there seemed to be a real bias about "just say no to drugs during labor and just say no to a C-section." That can be very misleading and even scary for women to read.

JILL: What is the recommendation for women with higher-risk pregnancies if they are in small towns seeing their local OB?

DR. AGNEW: If there is a twin pregnancy that is going along just fine in the obstetrician's view, they might bring in a consultant for a particular issue or maybe some diagnostic ultrasound. Usually the patient will need to travel to the urban area. Most of the time, nature does it just right and the babies are healthy and mom is fine. Twins have a tendency to come early, but many times it is not early enough to cause significant problems. When a patient tells me they are moving to a new town and want to know how to find a doctor, I tell them to call the labor/delivery unit of the local hospital and ask the nurses who they see. You can get terrific information that way.

JILL: Did you feel ready by the time the babies were born?

KATE: I'm a twin and my mom came the day we got out of the hospital. They were able to come home right away and we had nothing done. Through the hospital, we hired one person to come and do house cleaning so I could try to get organized.

TOM: Ours were in the hospital for a long time. They were born at the end of June and first it was, "They'll be home by Christmas." That seemed so far away. A few months later they said, "Maybe Thanksgiving . . ." A few weeks later we took the CPR classes because they said the babies might be coming home in a few weeks. The next day they told us the babies would be going home tomorrow! So after all that waiting, suddenly we were running around, getting cribs and everything. It just got frantic.

LAURA: Even though it was early, my mom suggested that I pack a bag, and the next day my water broke.

NICK: And I was really glad we'd taken those childbirth classes. I didn't want to go but I'm glad I did.

LAURA: We ended up having classes at home, because all the classes were booked and by the time they were available I was on bed rest. Our instructor was great and actually ended up attending the birth. She wanted to be with us.

KATE: I figured they would tell me what I needed to know at the hospital. I was going to have an epidural. . . . I thought, "Drugs are wonderful. Why should I have to learn how to breathe?" I didn't even have a tour of the hospital. I figured, "Don't worry. You walk in the front door, you go to the emergency room, and they send you up to labor and delivery."

MATT: I didn't have any intention of going into the delivery room but our doctor, who I thought was sick of me by now because I asked so many questions, convinced me. I told him that if he could find a surgical outfit that fit, I'd go in. He did, so I did. I was really thinking my presence might be counterproductive in there. I hadn't really thought about those classes. I figured it was the doctor who needed an education and he had gotten it. I just tried to stay out of everyone's way. There were wires everywhere and no escape route. Thank God my wife cooperated, and five minutes later one was being born. They introduced me to my son, and three or four minutes later the other one was coming out.

LAURA: I'll say one thing for the classes—our instructor would fully describe a process and then I'd ask, "But how does that work for twins?" I was afraid it would bore everyone else, but our instructor was great about it.

JILL: Did you realize you needed to look for a class early because you were pregnant with twins?

LAURA: I was neurotic enough that as soon as I got the paperwork from the hospital I started thinking I should get it all ready right away. It wasn't like I was worrying because it was twins, I'm just neurotic . . . When I tried to book a tour they told me they could do it in December. They said wait till you're five months to call. I was at four months and they were already booked. They found a spot for me.

MATT: At thirty-two weeks, Kate started exhibiting signs of premature labor and we got the forty-eight-hour speech. . . . Our OB was always saying the same thing: "Try to get to thirty-six weeks. If you can make it through March I'll be thrilled; I'll take you out to dinner." We didn't expect to make it past thirty-six weeks. Psychologically speaking, we were set for somewhere between thirty-two and thirty-six. She lasted until week thirty-four. The concern was for the babies. We never questioned Kate's safety.

GRACE: Our OB always said twins could deliver at thirty-six weeks as opposed to forty.

11

32 to 36 weeks

your developing twins

For twins, this is an especially remarkable period of development. Weight gain is now a little bit slower than for a singleton. This is the time they are relying on their mother's nutrition to help them put on the final layer of fat that is so important to the early weeks following birth. They will grow from 1,800 to 2,500 grams. Usually, a baby must attain a weight of 2,000 grams before it is discharged from the hospital, so the twins born closer to thirty-two weeks may need to spend some time in the intensive care nursery.

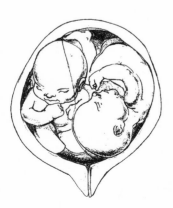

The twins' motor development is now far more sophisticated and less reflexive. This is the point that the lung development surges ahead. The alveolar cells of the lungs begin to produce surfactant and phospholipids. These substances will help the babies' lungs to expand for their first breath. They will also help the babies to exchange gases with the air—dissolving oxygen into the blood and extruding carbon dioxide back into the lungs. The placenta is continuing to function remarkably well, but the twins are having to share a little bit. They are truly cramped now and are

Twins' development at thirty-two to thirty-six weeks.

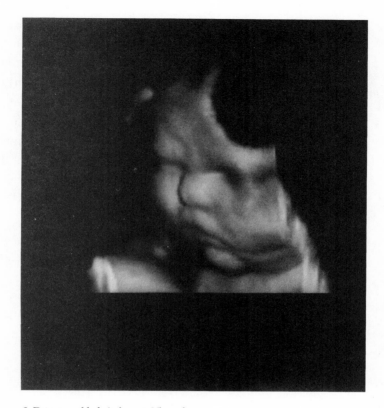

3-D image of baby's face at 35 weeks.

molded against each other. Your practitioner will be carefully monitoring the twins' positions to see if their heads are down. The positions they assume now are not likely to change.

your pregnant body

You may feel as though your hips are actually spreading, and the diameter of the pelvis probably has increased somewhat by this time. The ligaments supporting the pelvis are really stretching now to accommodate the babies as they move ever lower into the pelvic area.

The babies' movement is still as frequent but does not feel as intense, because the cramped quarters restrict it.

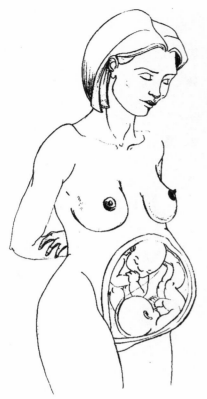

Your pregnant body at thirty-two to thirty-six weeks.

Braxton-Hicks contractions may be very frequent now. Continue to use the same rule of thumb: Any more than four contractions in an hour means you should call your practitioner.

Sleep is difficult due to increased frequency of urination and difficulty finding a comfortable position. The babies still need a lot of fluid, so it is important to keep up your own fluid intake.

Appetite may decrease as a result of your stomach having limited space due to the increasing size of your uterus.

Swelling of your lower extremities may grow more pronounced, so try to get your feet up as much as possible.

You may experience very vivid dreams or find yourself daydreaming with greater frequency about the impact the babies will have on your life.

symptoms that may be ongoing:

backache	nasal stuffiness
sensitivity to sun	bleeding gums
constipation	anemia
breathlessness	increased heart rate
change in sexual desire	leakage from nipples
change in appetite	glow of pregnancy
leg cramps	fatigue
heartburn	overheating
stretch marks	hemorrhoids
carpal tunnel syndrome	edema

transitions

okay, enough is enough

This is the point at which many practitioners report that their patients are starting to beg them to induce labor. No doubt about it, the woman carrying twins is ready to move on to a new role—from temporary shelter to dairy bar! No matter how frequently you've fretted as a couple that you just aren't ready, your body is telling you it has had enough. This is the time to summon all your resources to prepare for birth. That may mean being absolutely faithful to your practitioner's instructions if you are on bed rest, or finishing your research with the local twins club on which is the safest car seat.

Roundtable Talk

PRESENT AT THE DISCUSSION ARE:
Dr. Connie Agnew
Jill Ganon
Tom & Sarah
Nick & Laura
Joan & David
Robert & Grace
Kate & Matt

TOPICS FOR DISCUSSION ARE:
Surviving as a Couple
More Kids?

JILL: How is your intimate relationship now that you have the babies?

NICK: When we do end up with both babies in the bed—everyone sprawled out—we have found a way that I can be here, and Laura can be here [he gestures, creating a diagonal with his hands] and our feet are touching each other. Sometimes that is our intimacy. But these two little guys are the most joyous thing in the world. It's triple the work but it's quadruple the fun. I don't think our relationship has suffered.

LAURA: We joke . . . saying we're on the nine-month plan. We knew each other for nine months before we got engaged, we were engaged for nine months, then we were married for nine months when I got pregnant with twins. They should have been born nine months later, but they were born at seven months. Sometimes you just have to carve out some space to be together. Just say, "The babies are going to the sitter for an hour or two. . . . Let's watch a movie or just rediscover the couple."

NICK: As far as our intimate relationship goes, it's less than before and you don't have as long. It's sort of whenever you have the opportunity, like when they're napping or late at night, if you can keep your eyes open.

JOAN: At the end of a day we just sort of pass out together and say, "Look what we've done. . . ." There's a lot more cuddling [now].

LAURA: I think the key is patience and knowing the twins are going to take a lot of time. You need to understand that you are redefining your relationship. You're a family of four and not a couple of two. You just work with it.

NICK: You can get bogged down on a day-to-day basis, but when we are away from it all or if we're overnight somewhere alone, it's just like old times. It's the most fantastic thing in the world.

ROBERT: It doesn't sound very romantic but I think in a good marriage, you have to make appointments with each other and keep them. If the marriage is strong, it is good for the kids. It's easy to say, but it's much harder to do. Sometimes one says, "I don't want to keep this appointment. I'd rather go to sleep." But if you force yourself to stay with it, you get your second wind. . . . Whatever it takes, its crucial to the marriage and the children.

GRACE: Every two months we try to take off for four days together.

ROBERT: At least we try. In everyday life, everything seems to center around the children. I wonder about the divorce rate for parents of twins. I'm not sure it's separated out from the rate of parents of premature babies. The stress of dealing with prematurity must create a higher divorce rate. My question is, would they have ended up divorcing anyway? Maybe the relationship was too tenuous in the first place.

DR. AGNEW: Coping with prematurity brings out who you are as an individual and as a couple. It is a defining experience. The pressure is so great that you have to see yourself as a unit battling together against a struggle, rather than succumbing to the frustration and inconvenience it causes in the couple relationship. You really have to go into it as a couple and face it together.

JILL: Speaking of together, anyone thinking about more babies?

LAURA: As long as we work it around my ten-year high school reunion. . . . I want to be skinny when I go [laughter].

TOM: Well, kids are great. Our situation is somewhat unique because Sarah is working and I'm home with the kids. I'm a musician and when you're not playing, you're not really yourself. So I am trying to get out a little more now to work at night after Sarah gets home. That means we see less of each other. But you just have to have faith. On some level, you need to get yourself back before you can get back together as a couple. I feel complete with what we have, but if the Lord blessed us with another baby, that would be fine, too. My kids have been through so much, and they are so strong.

SARAH: We're moving next week and we have all their bassinets and stuff. Do we get rid of them? It's up in the air, but I would not do fertility treatment again. If it's meant to happen, it will.

DAVID: I understand what Tom said. When our boys came, we both lost ourselves. A hundred percent of everything went into taking care of our boys. We are now dealing with rediscovering who we are, and finally realizing that as a couple you have to make a very conscious effort to make time together. I think there was a time that Joan felt I didn't care about us as a couple . . . that I was more interested in the boys.

JOAN: It's like Nick said . . . He missed the boys so much, when he came home he just seemed to want to be with them. Now maybe every other week we get out to dinner together and it has been wonderful. Ultimately, I think we've grown closer. But there was a time that I felt we were living parallel lives, not really connecting. We were married twelve years when the babies were born and though we loved each other very much, we both had big jobs that seemed to take us away from each other. But it's funny—there was a time that I didn't think I would have children. Now we have the two boys, two cocker spaniels, not a clear space to put your foot on the floor, and I think, "How much difference would it be with one more?"

DR. AGNEW: At one point I had three kids in three different-size diapers. I'd push my cart up to the cash register and the guy would say, "Oh great— your own little landfill." I had a three-year-old, a toddler, and an infant. I agree with Joan—I didn't see much change going from two to three. Three to four was not planned, and that kind of threw a stick of dynamite into the house. If you do it while the kids are still little I think it's easier than wait- ing . . . and then heaven forbid you have another set of twins. That would be wild.

labor and delivery to postpartum

your developing twins

In twins, the average term weight is a little lower than that of a singleton, 3,200 grams as opposed to 3,400. Twins that get to thirty-seven weeks are considered term. They may attain as much as fifty centimeters in length. During these weeks the lanugo (the soft, downy hairs that develop on a baby's body in utero and that may be observed at birth) starts to disappear. Your babies use this time to continue storing the vital body fat that will help them to maintain their body temperature after birth. Ultrasound assessment of the twins grows increasingly difficult, because they are packed so tightly into the uterus.

labor

In the majority of twin pregnancies, labor will begin before thirty-seven weeks. Nature is telling you that the babies are ready and your uterus has reached its maximum capacity. Over a period of several days there are several signs that may alert you of your impending labor:

• *Increase in Braxton-Hicks Contractions*

You may be lying on the sofa watching David Letterman and conscientiously timing your contractions, only to find that you've fallen asleep and the contractions have stopped. This makes perfect sense. Labor rarely starts out of the blue. It likes to have a few little test runs before beginning in earnest. Don't be surprised if you have several evenings of increasing contractions, only to fall asleep. Remember, practice makes perfect.

• *Definite Sensation of Fullness in the Pelvis*

This may include pressure on the pelvic bone and even feeling like your hips are stretching wider.

• *Change in Vaginal Discharge*

You may notice that vaginal secretions are thicker and may be present in increased amounts.

• *Spotting or Bleeding*

There may be some appearance of blood as the cervix begins to become effaced or dilated.

• *Leaking of Amniotic Fluid*

A woman who is consistently having four contractions an hour could be going into labor. With twin pregnancies, there is no doubt that your practitioner needs to hear from you under those circumstances. If you notice anything unusual about the way the babies are moving, you should share that information with your practitioner as well. At your examination, you will be assessed in much the same way you have been at every exam of your pregnancy. Your vitals will be checked. If everything is fine, you will also have a pelvic exam at this point. If you are in fact in labor, there are three terms used by your medical team to note its progress:

• *The Station*

The station describes how far the head (or other presenting part) of the baby has progressed through the birth canal. A negative station (−3 or −4) is above the ischial spines on either side of the pelvis. The fully engaged baby is at zero station in the pelvis and the final descent continues, from +1 station until the baby crowns at +4 (the appearance of the baby's head at the vaginal opening).

• *Effacement*
This is the thinning out and shortening in length of the cervix.

• *Dilation*
In labor, the cervix will need to dilate from zero to ten centimeters in order to accommodate the vaginal delivery of your babies.

the three stages of labor

stage one: latent labor

Latent labor describes the period of time that your contractions are beginning: The cervix is not particularly dilated, but rhythmic, active contractions are persistent for a matter of hours. This stage of labor can last from twelve to twenty-four hours. The cervix is continuing to efface and dilation will reach three centimeters. Women who are pregnant with twins can expect their practitioners to follow them closely, even in this earliest phase of labor. Contractions may

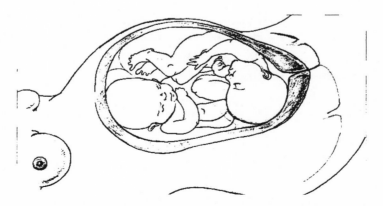

The cervix has begun to efface (get thinner), but there is no dilation.

last up to forty-five seconds and may or may not be painful. Your symptoms may include:

- leaking fluid from rupture of the membranes
- diarrhea
- a mucous discharge (mucus plug), which may be tinged with blood

stage two: active labor through delivery

There is evidence that in a twin pregnancy, your babies may benefit by being followed very closely through labor. At this point it is almost certain that you will be in the hospital and that both babies will be monitored with external fetal monitors. These are the same instruments used to measure the babies' heartbeats in your practitioner's office. The monitors are placed on your abdomen in a belt form, one for each baby. The use of fetal monitoring in high-risk pregnancies has greatly improved the outcome of these births. A third belt will be used to monitor the frequency of uterine contractions.

There is a tremendous amount of physical effort involved in labor, and you still need adequate nutrition during this time. But eating, even in little amounts, is likely to result in vomiting, which is unpleasant at any time and ter-

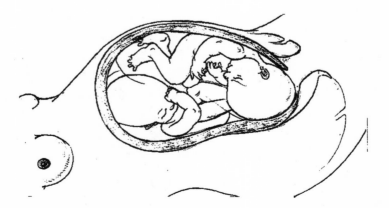

The cervix has dilated to 5 centimeters, and the first baby's head begins its descent through the birth canal.

ribly uncomfortable during labor. Intravenous fluid and glucose is usually in the mother's best interest, keeping her from becoming dehydrated and allowing her to have some fuel for her extraordinary effort. It is not unreasonable to expect your practitioner to order an intravenous line.

As labor is progressing, the couple can call on all the skills they learned in prepared childbirth classes to decrease anxiety, relieve pain, and work together through this remarkable process. But contractions can be painful and unrelenting. (Neither member of the couple will ever have more respect for their own mothers than they do during this period of labor.)

Your labor nurse will be working with you throughout, helping you with tips about relaxation and offering expert guidance. Long before you go into labor, you will have spoken with your practitioner about the opportunities available to you for pain relief. The most prudent approach takes into consideration the risks and benefits of each option before going into labor. Once you are in labor, your nurse will be able to help you to evaluate your options for pain relief and the impact they will have on you and your babies.

After a woman has dilated to between three and four centimeters, an intravenous or intramuscular pain reliever can be offered. Meperidine hydrochloride (Demerol) is safe and effective but can induce drowsiness. The effects wear off in about ninety minutes, but Demerol will not be offered if you are too far along because it could interfere with your ability to push the babies out when the time comes. Demerol is a powerful analgesic, but it crosses the placenta and will have an effect on the babies. Your practitioner will not want the babies to have their respiration depressed at delivery. Therefore, it is not recommended for use if delivery is expected in less than two hours.

dr. agnew on the value of epidural anesthesia

"I am a tremendous advocate of the use of epidural anesthesia because I've seen how much more pleasant the birthing experience can be for a woman who is not overwhelmed by pain. I had delivered hundreds and hundreds of babies and when it came time for me to give birth to my first child, I wasn't sure I'd need anesthesia. Well, when I was dilated to two centimeters I thought I was going to die but I wanted to just handle it. I was rigid as a board—I couldn't even unflex my fist. That was the way I was dealing with my pain. I agreed to an epidural when I was at three to four centimeters. Once I was relaxed, I stopped fighting the labor and in an hour I was fully dilated. In my second pregnancy, it took forever to dilate to four to five centimeters. At that point I had an epidural and once again, in an hour I was fully dilated. I am convinced that, at least for me, the epidural had a relaxing and positive effect on my labor."

Keep in mind that everything you learned in your prepared-childbirth classes will continue to be of tremendous benefit to you in labor. Another option for pain relief is epidural anesthesia. This is a regional anesthetic injected by an anesthesiologist into the space outside the spinal column. First, a numbing medicine is administered. Depending on the levels of anesthesia to be used, a catheter may be placed in the area so that the anesthesia can be administered on a continuous basis. This epidural anesthesia can significantly alter your perception of pain from the umbilicus down. But it does not impede the progress of labor. And since it does not enter the bloodstream, it does not affect the babies and is considered very safe.

Epidural anesthesia can be administered at different levels. The level needed for a cesarean section can cause a patient to be numb from the waist down, having very little control over her extremities. A lower level can be administered in such a way as to block the pain of contractions, while allowing the mother to remain aware of the sensation. She can feel the pressure, but it doesn't hurt. This enables her to be a very active participant, perfectly capable of pushing when the time is right.

It very important for the doctor delivering the babies to be an active participant in the decision-making process of pain management. The presentation of the babies is of paramount importance here. In particular, the position of the second baby is very meaningful when pain management is discussed. Epidural anesthesia can be very effective during complex deliveries. If, for example, the second baby is to be delivered in the breech presentation or by total breech extraction, the relaxing effects of the epidural will make the birth canal less rigid.

Another advantage of epidural anesthesia is that once it is in place, it can be administered in a matter of seconds. This can be vital in the event of cesarean section, particularly if there are signs of fetal distress and the practitioner wants to deliver one or both babies very quickly.

If the frequency of your contractions should decrease during your active labor, your practitioner may feel it is necessary to administer a hormone called oxytocin to help the uterus contract more efficiently. The rationale behind a decision to augment labor is clear: It is not in a baby's best interest to remain in the birth canal for an extended period of time.

Now that you are completely dilated to ten centimeters, your first baby's head descends into the pelvis and through the birth canal to be delivered through the vagina. Your contractions are continuing and now you are being encouraged to push. This process can last anywhere from five minutes to several hours. As baby number one nears delivery, your practitioner will determine if an episiotomy is needed. This is a small incision in the perineum to temporarily enlarge the vaginal opening to accommodate the passage of the baby's head. The thinking is that a clean incision is preferable to the ragged tear that could result if a good-size baby is allowed to deliver, forcing the tissue of the perineum to lacerate spontaneously.

These are three of the positions in which twins might present for delivery. If the first baby is vertex, and your labor is proceeding well, your practitioner is likely to recommend that a vaginal delivery be attempted. If the first baby is breech or transverse your practitioner will discuss the possibility of a cesarean delivery for both babies.

This is often a time of increased communication between the mother and

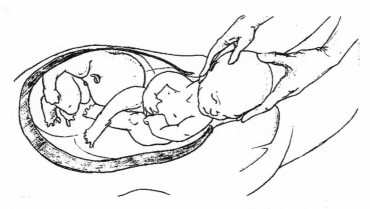

The head, which is typically the broadest circumference on a newborn baby, has passed through the vagina. Delivery of the rest of the baby's body can be expected to follow soon.

her birth coach. The dose of epidural anesthetic may be reduced at this time, and mothers report feelings from elation to fear to steely determination at this point. There are numerous positions that may feel right to the woman at this stage of her labor. Some women feel pushing in a supported but upright squatting position offers them the benefit of gravity. For others that requires too much energy, and they prefer to be in a birthing bed or seat. It is now that you truly understand why they call it labor: You are working very hard.

You are being guided by your medical team. The urge to push may feel uncontrollable at times. You are attuned to the laboring out of this baby and your body will assert its tremendous will to expel its first passenger. Again, everything you worked on in your birthing classes is coming into play. Many women describe an extraordinary sense of being connected to the voice of the practitioner who is directing the delivery of the babies. You'll rely on breathing techniques you've learned to help you to refrain from pushing when your practitioner tells you to hold off. As the first baby's head crowns and is then delivered completely, the rest of the body follows very quickly.

These are three of the positions in which twins might present for delivery. If the first baby is vertex, and your labor is proceeding well, your practitioner is likely to recommend that a vaginal delivery be attempted. If the first baby is breech or transverse your practitioner will discuss the possibility of a cesarean delivery for both babies.

Labor of the second baby will continue, and baby number two will slowly move lower in the birth canal. After delivery of the first baby, there is a brief opportunity to enjoy the overwhelming sense of relief. The first baby's cord is double clamped, and the father can cut the cord if he likes. Then it may seem as though the baby is swept away to be quickly dried off and swaddled. The baby may then be handed to the mother, who may already be involved with pushing out baby number two. The father may hold the first baby while the mother continues her hard work of delivering the second of the twins.

The interim between delivery of the first and the second baby is seventeen minutes on average. But your time may be shorter or longer by several hours. Your obstetrician will quickly evaluate the position of baby number two by pelvic exam. Second babies can appear in many different positions, so frequently an ultrasound is performed to get the most accurate view of how the baby is lying.

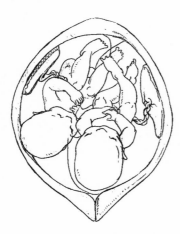

1. *Babies in vertex/vertex positions.*

If the baby is transverse or breech, the obstetrician might try to externally palpate your abdomen, gently guiding the baby into a vertex position. Sometimes the baby is not cooperative and will remain in breech position. At this point, your obstetrician will quickly decide whether or not to do a total breech extraction. Breech extraction is accomplished by the obstetrician reaching through the vaginal opening to where the baby's feet can be felt, grabbing the feet, and directing the second baby through the birth canal for complete delivery. The time factor is very important, because your obstetrician wants to complete the delivery before the cervix begins to close down. If the cervix has closed down to eight centimeters, the OB is likely to wait for you to labor out the second baby, a process that can take another two hours. If the baby is presenting in a position known as a frank breech—hips flexed, knees extended, and the heels near the ears—the obstetrician may allow a breech delivery. There are several mitigating factors when considering cesarean delivery for the second baby:

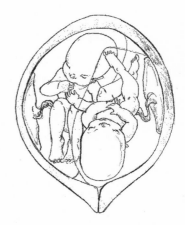

2. Babies in the vertex/breech positions.

- What is the size of the second baby? If it is smaller than the first, it should negotiate the birth canal without undue stress. However, the doctor may not permit a vaginal delivery if the second baby is larger than the first.
- What does the monitor tell us about how well the baby is tolerating labor? If the heartbeat monitor and ultrasound indicate that the baby is in a precarious position—lying transverse with its shoulder first, or with the umbilical ahead of the baby—a cesarean section may be indicated for the safety of the baby.

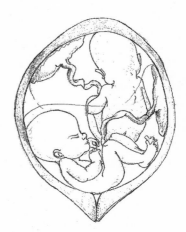

3. Babies in back-down-transverse lie/breech positions.

• Cesarean Section

We can see how a decision might be made to deliver the second baby by cesarean section. There is also the possibility that a woman will enter labor with an ultrasound showing both babies in breech positions. There might be significant risks in labor with one or both babies entangled in the cords. Or there may be the concern that the first baby will be unable to complete its journey through the birth canal without its head being obstructed by the other baby's feet. It may be the obstetrician's best call that a cesarean is needed because the two babies might interfere with each other. Cesarean delivery will also be discussed if a mother has an active herpes virus, risking the the babies' exposure to the virus through contact with the vagina. Newborn babies do not have tremendous resistance to infection. Other maternal medical scenarios—such as diabetes, or preeclampsia that has not adequately responded to treatment—may call for a cesarean section to be performed. Placenta previa will always require a C-section to prevent the risk of life-threatening bleeding during labor.

If a woman knows that she will be delivering by cesarean, there are several options for anesthesia:

- Epidural anesthesia, the process we've already discussed.
- Spinal anesthesia, in which the anesthesia is placed directly in the spinal canal without the use of a catheter. This allows numbness, no sensation, and adequate anesthesia for a finite period in order to accomplish the surgery.
- General anesthesia of the type is used in most surgical procedures in this country. This will put a woman to sleep and is not considered optimal for a normal cesarean section. General anesthesia is used only where epidural or spinal anesthesia are contraindicated, such as in the case of prior back surgery or other medical problems. In most cases, the mother is awake and will feel pressure, but not pain.

The personnel present for a cesarean section will include:

- the anesthesiologist, who places the anesthesia and sits at the head of the bed
- the obstetrician/surgeon, who will deliver the babies
- the scrub nurse, who hands instruments to the obstetrician
- a pediatrician for each baby
- a pediatric nurse

- a respiratory therapist (particularly for premature delivery)
- a circulating nurse, who is not scrubbed and circulates through the room, acting as a coordinator

If you were not about to deliver two babies, you could probably field a soft-ball team with the personnel present.

To begin the procedure, the mother's abdomen will be swabbed with iodine soap. An incision, popularly known as the a "bikini cut," will be made low down on the skin of the abdomen. The uterine incision—whether transverse or vertical, depending on the obstetrician's best judgment for the safest delivery of the babies—is made in the uterus. The first baby will be delivered out of the uterus and the cord will be clamped and cut. That baby will be handed off to the pediatrician or nurse in attendance while the second baby is delivered and the same procedure follows. In most circumstances, the first baby will be shown to mother and father very quickly and the parents will meet their second baby shortly thereafter.

The birth of the twins is an experience in which the father can actively participate. Dads should not avoid cesarean delivery for fear of being queasy or uncomfortable with the surgical procedure. Whether vaginal or cesarean, the birth of your babies is nothing less than magical, and every father should have the opportunity to share in the experience. Whether or not you wish to include any other family members is something you should discuss with each other and with your obstetrician. Find out what the hospital policy is regarding spectators before you broach the subject with your family. There are many ways in which you can arrange for your family's participation that do not include being present at the birth itself. Your older children might be able to visit you in labor and visit the babies while you are in recovery. They might want to be the ones to call the grandparents or others in the extended family.

stage three: delivery of the placenta

With a twin pregnancy, the placenta is likely to weigh about a pound and a half. That is a substantial amount of material to be expelled from the uterus, so there is likely to be continued cramping. Your obstetrician will hold the umbilical cords and help to guide the placenta in conjunction with your contractions. You will deliver the placenta within thirty minutes. Then your uterus will be massaged somewhat vigorously to enhance the contraction process in order to limit any additional blood loss. You may receive intravenous oxytocin to further stimulate your uterine contractions, or a shot of prostaglandin to expedite uterine contraction. Your obstetrician will carefully examine the inside of your vagina for any tears that may have occurred. A rectal exam will make sure that your rectal sphincters are intact and that there is no tear from the vagina into the rectum. If you had an episiotomy, that will be repaired with absorbable suture.

Following this, the obstetrician may examine the placenta to look for any unusual shape or membranes that might indicate unrecognized communication of blood vessels. The umbilical cords will be examined to make sure they appear normal and that there are three blood vessels within each cord. The presence of only two blood vessels can be a sign of kidney problems or other structural abnormalities.

The Apgar Test

Within the first minutes of each baby's life, he or she will be evaluated by the pediatrician and given an Apgar score. The Apgar evaluation is a method of assessing well-being in a newborn term baby using five criteria:

- heart rate
- respiratory rate
- skin color
- muscle tone
- reflex irritability

The baby can obtain up to two points for each category. The Apgar is performed at one minute and five minutes, and occasionally there is a third measure at ten minutes. While accepted as a standard for term babies, it is of limited value in assessing premature infants.

following delivery

Depending on what type of delivery you had, your hospital stay will be from two to five days. It is very important to understand that your body will need time—at least six weeks—to begin to feel "normal" again. If you have had a cesarean birth, be alert for any redness or swelling in the vicinity of your incision. Your practitioner will discuss the need to remove any staples from the incision. Your checkup visit will be scheduled for about two weeks postpartum. Your diet should stay about the same—don't think about a reducing diet at this point. The nursing mother will need a lot of energy to produce milk for two hungry babies, and every mother of twins has extraordinary demands made upon her body in the early months of their lives.

Fluid shifts in your body will begin right after delivery. In the first few days you will notice a significant and very welcome decrease in edema as your body begins to flush out its excess fluids. Your urination will increase, and you are likely to notice increased thirst. Be sure to stay very well-hydrated. Immediately postpartum, your bleeding can be heavier than what you'd experience during a heavy period. The lochia (bloody vaginal discharge) may require you to change your sanitary napkin at least every few hours. Vaginal bleeding may continue for several weeks. If you had a vaginal delivery, your nurse is likely to offer you cold packs that fit right on your sanitary napkin and provide excellent relief of the soreness present in the vaginal and rectal areas. As your uterus contracts you may continue to feel contractions, and they can be painful. Your medical team will help you figure out how to best manage any pain.

feeding your twins

Now—with some guidance from nurses and possibly a breast-feeding coach on staff at the hospital—you will attempt to nurse your babies if you are going to breast-feed, or to feed them their bottles if you will be using formula. The second, pediatric section of this book discusses in detail the pediatric implications of premature delivery and the feeding options you may face. For purposes of examining the parents' role in nourishing newborns, we will assume that your babies are prepared to begin nursing from the breast or bottle.

Every mom should be reassured that it takes time to get comfortable holding a newborn and finding just the right position for the baby to begin to latch on to the nipple to begin nursing. The new mother of twins needs extra encouragement from her husband and the nursing staff. Perhaps most important, she needs to be patient with herself. Term babies have a terrific suck reflex, and babies born a little early will catch up pretty quickly. The babies' first nutrition from the mother's breast is called colostrum. It is a clear liquid that is produced in the first forty-eight hours after delivery and has considerable immunologic proteins within it that can help to support the twins' immature immune systems. Follow the instruction from the nursing staff, who will probably explain that frequent nursing stimulates milk production.

As your milk begins to come in, you may notice a very obvious increase in the size of your breasts and they may be somewhat painful. Let your twins feed every few hours for up to fifteen minutes on each breast. The response of your breasts to your hungry babies is remarkable. These organs that you may have perceived as being rather decorative or cosmetic are suddenly pressed into service as the functional source of your babies' complete nutritional needs. Amazing! Mothers will find that their breasts anticipate feeding time by tingling, or sometimes "letting down" their milk in response to the cry of their hungry babies—or any hungry babies, for that matter. The pressure can be slight, or extreme enough to make you race for your babies just to relieve the urgency of an overabundance of milk.

You will want to take great care not to let your breasts become engorged, a term that describes breasts that are filled beyond their capacity. An engorged breast will feel almost rock hard and be terribly painful. You may need to pump some milk if your babies are not interested in nursing. You can use a breast pump or simply express some milk by hand as you shower. The second section of the book will address the use of breast pumps, storing milk, and the health implications for your twins. But there are important concerns about careful hygienic care of your breasts for your health as well. Your nipples contain numerous tiny openings from which the milk is released. These openings are more dilated now than they are at any other time. If bacteria enter a milk duct and infection ensues, you can get mastitis. Mastitis can be very painful and may be accompanied by fever, chills, and overall malaise. If mastitis is suspected, alert your practitioner and examine the color of your breast milk. Your babies should not drink any milk if it is not white in color. A yellow cast to the milk is a sign of infection. You will be administered an oral antibiotic and will need to pump and discard the milk from the affected breast. Your practitioner may administer an antibiotic that is compatible with breast-feeding so that you can continue to nurse from the unaffected breast.

Your nipples will take some time to adjust to the demands of two hungry babies. Some moms say that childbirth was a snap, but getting their nipples accustomed to nursing was really the hard part. Lanolin cream is a must for the bedside table of every new nursing mother. Between feedings, remember to rinse your breasts with warm soapy water. Be sure to rinse with clear water afterward, as the babies will taste the soap.

If you are not going to nurse your twins, your best course of action is to wear a somewhat binding bra and avoid any stimulation of your breasts. Some practitioners may use medication to inhibit the production of milk.

postpartum depression

There is a wide range of emotional reactions that follow birth. Most of us have heard about postpartum depression, or "baby blues." It is possible to break down this range of reactions into three categories that may help a mother to self-appraise and begin to address her own emotional condition:

- The first is a sort of mild and transient depression that we call "baby blues" or "maternity blues." It is very common and is probably present in 50 to 70 percent of mothers delivering twins. There can be teariness, anxiety, irritability, and restlessness. The condition usually manifests within ten days postpartum and will subside within a matter of days. It is tempting for the medical community to associate this blue period with shifting hormones, but we don't really know if there is a clear connection. There is the suspicion that it is related to altering levels of the hormone tryptophan, which is present in the neurotransmitters of the brain. On the other hand, many experienced mothers will tell you they believe it is associated with sleep deprivation in the early weeks following the birth of the twins.
- The second category is classic postpartum depression, and it appears in 10 to 15 percent of mothers of twins. It seems to occur more commonly

in women who were previously diagnosed with depression at some point prior to pregnancy. It also seems to be more present in women who had some degree of complication in the pregnancy, who were taken by surprise on the day of the twins' birth with a complicated delivery, or who experienced an unrelated problem, such as the death or severe illness of a member of the extended family.

- The third category is an overt psychosis, which is exceedingly rare.

So how do you know if you have some degree of depression or if you are just more exhausted than any book, friend, or doctor could possibly have prepared you to be? Symptoms such as weight loss and fatigue may very well be just a part of the postpartum package. Low thyroid function (hypothyroidism) can occur after pregnancy, and some practitioners will be inclined to check their patient's thyroid function. Replacing thyroid hormones can cause a dramatic improvement in mood. But add to these signs feelings of ambivalence toward your children and husband, and most practitioners will be inclined to see this as a red flag and want to look further into the need to treat you for postpartum depression.

It can be very uncomfortable for a new mother to acknowledge these symptoms. The first course of action is unlimited support from the family and understanding from her practitioner. A new mother's ability to acknowledge her feelings of guilt, fear, or uncertainty are the first steps back to sound emotional health. Continued follow-ups in the form of support groups, a therapeutic environment, and the possible use of medication are vital to the well-being of the mother and her whole family.

When Postpartum Depression Is Beyond the "Baby Blues" One Family's Success Story

Joan and her husband, David, had been married for twelve years when they got pregnant with twins. Joan, a psychiatric nurse, considered herself to be an extremely focused, competent, and independent woman. Her pregnancy was not without complications and she describes having felt anxious, ". . . but I still don't feel like it was inappropriate . . . I was having twins, I was on bed rest. . . . It provoked some understandable anxiety." After the babies were born, however, she began to feel far more distressed.

I felt constantly overwhelmed and terribly sleep-deprived those first few months. But the depression really hit about four months postpartum and coincided with my first postpartum menstrual period, though I don't think I made that connection at the time. I cried all the time. I didn't have any interest in doing the things I normally loved to do. I remember thinking how odd it was when I did not want my closest friend to come and see us for New Year's Eve. I did not feel suicidal, but I remember feeling I wanted to make sure the babies were fine; call my husband or my mother and say, "The boys are safe, but you have to come and take care of them," and walk out the front door. I wanted desperately to get away. Remarkably, I never had any thoughts about harming the children, though many women in the throes of depression do.

No matter how capable I'd been in my professional life, and no matter how well I'd cared for my father when he was ill, I did not really feel confident about caring for a baby—let alone two. My friends either had grown children or had decided not to have children, so I did not have a natural circle of peer support. My husband had stayed home for three weeks and my mom helped during that time, but now it was pretty much me and the babies. I was extremely anxious. I worried all the time that something would happen to them: that they would get sick, or I'd drop them . . . something horrible would happen. Now I understand that excessive worry is a classic symptom of postpartum depression. But at the time, all I knew was that I just didn't feel good. I didn't feel happy. I mean, I had a deep feeling of happiness at having these two beautiful babies, but I felt sad all the time. If you were to look at me, you would have seen a very sad person. And the feeling that was with me constantly was that I was not a good mother: I saw all these other mothers who looked great and seemed to have lots of energy.

Right about that time, the babies started sleeping through the night a little bit more—but I didn't. It was a horrible irony. I could not turn off my mind. I have always had very high expectations of myself, and I felt I was failing to live up to my
(continued)

own standard of "being a good mother"—though what that meant, I couldn't have really said. The one exception to all of this was my experience in nursing the boys. I loved nursing and it seemed to go well for us. It was also the only time I got to devote to one baby at a time. Sometimes I nursed them at the same time but I preferred to nurse them one at a time. When I complained about being tired and generally overwhelmed, my pediatrician tried to guide me to nurse them at the same time, and I was able to, but that took much of the joy away. I must say that he was very supportive of my desire to nurse the boys. And it meant a great deal to me to feel that he really heard me and my commitment to nursing and didn't waver in his support of my decision.

My mother finally came to me and told me she thought I was experiencing postpartum depression. She had found a book called Mothering the New Mother, *and as I looked at the book I came to agree with her. I called Jane Honikman, the author of the book, who, it happened, was the leader of a support group in Santa Barbara. That was the beginning of my identifying my depression and actively seeking help. Jane told me to write down several statements: "I will get better"; "This is not my fault"; and there was a third, but those were the ones that were most important to me. I read them over and over. I began going to a support group where there was a room full of women who shared my experience. I was the only mother with twins, but I know that there is a significant incidence of depression in mothers of multiples that can go undiagnosed because they may have the expectation that they are going to feel overwhelmed and that is just the way it is. . . . I know that for the first four months of the boys' lives I constantly compared myself to the mothers I saw and assumed my problem was just that I had two, so naturally it was tougher. It was so important for me to finally have a diagnosis: This was postpartum depression and I would get over it. In addition to the support of the group, I saw a therapist who was familiar with postpartum depression and that was important, because the therapist I'd seen earlier suggested my depression had nothing to do with the birth of the babies . . . that I was unhappy about the loss of autonomy and career. . . . This second therapist recommended that I see a psychiatrist to be evaluated for medication. I was unwilling to do so at that point because of my belief that I could not nurse and be on medication. I started to feel a little better and resolved to take really good care of myself. In retrospect, it was* kind of ridiculous. I joined a gym and went one time! But I was determined to "handle this myself." I went to the group and saw my therapist weekly. My symptoms continued, but they were no longer constant. I felt I was improving.

Then, at nine months, Robert weaned himself and I was devastated. I got my second postpartum menstrual period and entered another cycle of depression that I can only describe as being in hell. There were mornings I couldn't get out of bed. At that point I agreed to be evaluated for medication. I saw a psychiatrist who was very familiar with this type of depression. I think the most important thing I can share with moms of twins who might be experiencing this awful dilemma is that I came to understand that what my boys really needed was me. More than they needed my breast milk, they needed me to be their mother. They had a person who nursed them, but couldn't sing them a nursery rhyme, or even play with them. My psychiatrist explained to me that the type of antidepressants that would enable me to continue nursing would also have more side effects. The ones that were most effective in treating my kind of depression had not been adequately assessed as regards [to] their effects on nursing babies.

Once I'd decided to begin medication, my pediatrician guided me in how to manage weaning. On my fortieth birthday, I nursed Paul for the last time and Robert had pumped milk in a bottle and it was really extraordinary—all of a sudden it just felt okay to stop nursing.

My understanding of the protocol for handling medication in postpartum depression is that the most significant relapse of symptoms is most likely to occur twelve months from the time of remission of symptoms. So they like to keep you on antidepressants for up to eighteen months. This is for those who, like me, don't have a prior history of depression. So I continue with my therapist every other week and my husband and I sometimes see her to discuss the impact of all of this on our marriage. I really want to stress the importance of support groups for any woman dealing with postpartum depression. I feel I lost a significant part of my boys' first year because I was sort of lost in this sense that it was just the "baby blues" and took so long to recognize my condition as treatable. I now have every expectation that I am going to come through this to feel better than ever.

a few parting words

You have taken the extraordinary first steps in your journey with your twins. The substance of this book is about to shift into the next epic segment of your travels: the first year of life with your two, new babies. Your regular visits to your practitioner will change to regular visits to the babies' pediatrician. And you will begin to take the postpartum pulse of your family:

- First of all, how is the new mother? Are you able to sleep at all? How is your appetite? Are you feeling increasingly competent about nourishing your babies? Have you begun to establish a list of resource people to help you through these early months with twins? Do you have some sort of routine going in the house?
- How about the couple relationship? Are you finding a little time to communicate each day? Do you each feel supported and recognized for your extraordinary efforts?
- Are your other children finding their place in the newly redesigned family? Are the young ones acting out? Is there a little of your time each day that they can count on to be just for them?

You will find that there is some natural crossover in the discussions that follow. Just as there is no discussion of Mom's pregnancy without looking at her two passengers, there can be no reflection on the twins' first year without placing them in the context of the family. As we shift from a maternal to a pediatric focus, we wish you and your beautiful babies continued safe travels.

the first year of life

ready . . . set . . . twins!

preparing for your twins' arrival

The first section of this book looked at multiple pregnancy from the parents' point of view, taking us through prenatal counseling to the birth of your twins. Now we need to back up a bit in order to examine your babies' impending birth from the pediatric angle. In one of nature's exquisite ironies, parents of twins have less time to prepare than their singleton counterparts. On average, gestation for twins is two to three weeks shorter than it is for singletons—thirty-seven weeks rather than forty—so forget any ideas you may have about last-minute preparation: By the time you approach delivery, everything will feel like it should have been completed yesterday! Once you've entered your third trimester, you have limited time to think about some very basic questions:

- Will we get two cribs or co-bed our twins?
- What is the best twin stroller for us?
- Will we dress the babies differently from the start?
- What do we want to name our twins?
- Should we try to hire help, or would it be better to ask our extended families to pitch in for the first month?

And this is just the short list, the specialized questions that you, as expectant parents of twins, need to resolve. You also need to make the basic preparations common to all prospective parents. The list goes on and on, easily outpacing the last weeks of your pregnancy. So let's take a look at what you need to do, keeping in mind that your schedule is likely to be a few weeks shorter than that of parents expecting a singleton delivery.

choosing your pediatrician

Among the many important decisions you'll be making, your choice of a pediatrician is right up there at the top of the list. While parents of singletons often wait until thirty-five weeks' gestation to start looking for a pediatrician, families expecting twins should start early, about thirty weeks or even earlier if recommended by their obstetrician. Sometimes this process has to take place from the mother's hospital room by telephone while she is on bed rest, or the father can start it by asking the prospective pediatrician to visit the mother in the hospital.

Talking to your obstetrician, or friends who are parents of young children, is a good way to develop a short list of pediatricians who might be right for you and your twins. Of course, where friends are concerned, you must consider the degree to which their child-rearing philosophy mirrors your own. You can have a great pal with exactly the same taste in movies and books, yet if you think she is nuts when it comes to raising her children, her taste in pediatricians is not likely to work for you. Your obstetrician or members of a local twins club may be able to supply you with a list of pediatricians whose practices have a high percentage of multiples. Call the pediatric practice and find out if they offer prospective parents an opportunity to interview the doctor.

Many pediatricians with substantial "high-risk" practices have had a lot of experience in dealing with premature infants and twins. In the case of premature twins who may need to spend some time in the hospital before being discharged, it is best if the general pediatrician who will care for them after they go home is involved in their care as much as possible while they are still hospitalized.

Should you be preparing to start your family in an unfamiliar city, call the neonatal unit in the local hospital, explain that you are pregnant with twins, and ask the head nurse to recommend several pediatric practices for your consideration. If the nurse you speak with has a child, ask which pediatrician he or she sees. This gives you a good jumping-off point for interviewing pediatricians. Of course, insurance and financial considerations may play a big role in which doctors are available to you and in what capacity.

As new parents, it makes perfect sense for you to look to an expert for an endorsement of your emerging parenting skills. Many parents, reflecting on long-term relationships with their pediatricians, have acknowledged their desire early on to do well, noting the importance of receiving their doctor's approval for good parenting. Frequently, the most successful doctor/parent relationships acknowledge that phase and then go beyond it. Even at the outset of your association with your pediatrician, it is important to voice any questions you may have about specific recommendations, or even a general approach to child care. Open communication will often clear up any misunderstandings that you may have and will also serve to enhance your trust in your children's doctor. This relationship usually works out best when parents and doctor are on the same path, even though they may not be in complete agreement on everything. For example, it will be frustrating for you and your pediatrician if you continue to ask that your child be put on medication when the pediatrician doesn't think it is necessary. So it's a good idea to find out from the beginning if you are all in agreement about your doctor's general approach to medication, or any other aspects of care that you feel strongly about.

The pediatrician is an important source of information for your family. Some of that information is absolute: Your children's health and sometimes their very lives are at stake. Your pediatrician's directions on subjects such as the use of car seats or fevers must be followed to the letter. Other information, however, is more like guidance and may need modification to work for your family. Issues such as feeding schedules or sleeping arrangements need to be flexible. With this type of information, you should do what feels right for you. If you are in doubt about whether a particular recommendation from your pediatrician is doctrine or simply a suggestion, you should always feel comfortable enough to ask.

questions to ask at the pediatric interview

A pediatric interview can be conducted in several ways. Some parents start out by asking the pediatrician to describe his or her practice, and follow up with questions that have either been generated from comments or prepared earlier. Other parents prepare a detailed list and begin the interview by asking their own questions. The goal here is to get practical information about this doctor's approach to pediatrics, and to assess your gut reaction to the practitioner who will be caring for your twins.

These are some of the questions you might want to pose to a pediatrician you are considering. You may not be interested in all of them, but they will give you an idea of the range of subjects that you should be able to discuss comfortably with a prospective pediatrician. It's a good idea to discuss these questions with your mate beforehand so that you have some idea of the answers you both are seeking before the interview takes place.

- How soon after our twins are born will you see them?
- Do you see a lot of twins in your practice?
- What is your schedule for well-baby visits?
- What happens at a well-baby visit? How do you handle the visit with twins?
- How much time do you spend with a patient at a well-baby visit?
- Do you have a different schedule for premature babies?
- Who will answer my questions if I call the office?
- What are your office hours?
- What happens if we call after office hours?
- Is this your own practice, or are there other pediatricians we might see in this office?
- If it is a group practice, can we request to see you exclusively?
- What is your philosophy about immunizations?
- Can you talk to us about feeding our twins?
- What is your philosophy regarding medication and the use of alternative approaches to health care?
- Where did you take your training?

- Do you have children of your own?
- What do you think about circumcision?
- What hospitals are you associated with?
- Are you board certified?

dr. klein on his well-baby visit schedule

"I see the babies two to three days after they are released from the hospital; then at two weeks of age; and then at one, two, three, four, five, six, eight, and ten months of age. Immunizations begin with the one-month visit and continue at the two-, three-, four-, five-, and six-month visits. At the eight- or ten-month visit I give additional immunizations and do a hemoglobin and a TB test as well.

For premature babies, I may see them every week until they reach their actual due date, and then, unless they have some special needs that require additional medical attention, they go onto the same schedule that I use for term babies."

a word about the team approach

As you move toward a due date, there are questions about your babies that will be on the minds of your physicians (obstetrician and pediatrician), yourselves, and anyone else you have brought into the twin loop. This is a good time for parents to make sure that they are talking with each other and attempting to reach consensus about just who is in that intimate circle that makes up "the team." Successful communication with each other and with your physicians is all-important now as your due date approaches and you can no longer postpone any important decisions.

The practice of medicine in the United States does not exist in a vacuum. Like theories in education or techniques in child-rearing, medicine exists within the framework of popular culture and the broad scope of its influences. There might be several protocols for treating a particular symptom of your pregnancy, or even your child's illness. Medical practice can range from instruction in relaxation techniques to use of the newest drugs. Patients are becoming educated consumers of health care, and are far more likely to question their practitioners today than they were thirty years ago. The Internet is one of the most convenient places a pregnant woman can go for information. There she can communicate with everyone from internationally recognized obstetricians to other moms whose twins are old enough to be asking for the car keys. All may offer valuable advice. But what do you do when you have conflicting information and the stakes are so high?

This is what the team approach is all about. Has a friend recommended an herbal tea to treat sleeplessness? Perhaps you are anticipating raising your twins as vegetarians. You need to discuss these things with your doctors. Just as it is imprudent to make an assumption about the tea ("Well, it's only an herb"), it is equally unwise to make presumptions about your doctor's attitude. Is the doctor willing to look into a vegetarian diet for your seven-month-old twins? If not, is there a colleague the doctor can consult or recommend that you see?

It is interesting to note that we live in an age that seems to support extreme views of the medical community in general, and birth and delivery in particular. Certainly it is true that women were experiencing "natural childbirth" long before medical schools entered the picture. But along with advances in medicine have come enhanced diagnostic capabilities for both mother and fetus. The result has been a dramatically reduced rate of infant mortality. The medical team delivering twins is as delighted as the expectant parents when both deliveries take place without complications. But they are also understandably pleased to have the very latest in technological support when it is needed.

People who flee the mainstream of medicine may embrace a natural philosophy that can be somewhat reactionary. For example, there are vocal critics of the medical establishment who feel that doctors are out of step with the needs of today's parents of twins. They maintain, for example, that medical intervention is frequently introduced to satisfy the comfort level of the physician and has no proven benefit to the outcome of the birth of the twins. But the truth is that in the case of high-risk pregnancies of twins or higher-order multiples, there has been a significant decrease in infant morbidity when the babies are monitored during labor. Medical intervention may very well be the only responsible alternative if the natural approach is not the safest possible one for mother or babies.

before your twins arrive

Again, parents expecting twins need to be a few weeks ahead of the singleton parents' schedule when it comes to getting ready for their babies' arrival. Later on in this book we will discuss the specifics of baby-proofing your home and the safety concerns of those products you'll need for your growing babies. For now, let's limit our discussion to what needs to be in place for bringing your newborn twins home after delivery.

You may find it helpful to make a list of the material objects you'll want to have on hand once you bring your babies home. Heading this list, of course, will be your two car seats.

• Car Seats

Every state in the United States requires the use of child car seats. All car seats manufactured today must meet the Federal Motor Vehicle Safety Standards set for crash-worthiness established in 1998. Do not use a car seat manufactured before that time, and never use an infant carrier for a car seat! When purchasing your car seats, make sure that they both fit correctly into your vehicle. If you have two cars, even if one will be used more frequently for transporting your babies, make certain that the car seats fit correctly into both.

The safest place in your vehicle for your car seats is the backseat. *The car seats of babies weighing less than twenty pounds and under one year of age should be secured in the backseat, facing backward—do not turn either baby's car seat around to face forward until he or she is one year old and weighs at least twenty pounds.* One car seat should be anchored in the center of the backseat, and the other should be behind the front right-passenger seat, allowing you optimum visual access to both babies in their car seats. Follow the precise instructions of the car seat manufacturer, and call the manufacturer if you have any questions regarding safe installation of the car seats in your vehicle.

The National Highway Traffic Safety Administration (NTHSA) has stated that the most frequent cause of injury during an accident to a child in a car seat is improper use and/or installation. The NTHSA web site (see the Resource Guide at the back of this book, under Car Safety Seats) can direct you to Child Safety Seat Inspection Sites all over the country, whose goal is to assist you in the safe installation of your children's car seats. These sites, listed by address and telephone number, are located at a variety of places such as local fire, sheriff, and police stations, hospitals, social service organizations, and auto shops. These inspection sites may be free of cost, they may accept a suggested donation, or there may be a fee for their service. Call ahead to find out their policy. Some sites may offer alternate seats when there is a need to replace damaged or recalled models.

Never use a car seat in a seating location that has an activated airbag, and never travel in a vehicle with your babies without having them securely strapped into their car seats. It is strongly recommended that you purchase your car seats new. A car seat that has been in an accident may have developed hairline cracks that will not be apparent upon a simple visual examination. And be sure to hold on to your receipt until you know that both car seats can be safely installed in your particular car model.

• Cribs and Bedding

First you will need to decide whether you prefer to put your twins in two cribs or co-sleep them in one. Crib slats should be no more than 2⅜ inch apart. End posts should be no higher than 1/16 inch above the crib's end panel, as older babies can strangle if their clothing gets caught on a corner post. Apply these guidelines to cribs offered by friends or family, or that you might wish to purchase secondhand.

The crib mattress should fit snugly, and bumper pads should fit securely around the entire crib. Snap or tie bumpers into place, trimming any excess length from ties to prevent your twins from strangling or becoming entangled. Remember, when you put your babies down to sleep, place them on their backs on a firm mattress without any pillows.

• Strollers and Carriers

One of your biggest challenges will be getting out and about with your very young twins. Most parents of twins get many hours of use from their strollers, so you want to buy the right one. If you already have a pram or carriage, both your newborn twins are likely to fit in it comfortably, so you may have a brief reprieve from purchasing your two-seat stroller. You will have some choices to make: There are limousine strollers with seats facing each other, side-by-side strollers, and even three-seaters in case you already have a toddler at home. If you have not yet made contact with a local twins club, this is the time to seek opinions from parents who have been there.

The baby carrier, a soft, shoulder-slung "front pack" for holding your baby while freeing your hands, can also be very helpful. Some manufacturers make baby carriers designed for twins (see the Resource Guide at the back of this book), though not all parents choose to use them. Any soft carrier you choose should be washable, sturdy, and have adjustable straps. Many moms (and dads) are reporting great success using one or two baby "slings." These are wonderfully conducive to achieving and maintaining that special closeness to your babies for many hours throughout the day. You will find that there are quite a few manufacturers offering these front-wearing wide fabric bands that slip over your head and one shoulder and provide you with a comfortable, cozy means of walking around with one or both babies, holding them close to your chest, while leaving your hands free. Some slings are designed to allow you to comfortably and safely carry both babies in one sling while they are small, while some parents wear two slings—one over each shoulder, comfortably transporting the babies that way until they are several months old. Another advantage of having two slings is to allow each parent to carry a baby out walking, while leaving the stroller behind. Regardless of the carrier method you choose, your babies' heads should be supported and their weight evenly distributed. A soft carrier or a sling is for walking with your babies and should never be used to transport your twins on a bicycle or in a car.

basic supplies

Bath Time

Two soft, hooded, cotton baby towels for each baby will get plenty of use. You may want a portable bathtub or bath seat to hold your baby securely in the bath. Since you're likely to be bathing your young twins one at a time, one tub or seat will do. Several soft, cotton baby washcloths for each baby will come in handy at feeding time as well as in the bath. Placing the bath seat in the sink or on a counter may save on back strain. Of course, never leave your babies unattended, even for a moment, at bath time.

• Diapers

Anticipate an average of ten a day for each of your newborn twins. You may choose to use cloth or disposable diapers, or to use cloth diapers at home and disposable diapers when you are out and about. Should you decide to use disposable diapers, don't load up on them until your babies are born and you see which brand and size will work best for you.

If you do plan to try cloth diapers for your twins, a year's worth of diaper service would be a significant gift from a group of friends, coworkers, or family members. Don't be shy about making such a request of people who are hoping to give you a gift. Baby registries, like bridal registries, are increasingly common, and friends and family are often happy to know that their gift will be so helpful to you as a new mother of twins. Cotton diapers make perfect shoulder protectors for keeping spit-up away from your shirt or blouse. Always have a dozen extra cloth diapers on hand.

• Clothing

The more of each necessary item you have, the less frequently you'll have to launder them. On the other hand, too much clothing makes for storage and organizational headaches. When you think about the basics for your twins, balance the monetary cost against the price you pay in creating extra work for yourself. This is also the time to confront the question of whether or not you will dress your twins alike. You may have strong feelings about this, or you may want to talk to other parents of twins to find out what has worked for them.

Your babies' wardrobe might include:

- six cotton snap undershirts for each baby
- six one-piece, leg-snap pajama sets for each baby
- six receiving blankets for each baby
- two blanket sleepers for each winter baby
- two snowsuits for each winter baby
- two sets of booties (especially for winter babies)
- two hats, suitable to the season, for each baby

While these basics will get you started, few parents or their friends and family can resist the adorable clothing that is out there for little babies. Enjoy this wonderful opportunity to purchase or receive those special gifts, such as handmade sweaters or baby blankets, for your beautiful, new babies.

• Twin-proofing

Your newborn twins will, of course, be unable to get around on their own at first, but "twin-proofing," the process of making your home safe for your babies, can and should be started before they arrive. We will go into greater detail about twin-proofing later in this book, but by the time you go to the hospital to deliver your babies, you ought to have completed the first four items on this list:

- Have the telephone numbers of your pediatric office, poison control center, fire department, and, of course, 911 posted at every telephone.
- Be sure that the twins' sleeping spots are not next to any curtain cords or electrical wires that they could grasp or become tangled in.
- Consider any special arrangements that you may want to make regarding your pets.
- Check with the local nursery to be sure that none of your houseplants are potentially dangerous to your babies.

It may seem a little early to be worrying about these next twin-proofing steps, but if you can manage to get them done before the babies are born you'll be glad you did.

- It is not too early to count the number of electrical outlets in your home and purchase safety caps to cover them from exploring baby hands.
- Even if you don't yet have them installed, start thinking about baby-safe latches for cabinets, as well as safety gates at the tops of stairs and between rooms you won't want your exploring twins to enter.
- Begin to think about storing all poisons, medications, and any other dangerous or toxic substances in high, locked, inaccessible places.

There are many topics you and your partner will want to discuss with each other before the babies come home. Total agreement between parents on all areas of child care is highly improbable, but you are far more likely to have reasonable discussions about all issues, including any hot-button topics, before you are confronted with your two very special deliveries.

things to think about

• *How much time will you be able to take off from work when the babies come home?*
The Family and Medical Leave Act guarantees covered employees up to a total of twelve weeks of unpaid leave per year for several family and medical circumstances, including the birth of a child. The FMLA also requires covered employers to continue to supply health insurance benefits during that time if benefits were in place prior to the leave. You may want to consider the longer-term implications of Dad staying home for the first two weeks or so. If, as would be the case under the FMLA, it means loss of income, will that be manageable? If you are not covered by the FMLA, can you be assured that time off will not jeopardize your job security? Many employers will be sympathetic to the extraordinary demands of twins, but you need to figure these things out ahead of time. (See the Resource Guide at the back of this book under Support for Families with Twins.)

• *Do either of you have parents or other family members who could help out for the first month?*
If ever there was a time to call out the troops, this is it. However, both parents need to understand the implications of asking family to help out at such a highly emotional moment in your lives. If your mate has a hard time with your mother or you are uncomfortable with his older sister, talk about it ahead of time.

• *Are you comfortable with family help if it means they will have to move in with you for a while?*
The apartment that seemed so spacious to you as newlyweds may feel very cramped when you bring two babies home. Are you prepared to wait in line for the bathroom or have your in-laws camped out in the living room? If having

your extended family in your home makes for too-close quarters and the cost of hotel living for out-of-towners is prohibitive, maybe you have friends who can provide a temporary home-away-from-home for visiting family.

• *Can the family budget be manipulated to allow for hired help in the first two weeks or first month, if that is desirable?*
Some people simply do not have family to help out. While the cost of hiring a baby nurse is too high for many families, it is far less costly to hire someone to come in for three or four hours a day to clean, do laundry, and prepare meals that can be frozen and served at your convenience. Even families who can afford a nanny for their newborns may prefer to care for the babies themselves while handing off the household chores.

If any hired help is out of the question, this is another opportunity to interact with your community of friends. There may be a local twins club that would be happy to supply some support, or members of your church, synagogue, or mosque who will willingly step in once they are made aware of a need.

• *Have you thought about the implications of naming your two babies?*
Parents are all over the map on this question. Some seek to emphasize the miracle of a twin birth by choosing rhyming or alliterative names for their twins: Jill and Bill, Marie and Michelle, or Annie and Andrew. Other parents choose to honor a family member on either side of the family in their name choices. Still others seek from the outset to emphasize their twins' individuality by choosing completely unrelated names. Each of these choices has implications in the lives of your unborn babies, so it is wise to talk them through ahead of time.

• *Have you read your health insurance policy from cover to cover?*
Many parents of twins report frustration over dealing with their insurance carriers. It is not uncommon for insurance companies to refuse payment on a claim that appears to their computer to be double billing. First, read your policy! Take notes, then speak with a representative of the insurance company and alert them to the fact that you are having twins, so what may appear to be double billing is, in fact, care for two babies. If both parents have insurance before be-

coming pregnant, think hard before dropping one policy to save a little money. Often, with two policies your coverage for the babies will be more comprehensive. Some companies cover well-baby visits while others do not. Some companies will not cover two claims for the same diagnosis if they occur within too short a time period. Parents of twins have to be vigilant consumers.

The birth of your babies is an exciting and complicated time. You may have been told that the babies are covered by your policy for the first thirty days of their lives. But in the frenetic time surrounding the birth of the twins, don't forget: *You need to put your babies on the policy before those thirty days are over.* You should make that call to your insurance carrier as soon as the babies are born, because some carriers will refuse to cover them after the first month if they have not been notified of the births within thirty days. This is of particular importance in the event there are any medical complications. You do not want to give your insurance company the right to deny coverage because you failed to notify them of the births within the designated time period.

Your Older Children at Home

Women with twins are often on bed rest for extended periods of time. Whether it is in the hospital or at home prior to delivery, a twin pregnancy often presents greater family stress than an impending singleton birth. First of all, in all discussions with your other children, it is important to make your explanations age-appropriate, as well as suitable, to your older child's experience. If your four-year-old's grandmother has just had an extended stay in the hospital for an illness, imagine what it might be like for her to hear that Mommy is going to the hospital and we don't know exactly when she'll be coming home. Be sure to explain your absence in terms that are both clear and comforting. For mothers on bed rest in the hospital, schedule regular play dates there for mother and child. If you are on bed rest but not confined to the hospital, these special play dates can be a time when you are together at home, focusing needed attention on your child before the twins arrive.

After delivery, maybe Dad can take the time he is not at the hospital with Mom to be at home with the older child. Find out ahead of time if your children will be allowed to visit you in the hospital, and ask if they can tour the nursery and/or birthing room several weeks before you're due. If it is your child's preference to stay at home for the days you are in the hospital, try to accommodate that wish. It is best for very young children to stay in their own homes with a family member or trusted friend whom they know well and who has baby-sat them in the past. Your nine-year-old may be delighted to go to Grandma's for several days until Mommy comes home, but that is not likely to be the case for a younger child.

One Mom's Tale
On Bed Rest in the Hospital for Seven Weeks with Two Small Children at Home

Annie and her husband, Paul, had two young children when they became pregnant with twins. At twenty-eight-and-a-half weeks, Annie was experiencing several symptoms of premature labor. With two children under four, she had to agree with her obstetrician that any bed rest would be pretty much impossible at home. She was admitted to the hospital and placed on complete bed rest. Fortunately, that did not include her dialing finger, since her telephone would become the command post for seven weeks of marshaling the troops to help care for her three-and-half-year-old son, Ben, and sixteen-month-old daughter, Emily.

At twenty-eight and a half weeks, my obstetrician gave me less than a day to prepare for a hospital stay that would turn out to be seven weeks long. I was pretty much in a panic. I had two little kids at home and had to try to explain that Mommy had to be in the hospital but it was going to be all right.

It was over ten years ago, but there are some things you just don't forget. In my seven weeks I had thirteen roommates, and every one of them had something else going on. They never put a woman who had delivered a baby in with me. But I tell you, by the time I got out of there I felt like if someone had given me a stethoscope, I could have walked the halls and seen patients. There were two other twin moms there during my stay. We were all due about the same time. They were discharged, but we all ended up back in the hospital to deliver within forty-eight hours of each other.

(continued)

One of the hardest things was not being able to see my kids as much as I wanted to. We spoke every night, but they only came to the hospital about once a week. I had a whole wall of their scribbles and pictures right there with my calendar marking off each day. My friends were incredible. I got on the phone and really tapped every resource: There were families we knew from my husband's job, moms from my son's preschool, church friends. A great young girl who baby-sat for us made sure to be at our house every day at five o'clock so the kids could come home. Emily would spend the day with one of our friends and Ben was at preschool. We set up a week at a time. There was an incredible food-preparation detail. We had a freezer filled with casseroles, even when I came home! Amazingly, the kids ate dinner at home every night I was away and slept at home, too.

It was pretty tough on my husband. In fact, the first night I was in the hospital, Paul had both kids out shopping. Emily was in the cart and Ben was riding underneath. He somehow got a finger stuck in the wheel and they had to race off to the emergency clinic. Not a great first night without Mommy. . . . Paul had so much to deal with and he had bronchitis during that time. I felt absurd—here I was in the hospital, the picture of health, imposing on every person I knew. . . . I was not allowed up or out of that bed at all. I had a million things to do and was not able to do a thing. . . . They were managing the contractions with muscle relaxants and told me that if I could get through seven weeks they would probably let me go home. I have never been more motivated in my life.

When they did let me go home, as eager as I was, it was kind of scary. I was so huge. . . . My mom and dad came and we really worked to keep the kids from jumping on me. I sort of camped out on the couch. We had a friend who continued to come and clean out the fridge each Monday and help with laundry. . . . She was incredible.

"One Mom's Tale" will resume in Chapter 15 with the birth of the twins.

preparing for delivery and birth

where to deliver your twins

The delivery of your babies should be discussed and prepared for well ahead of your due date. This means talking about who will be present at the delivery and where it will take place. It is very much in your interest as advocates for your twins to find out what will happen before and after delivery and what support services are available for families with twins. If you have not yet done so, be sure to read your health insurance policy from cover to cover.

things you may want to know about the hospital

- Can the father be present in the delivery room if you expect to deliver by cesarian-section? Does that same policy hold for the unanticipated C-section?
- What is the hospital policy regarding the babies being with you in your room?
- Are there staff members specially trained to help you begin to breast-feed your twins?
- Does the hospital offer any financial discounts in the case of multiple births?

- Discuss the conditions associated with visiting the babies in the event that you are released before one or both of them: visiting hours, the number of visitors at a time, etc.
- Can you sleep over in the hospital if you are released before one or both of the babies?
- Is there a hospital tour available for your older children while you are pregnant?
- Can your older children visit you and the babies in the hospital?
- Does the hospital provide any ongoing programs for parents of twins?
- Are they able to recommend any resources in the community for parents of multiples?

It is also important to inquire about the capabilities of the facility itself. On average, gestation for twins is two to three weeks shorter than it is for singletons: thirty-seven weeks rather than forty. Many hospitals are equipped to handle healthy multiple births after thirty-four weeks' gestation. If your doctor anticipates that your twins will be born earlier, it is best to give birth at a medical center that has a specialty-care (level II) or subspecialty-care (level III) nursery. These facilities will have a neonatologist on call twenty-four hours a day to handle immediate problems. The neonatologist is a pediatrician who specializes in working with premature infants or full-term newborns who are ill. There is an expanded discussion of these levels of care a little later on in this chapter.

preterm labor

The presence of any of the following conditions in pregnancy may increase the chances of early labor and delivery of your twins before thirty-four weeks. Be sure to discuss with your doctor the pediatric implications of these conditions:

- polyhydramnios—the presence of excess fluid in the gestational sac
- bleeding episodes or change in vaginal discharge that include blood or mucus

- concerns about the health or growth of one or both babies
- increased frequency of uterine contractions
- a prior obstetric history of preterm delivery
- pregnancy with high-order multiples (triplets or more)
- evidence of twin-to-twin transfusion

how far from home to hospital?

Having babies, especially twins, is an inexact science, and your possible early delivery must be kept in mind. Consider a situation in which the physician doubts that a pregnancy will go beyond thirty weeks. The parents live in a suburb, forty miles from the nearest subspecialty (level III) urban medical center. The discussion here should focus on the options available to the family. The expectant mother could stay at home anticipating giving birth at the local facility, or she could arrange, possibly with considerable inconvenience, to reside in the city where the hospital has a neonatal intensive care unit. Many smaller hospitals use transport systems that will take the babies by ambulance, plane, or helicopter to the more sophisticated facility.

All the factors must be considered. Is the mother on bed rest, and can or should she be checked into the larger facility to await the birth? Are there small children at home who need to be cared for to guarantee the mother's bed rest at any site? Should the parents take their chances and anticipate making the drive when she goes into labor? What is the data on survival rates for infants who must be transported immediately after birth? Common sense tells us that separating the mother from one or both of the babies is not going to be easy on any of them. Once again, communicating with your doctor about your options can make the difference between calm resolve and anxious uncertainty.

Throughout the country, there is a movement toward regionally designed perinatal care that is based on the capabilities of hospitals to provide for the particular medical needs of newborn babies. For many years this system utilized a three-tiered description of perinatal care—level I, II, or III. Those designations have been replaced with the terms *basic, specialty,* and *subspecialty,* which provide descriptions of the services provided at each facility. You may discover that in your area, "levels I, II, and III" are still in common usage, so the descriptions below use both terms.

The Right Level of Care
for You and Your Babies

The following information is adapted from Guidelines for Perinatal Care, Fifth Edition, American Academy of Pediatrics, American College of Obstetricians and Gynecologists

BASIC CARE (LEVEL I)

- Surveillance and care of all patients admitted to the obstetric service, with an established triage system for identifying high-risk patients who should be transferred to a facility that provides specialty or subspecialty care
- Proper detection and initial care of unanticipated maternal–fetal problems that occur during labor and delivery
- Capability to begin an emergency cesarean delivery within thirty minutes of the decision to do so
- Availability of appropriate anesthesia, radiology, ultrasound, laboratory, and blood bank services on a twenty-four-hour basis
- Resuscitation and stabilization of all neonates born in the hospital
- Evaluation and continuing care of healthy neonates in a nursery or with their mothers until discharge
- Adequate nursery facilities and support for stabilization of small or ill neonates before transfer to a specialty or subspecialty facility
- Consultation and transfer arrangements
- Parent–sibling neonate visitation
- Data collection and retrieval

Some basic care facilities may provide continuing care for neonates who have minor problems. Many basic care facilities provide care for convalescing neonates who have been transferred from specialty and subspecialty facilities.

SPECIALTY CARE (LEVEL II)

- Provision of some enhanced services as the well as the basic care services described above

- Care of appropriate high-risk women and fetuses, both admitted and transferred from other facilities
- Stabilization of severely ill newborns before transfer
- Treatment of moderately ill larger preterm and term newborns
- Data collection and retrieval

Care in a specialty-level facility should be reserved for stable or moderately ill newborns with problems that are expected to resolve rapidly and that would not be anticipated to need subspecialty-level services on an urgent basis. These situations usually occur as a result of relatively uncomplicated preterm labor or preterm rupture of membranes at approximately thirty-two weeks' gestation or later. Although some specialty-care hospitals also have neonatal intensive care units with subspecialty capability, the available perinatal subspecialty expertise is often neonatal medicine and not maternal–fetal medicine. Availability of pediatric subspecialists, such as in cardiology, surgery, radiology, and anesthesiology, in specialty-care facilities with advanced neonatal care units is variable. Anticipatory planning and agreement on situations to be managed should be established and consideration should be given to regional or system needs and resources. Preterm labor and impending delivery at less than thirty-two weeks' gestation usually warrants maternal transfer to a subspecialty-care center, as do gestations of less than thirty-two weeks.

SUBSPECIALTY CARE (LEVEL III)
- Provision of comprehensive perinatal care services for both admitted and transferred women and neonates of all risk categories, including basic and specialty-care services as described above
- Evaluation of new technologies and therapies
- Data collection and retrieval

The services provided by a subspecialty-care facility vary markedly from those at a specialty facility. Subspecialty-care services include expertise in neonatal and maternal–fetal medicine. Both usually are required for management of pregnancies with threatened maternal complications at less than thirty-two weeks' gestation.

(continued)

Fetuses that may require immediate complex care should be delivered at a subspecialty-care center.

In circumstances where subspecialty-level maternal care is needed, the level of care subsequently needed by the neonate may prove to be at the basic or specialty level. It is difficult to predict accurately all neonatal risk and outcomes before birth. Appropriate assessment and consultation should be used that consider the potential risks of the woman as well.

who will attend the delivery?

It is important to take the time to speak with your doctor about the personnel who will be involved from the pediatric side. Full-term twins do not always have additional personnel in attendance, but it's different when premature twins are expected. Often, a pediatrician or a neonatologist will be called in to attend to the babies at delivery. There may be a respiratory therapist present, or additional nurses who are specially trained to assist with the newborn twins. In a teaching hospital, interns and residents are likely to be called in to assist. On certain occasions the obstetrician will want an anesthesiologist on hand. The position of the babies is a significant factor in determining who is best equipped to deliver them. If, for example, one of the babies is transverse and the other is breech, the obstetrician may need to do a breech extraction. You will want to know if your obstetrician is very familiar with this procedure. It is both wise and appropriate to ask your doctor about his or her experience with the various types of twin presentations. Years ago, there was a general consensus in the medical community that the second twin was more at risk for complications of birth and delivery. Today, advances in fetal monitoring have greatly diminished, if not completely eliminated, those risks. You want your own focus to be on delivering your babies, and this is best accomplished by feeling confident that experts trained to do their specialized jobs are handling the medical details. It may sound as though you are gathering enough people to staff your own clinic, but the intimacy of this moment is forged by your connection to your twins and theirs to each other; it will not be compromised by having what seems like a

Breech:
rear 1st

Transverse
Horizontal

small crowd in attendance. Think of it as a rare opportunity to socialize with grown-ups who are as interested in your babies as you are.

The Right Start

The likelihood of a successful outcome for a newborn needing intensive care is higher when the pregnant mother is transferred to a level III neonatal intensive care unit before giving birth than when the neonate is transported after delivery.

---

vaginal vs. cesarean delivery: what does it mean to your twins?

In a healthy, term infant—whether it is the first or the fourth pregnancy—there is some benefit to vaginal birth. When an infant negotiates the birth canal, its head, which is the largest part of a newborn baby, usually proceeds first, followed by the chest and abdomen. This mechanical compression of the baby's chest, in addition to the release of various hormones at the time of delivery, facilitates the removal of fluid that is present in the lungs so that when the baby takes its first, very important breath, there is less fluid to be reabsorbed. We know that the baby delivered by cesarean section is more likely to have some mild breathing problems—transient tachypnea of the newborn (TTN), caused by retained lung fluid. This breathing difficulty usually corrects itself within twenty-four hours, though some babies do need a little oxygen to help them through the first hours. In even rarer cases, they will need to spend some time on a respirator.

In the case of a premature baby, there can be benefits and risks to vaginal delivery. If a premature twin is in the breech presentation—that is, feet first—delivery through the vagina may not be appropriate. Keeping in mind that the head is usually the largest part of the baby, the breech delivery runs the risk of having the head somewhat delayed in its passage through the birth canal. If either the feet or rear end should deliver first, you don't have the benefit of the baby's head to dilate the cervix, and the head may not deliver as fast as it should.

As far as the implications of vaginal or cesarean birth for the second twin, there are many factors to consider. If the first twin has been delivered without incident, the cervix is completely dilated, and the second baby is about the same size, either a breech or vertex (head-first) delivery should be pretty uneventful. Most obstetricians are pretty confident of a successful second delivery if the second baby's head comes down and delivers vertex. All obstetricians would probably agree that the very-best-case scenario for a twin delivery is two babies who present vertex for a vaginal birth.

If the second baby is breech and there is concern about head entrapment, the obstetrician may perform a total breech extraction. This is an extraordinary obstetrical maneuver that has been in practice since the earliest records of birthing. It requires the obstetrician to reach up into the uterus and bring the feet down in a controlled, gentle fashion. The fetus is guided through the birth canal, feet first, after the delivery of the first twin. The obstetrician will make this decision regarding the delivery of the second twin after the delivery of the first baby.

There are also other alternatives. The obstetrician may be able to guide the breech fetus from the outside of the mother's body: Through the use of hands on her abdomen, the obstetrician will maneuver the baby to be vertex for a vaginal delivery. The mother is then allowed to complete vaginal delivery of the second twin. The use of ultrasound and other technologies enables your obstetrician to monitor the undelivered twin in order to make the best decisions regarding delivery.

after the twins are born

It is helpful to anticipate the changing of the guard as your team shifts from delivery of the twins by your obstetrician to overseeing their health after birth by their pediatrician. You may want to have one set of questions for your obstetrician and prepare another for your pediatrician. Most of your questions should be answered before delivery; however, some questions may persist, so it will be helpful to write down the few that are left or that pop up after the pediatric interview. After delivery, it's hard for parents of twins to think about anything but the miracle of their two babies in the here and now. It is not unusual to hear a new mother comment on the mental, hormonal, and emotional shift that takes place as she adjusts to the twins actually existing outside her body. Realizing that your twins now have a pediatrician, while you as a mother have your own practitioner, is one of the very first steps you take in granting your children their own identities in the family. Once your twins are born, your relationship with your pediatrician shifts instantly from abstract discussion to sharing the responsibility for the health care of two very real lives.

the premature twins

While forty weeks is the recognized gestation period for the human infant, any baby, singleton or twin, is considered term after thirty-seven weeks. Those delivered prior to thirty-seven weeks are considered premature. More than half of twin pregnancies deliver between thirty-four and thirty-seven weeks. This period is a gray area as far as discussions of prematurity are concerned, since most of the significant health issues associated with prematurity occur in babies born before thirty-four weeks.

It is important to understand that many of the pediatric health concerns about your twins are not due to their being multiples, but are more likely the result of their being premature. In the following discussion, we will briefly discuss the multitude of problems that are likely to affect twins born before thirty-four weeks, then discuss the few, less significant problems that may affect twins born after thirty-four weeks' gestation.

premature twins born at less than thirty-four weeks' gestation

A remarkable increase in survival rates for all infants born between twenty-four and thirty-four weeks' gestation has taken place over the last ten to twenty years. While it was once thought that twin infants born prematurely had decreased survival compared to singletons, more recent studies suggest that twin infants, compared to singletons at similar gestational age and birthweight, have similar mortality and complication rates.

Twenty-five years ago, babies born under one thousand grams and before twenty-eight weeks were often not viable. Now, almost 80 percent of twins born between twenty-four and thirty-one weeks survive. Today, insights into the physiology of premature babies, as well as advances in modern medicine, are keeping pace with the increase in multiple births. It's a wonderful time to be giving birth to twins!

Respiratory Function

The first and most obvious adaptation to life outside the womb is the baby's reliance upon its lungs to supply oxygen. What we look for is the newborn's first gasp, to be followed by a deep breath and the first cry. The lungs fill up with air and the baby begins to "pink up." One or both babies may require a little extra oxygen for a jump-start. Adequate support of pulmonary function is critical to the premature baby.

Respiratory distress syndrome occurs when the baby's lungs have not matured sufficiently to promote adequate breathing. A developmental deficiency in surfactant, a chemical that allows the lungs to expand and stay open, is primarily responsible for RDS. Recent replacement therapy with various commercial surfactant preparations has led to a much improved outcome of this formerly deadly problem. RDS tends to be more of a problem for male babies, probably because their lungs don't mature as quickly in utero as the lungs of a female. The symptoms of RDS can range from mild to severe. In the mildest cases, the baby will receive humidified oxygen. If that is insufficient to provide relief, continuous positive airway pressure (CPAP) is created by inserting a tube into the baby's nose to deliver oxygen. In the most extreme cases, a ventilator that controls the pressure and volume of air is utilized by inserting an endotracheal tube into the baby's windpipe.

In the case of babies born under twenty-eight weeks, there is almost always some respiratory problem, with 50 percent likelihood that they will develop bronchopulmonary dysplasia (BPD), a form of chronic lung disease. The earlier the gestation, the more likely the twins are to develop this problem. Fortunately, most babies can recover completely from this condition, but it does take a long time. The lung takes about two years to develop its full complement of airways and then increases further in size as the body grows, so there is a great deal of potential for improvement in the lung after the babies are born.

* Apnea

Apnea, which is not uncommon in premature babies born before thirty-four weeks of age, is defined as a temporary disruption in breathing. It may last for only a few seconds and not present much of a problem, or it may be more prolonged (more than twenty seconds in duration), be associated with a slowing of the heart rate called bradycardia, and be of much concern. There are many disorders that can cause apnea, and your doctor will want to make the appropriate clinical and laboratory evaluations to rule them out. Idiopathic apnea of prematurity is the presence of apnea in an otherwise healthy premature baby. Babies with this type of apnea will grow out of it as they mature. If this diagnosis is made, it can be treated with medication. It's interesting to note that caffeine, which stimulates respiration, is often prescribed to treat apnea. This irony has not escaped the notice of numerous mothers who have commented that they gave up coffee for nine months only to have their newborns become instant "coffee achievers." Typically, once the baby is apnea-free for five to seven days in the hospital, medication is discontinued and the baby is observed carefully. Treatment may be reinstated if significant episodes of the apnea recur. If necessary, parents may be able to bring their premature twins home with apnea monitors as well as caffeine, which is given once a day, or aminophylline, a similar drug that stimulates respiration, and is given three or four times a day.

* Home Monitoring for Apnea

FINANCIAL CONSIDERATIONS:

As soon as you and your twins' doctor anticipate that you'll be needing a home apnea monitor, you should discuss it with the appropriate hospital personnel (discharge planners). The most common delaying factor in the discharge process is funding. The hospital should look into which expenses will be covered by your health insurance carrier and discuss them with you ahead of time. They may also help to determine whether you are eligible for any government assistance. In the case of multiple births, you may find that hospitals, home health-care agencies, and/or medical rental companies will offer you some financial break. You'll never know unless you ask.

What You Need to Know

- Understand the diagnosis. What is the usual course of symptoms, and how long should you expect to be monitoring?
- Discuss the purposes, responsibilities, risks, and benefits of home monitoring.
- Have you learned how and where to place the monitor, how to attach it to one or both babies, and how to provide the appropriate skin care?
- What do you need to know to carry out a successful home-care plan? Do you have an adequate support system? Have you lined up additional caregivers to be trained in the use of the monitor system?
- Do you understand that you must use the monitor when your twins are sleeping, when they are in the car with you, or when they are unattended in a room at home?
- What are the appropriate interpretations of and responses to the monitor alarm? It can be difficult to distinguish true apnea alarms from those that are simply the result of a lead becoming dislodged from your baby's skin. What is your emergency medical plan, including names and phone numbers as needed?

the cardiovascular system

The cardiovascular system—the heart and the blood vessels that work with the heart—must also adapt to function in the extrauterine environment. In utero, before birth, the blood is obviously not shunted through the lungs for oxygenation. There is a channel called the ductus arteriosus that shunts blood from the right side of the body to the left side, bypassing the lungs. In a healthy baby, the ductus arteriosus will close within the first twenty-four hours. In premature babies this duct may not close naturally, and medication may be needed to close the patent ductus arteriosus. In rare cases, surgical closure is necessary.

other problems

Other problems that are more likely to affect your twins if they are born before thirty-four weeks include:

- Intraventricular hemorrhage (IVH), bleeding in the brain. Although it occurs in 10 to 20 percent of babies born before thirty-four weeks, it seldom results in severe long-term disability.
- Necrotizing enterocolitis (NEC), inflammation of the intestine that may lead to perforation and sepsis (infection).
- Retinopathy of prematurity (ROP), retinal damage that usually has little effect on vision.
- Twin-to-twin transfusion syndrome is thought to occur when blood from one twin flows into the other twin through vascular connections in the placenta. One twin then becomes anemic and growth-retarded as a result of decreased blood volume. The other twin, who is the recipient, has an increase in blood volume and is much larger at birth. Complications after delivery are primarily due to growth retardation and premature delivery. This problem occurs almost exclusively in identical monochorionic/diamnionic twins and is very rare.

(*See the Resource Guide at the back of this book for a referral to Dr. Klein's and Ms. Ganon's book* Caring for Your Premature Baby.)

twins born after thirty-four weeks' gestation

Twins born after thirty-four weeks' gestation are unlikely to have the significant problems mentioned above but may have some less serious problems that delay their discharge home.

jaundice

If bilirubin has not already been measured, your doctor will probably order a bilirubin count on the proposed day of discharge in order to assess the bilirubin level and determine if and when that level should be checked again. A high bilirubin count and the resultant jaundice is more common in premature than full-term babies and is therefore a frequent pediatric concern for many twins who are born early. Jaundice, which occurs in many newborns, is a yellowish discoloration of the skin. It results from the liver's inability to metabolize bilirubin (which is yellow) as quickly as it is produced.

After a baby is born, it begins to break down fetal blood cells, and bilirubin is a byproduct of that operation. The bilirubin is then processed by the liver and passed out through the intestines as waste. As the bilirubin level rises, the yellow color appears first in the face and eyes, and then moves down to the trunk and to the legs. Premature babies are more likely to become jaundiced than term babies because their systems are immature. Parents should be instructed to observe their twins' skin color. In the case of term babies, the pediatrician is likely to monitor the bilirubin count but may not recommend phototherapy (special lights that help the body clear the bilirubin) until the yellow cast to the skin has spread to the legs. In the case of premature twins (born between thirty-four and thirty-seven weeks), phototherapy may be appropriate as soon as the yellow color has spread to the baby's belly. In a full-term baby, bilirubin levels peak between three and five days. These levels are measured by the milligram per deciliter (mg/dl) of the baby's blood. If the bilirubin level reaches 19 or 20 mg/dl, phototherapy is likely to be recommended. In a baby born between thirty-four and thirty-seven weeks, the peak occurs between five and seven days, and it is appropriate to use phototherapy when the level reaches 15 mg/dl—a sort of preemptive strike against levels that are likely to rise. Some pediatricians may recommend phototherapy at even lower levels of bilirubin.

Either one or both of your twins may need phototherapy. This can be achieved by several effective means. If the babies are otherwise healthy, the use of fiber-optic blankets at home will enable parents to have their twins discharged from the hospital. The hospital or a medical equipment company will supply parents with these blankets and instructions for their use. By wrapping the babies in the blankets while they are being cuddled or fed, you are essentially encasing each baby in a layer of light. Fiber-optic blankets tend to work well and have the distinct advantage of enabling you to hold, feed, and bond with each twin during phototherapy. The more traditional option is to place the baby under a bank of fluorescent lights that are available in the hospital nursery or can be rented for home use. If home use of the fiber-optic blanket is not achieving the desired effect, one or both babies may be readmitted to the hospital, where intensive phototherapy using lights and a fiber-optic blanket is likely to succeed in lowering the bilirubin levels. A baby with a high bilirubin count will have blood drawn so that bilirubin levels can be monitored. This is standard procedure, as very high levels can have serious implications for your baby's health.

• *Home vs. Hospital Phototherapy*

You should feel comfortable about trying home phototherapy as long as your twins are feeding well, are active, and show no indications of other medical problems. A home health-care professional assigned to work with your family should be able to do the following:

- Assess the degree of clinical jaundice
- Draw blood for bilirubin determinations if needed
- Weigh each baby
- Set up and explain all aspects of the phototherapy system that your doctor has recommended for your use
- Conduct follow-up clinical assessments and blood drawing as directed by your doctor

If bilirubin levels do not decline, your doctor will recommend hospitalization and intensive phototherapy.

It is important to remember that approximately 60 percent of full-term infants become clinically jaundiced over the first week of life. Casual discussion with other parents in your doctor's waiting room or even on line at the ATM will confirm this; it can be reassuring to hear the veteran parents of year-old twins talk about the successful treatment of jaundice in their babies' first days of life. But those same casual chats can yield an abundance of misinformation. There have been instances where well-meaning neighbors told parents that the only thing their baby needed was some "sunshine" to cure jaundice. This led them to allow the baby to sunbathe, which exposed their newborn's tender skin to overexposure in the sun.

There is also a lot of misinformation about breastfeeding and its implications in the presence of jaundice in newborns. Doctors refer to some cases of jaundice that occur in nursing babies in the first week of life as breastfeeding jaundice. That is distinguished from breast-milk jaundice, which may occur later in over a third of all breast-fed babies and often lasts up to three months. Mothers who want to nurse twins with either of these forms of jaundice should be encouraged to do so.

In the case of breastfeeding jaundice in full-term babies, it is clear from several studies that there is a close relationship between frequency of nursing and a decreased incidence of elevated bilirubin levels in the first week of life. In other words, the more frequently you breastfeed your twins during the first days of life, the lower their bilirubin levels will be. This is probably because the more frequently a mother nurses during her twins' first and second days of life, the earlier her breast milk comes in. New mothers who are nursing their twins should try to feed them as soon as possible after delivery and continue to nurse as often as they wish during those first few days of life. Some mothers try to nurse the twins as frequently as ten to twelve times in a twenty-four hour period to ensure that their breast milk will come in by the third day. Typically, the baby's jaundice will then improve because the breast milk, which is rich in fluid and calories, causes the liver and intestinal function to kick in more effectively.

The bottom line, whether your babies are premature or term, is that you want to attempt to nurse them both as often as you can, because there will be periods of time—maybe as long as four to six hours—when the babies will not be interested in nursing, and that's usually not a problem for them. But when either baby is alert, crying, and awake and wants to nurse, you have to take advantage of the opportunity, perhaps nursing as frequently as every hour. In fact, as challenging as this may be, if you want to attempt to establish a simultaneous breastfeeding schedule, when one baby is awake and ready to nurse you can wake the other and nurse them together. (We'll talk with a mom about her experience simultaneously nursing her twin sons in the next chapter.)

Sometimes one baby is better able to latch on and begin sucking, while the other is slower to learn to nurse. It is natural to be concerned about both babies getting adequate nutrition, but you don't have to have both babies nursing in order to get your breast milk to come in. Remember, in the beginning, they're not getting much milk anyway, and the true focus of this exercise is to get your milk flowing.

regulating body temperature

Most healthy babies born after thirty-four weeks don't have trouble maintaining body temperature. Occasionally, one or both twins will be a little cold right after birth and need to be placed in a warming bed or incubator. The incubator is an enclosed, temperature-controlled, infant-size bed. It is usually made of transparent Plexiglas that has porthole openings to allow medical staff and parents to care for the baby. A baby born between thirty-four and thirty-seven weeks may need to be in the incubator from several hours to several days. At this age, infants are often taken out of the incubators for brief periods of time in order to be fed (either by breast or bottle) and held by their parents.

feeding your twins

Whether they are breast- or bottle-fed, it is important to remember that babies born after thirty-four weeks come in all sizes and degrees of maturity. Some twins born at thirty-five weeks are more like premature infants and others are more like full-term babies. Again, there is no exact cutoff; the timing of the last weeks of fetal development is not precise. The healthy premature infant develops the ability to suck, swallow, and breathe in a coordinated fashion between thirty-four and thirty-six weeks' gestational age. Most infants born after thirty-four weeks can accomplish this feat with little problem and are ready to nurse or bottle-feed immediately after delivery. Yet some infants born prior to thirty-six weeks need to be fed by a tube that goes into their mouth or nose and down into the stomach.

Mothers whose newborns cannot nurse right away will need to use a breast pump in order to bring in their milk supply. A pump should be available in the hospital, but a rental machine will be necessary for use at home. A new mother attempting to provide breast milk for premature twins before they are actually able to take the breast will initially need to pump her breasts at least six to eight times per day, and more frequently if possible. Colostrum and breast milk can then be given to her infants by tube until they are able to nurse. The prematurity of some infants may preclude them from sucking vigorously enough to maintain an adequate milk supply even once they have started nursing. A breast pump with a double setup allows you to pump both breasts at once so that you just might be able to have a few waking hours when you are not feeding or preparing to feed your newborn twins.

In a few days, these infants will develop the skills to breast- or bottle-feed at least once a day to start. A strategy that often works for the mother who wants to breast-feed her slightly premature twins is to have the twins nurse once a day when they are ready to start. Additional breast-feedings can then gradually replace the tube or nipple feeding until the infant can be totally breast-fed. There is no easy way to prepare yourselves as parents for the sight of your babies hooked up to feeding tubes, and this is a good time to use the resources that you have to find other parents whose twins have gone through the experience. Take a look at their rollicking one-, three-, or eight-year-olds and remind yourself that you and your beautiful newborn twins will get there, too.

In the case of some extremely premature twins, your physician may recommend commercially prepared human milk fortifiers in powder or liquid form that can be added to pumped breast milk to further enhance the babies' nutritional intake. Establishing a breast-milk supply for your premature twins takes some special preparation, but many parents have found it well worth the effort. The babies will get the nourishment they need in those early weeks and the mother will develop the milk supply to nourish them successfully as they become more enthusiastic feeders.

It is helpful for new parents to recognize that the first day after birth is a very dynamic time for a newborn's shifting body fluids. Even infants who are ready to feed (either by breast or bottle) immediately after birth take in only a small amount on the first day. Their weight decreases for several days and then as their fluid intake increases (and the mother's milk comes in if she is nursing), they begin to regain their birthweight. In fact, if a baby doesn't lose a little weight after birth, we may be concerned that there is some fluid retention.

Many new parents are under the impression that they should expect six to eight wet diapers a day for each twin right after birth. What usually happens, however, is that the number of wet diapers may actually decrease to two or three per day until their fluid intake increases and they start to have the expected six to eight.

dr. klein on good hygiene at feeding time

"Although it is well accepted that breast-feeding results in fewer colds, diarrhea, and illnesses in young babies, the exact mechanism that accounts for this phenomenon is quite complicated.

Apart from the fact that the immunoglobulins and cellular components found in breast milk protect against infection, the fact that breast-feeding moms tend to wash their hands very frequently may also be a contributory factor. Whether your babies nurse at your breast or take a bottle, cleanliness is very important.

If mom has a cold, she needs to take extra precautions as her hands touch her nipples or her baby's mouth. Simply stated, anyone feeding the twins should be sure to wash their hands first."

bringing your babies home

There are certain criteria that we look for when deciding whether your twins are ready to be discharged. The standards may vary, but this gives you a general impression of what to expect:

- Each baby must be able to maintain his or her body temperature at room temperature.
- Each baby must be taking all feedings—whether by breast or bottle—by mouth.

In the case of premature babies born prior to thirty-four weeks, we add the following conditions:

- They should have consistent weight gain prior to discharge.
- If they are off respiratory stimulants, they should be apnea-free for three to five days.
- If they are on respiratory stimulants, they should be apnea-free for three days, and the parents should be prepared for and capable of taking care of their babies at home on an apnea monitor.

Most babies born after thirty-seven weeks can be discharged after a day or two. While many babies born between thirty-four and thirty-seven weeks may also be discharged that soon, some may spend additional days in the hospital before they are ready to go home.

SIDS and "back to sleep"

Before you leave the hospital, it is likely that one or more members of your medical team will speak with you about the importance of placing both your babies on their back to sleep. *This is because sudden infant death syndrome (SIDS), which is defined as the unexplained death of a previously healthy infant, usually occurs when babies are asleep and is associated with sleeping in the prone (face-down) position.* Armed with this knowledge, the American Academy of Pediatrics (AAP) has stated that healthy babies, including premature infants (unless there are medical reasons that preclude it), should *always* be placed on their back at bedtime and for napping. It has been demonstrated that the risk of SIDS for twins is greater than it is for singletons. Risk is also increased for males and for those babies that are small for their gestational age. The AAP, in collaboration with other organizations dedicated to child health and safety, have created the "Back To Sleep" campaign to raise public awareness of the importance of safely positioning infants for sleep and nap time. This is not the information your mother heard from her doctor when you were a baby, but while the cause of SIDS continues to elude researchers, we do know that a "back to sleep" position has significantly reduced the risk of the syndrome.

Death from SIDS is unusual before one month of age, and the peak incidence occurs between two and four months. Almost all cases of SIDS (95 percent) occur by six months of age. While we have not yet been able to definitively state the cause of SIDS, we do know several facts of which parents should be aware:

- SIDS is not caused by suffocation or choking.
- The "back to sleep" position does not cause babies to choke, should they spit up.
- SIDS is not contagious.

- SIDS is not caused by the diphtheria, tetanus, or acellular pertussis (DTaP) vaccine, or other immunizations.

Parents should put their babies down to sleep on their backs, on a firm mattress, with no blankets under the baby. No pillows or stuffed toys should be in the crib of an infant. One light blanket is sufficient, and the room temperature should feel comfortable to you. Unless your doctor tells you there is a medical reason for placing your babies in another position, remember that they should always be placed on their *back to sleep*.

going home

priorities

Chaos is a term with which you'd better be very familiar. Writer Nora Ephron has said that bringing home a baby is like tossing a small hand grenade into a house. Draw your own conclusions about bringing home twins. The more you resist, the more likely you are to be overwhelmed by your newly chaotic environment. If twins are your first children, you cross the threshold of your home as a parent for the first time without the litmus test of previous children to help you gauge the big and little situations in the daily lives of two newborns. If you do have a child or children at home, you have their needs as a constant hum in the back of your mind: Are they feeling left out?

How will you plan William's birthday party? Has Jennifer finished her homework? Has she even looked at her homework? Some parents of newborn twins arrive home to a toddler who is suddenly displaced as the baby of the family. There is not a parent of twins who has not thought, "How will I survive this?"

The best advice to give any family with newborn twins is to prioritize. We've all experienced those moments in our lives when we see a family's devastating loss on TV, and even as we take in the news and share in their sorrow, we think, "Thank heavens my kids are fine; my family is safe; everything is okay."

For a brief time we get our priorities straight. All those nagging daily thoughts ("I could use a little more money in the bank" and "Will I ever lose those fifteen pounds?") disappear, and suddenly life is just great—"My kids are fine . . . my family is safe." But inevitably, that instant prioritization of what is truly important fades away and within weeks, days, or even hours, we return to the lesser

The First Law of Survival for New Parents of Twins
Designate! Designate! Designate!

- If Mom handles the family accounts, let Dad take them over. It could mean a nap to an exhausted mother.
- Ask your teenager to help you fold the laundry.
- Go over your weekly shopping needs with a friend or extended family member who might handle the family shopping for the first month. Have a friend take over for the next two weeks and pass the task along to volunteers for the first four months of the babies' lives.
- When friends ask if they can help, say yes first, and figure out what they can do later. (If you're really on top of this, you may have a list of tasks on hand, ready to designate. For example, pick up cleaning on Mondays, take the car in for an oil change, weed the garden.)
- Schedule a grocery trip with an older child to choose lunch supplies for her own school lunches. This gives the two of you some special time together and teaches her self-sufficiency. (Your designated shopper will take over in the weeks to come.)
- Ask willing friends or family to stock the freezer with ready-made meals for you to defrost and serve. It is more important that you sit down and eat with your family than cook for them right now.
- Let the babies become familiar with your extended family. If your sister-in-law can take them for a stroll twice a week, use that time to get off your feet.

Remember, people really want to help.

concerns that make up the complicated litany of day-to-day life. On the far side of all the exhaustion, and all the details of making it through each day with your beautiful new babies, is your deeply rewarding family life. Just try to keep your eyes on the prize!

Arriving home with twins carries the matter of prioritizing to a whole new level. Lists that used to start with "organize family photos" will not surface again for several years. Suddenly your priorities cry out to you quite literally, and with startling clarity. (It may, however, take a little time to distinguish the cry of one priority from the other.) The piles of photos will wait. You have two newborn babies who are utterly dependent upon you for their survival. However it may have been, there must now be a fundamental shift in focus.

growing comfortable with feeding your twins

The immediacy of your babies' needs will be loud and clear at feeding time. As parents, your approach to feeding your twins should be determined by what works best for your particular family. Many considerations enter into play when parents of twins are deciding whether to breast-feed, bottle-feed (using expressed breast milk or formula), or try a combination of the two. The way you choose to feed your twins is, in part, a family lifestyle decision. Keep in mind that there are possible advantages to the family in both feeding approaches. As is true with all newborns, your twins will respond best to the feeding method or methods that offer you the greatest opportunity to be successful as nurturing parents. Your babies will flourish as a result of your ability to relax and bond with them at feeding time.

The benefits of breast-feeding are undeniable, but the challenges of nursing your twins can be formidable as well. Included in this chapter is an inspiring talk with a mother of twins who, with a lot of help, made her way through those early nursing challenges and as of this writing is preparing to wean her twins after a year of nursing them simultaneously. Ultimately, parents should be encouraged to nourish their babies in whatever manner they decide is best for their twins, while being realistic for themselves. The impression that breast-feeding is the only right way to nourish your twins should not be the determining factor in feeding your babies. A mother who, for whatever reason, chooses to bottle-feed her twins should not be made to feel she is failing to do right by her babies. Modern formulas also provide excellent infant nourishment, and bottle-feeding can offer a father the opportunity to more fully participate in nourishing his twins. At a moment in his life when the responsibilities for providing for these two babies is thrust upon him, the father who takes the time out to feed his babies is given a sweet reminder of why he is on that often exhausting treadmill in the first place. Whether using formula or expressed breast milk, when a father shares in the feeding of the twins he is included in a very important aspect of their early life. It is interesting and comforting to both parents when they can compare notes on their twins' individual eating styles. Whatever decision you make, your deep satisfaction at cuddling your hungry babies and watching them thrive will tell you that you've made the right choice.

Where there is a strong history of food allergies, your pediatrician may restrict regular formula and recommend a predigested cow's milk–based formula if the babies are not nursing. Either or both nursing babies might also react to cow's-milk protein when the mother is drinking milk. Some breast-feeding mothers with particularly irritable babies may want to eliminate all milk and beef products from their diet for one week in order to see if this results in a calmer baby. Babies can react irritably to the taste or content of breast milk, depending on what a mother eats. The nursing mother who is taking in a lot of caffeine in coffee, tea, or soft drinks is likely to see the effects of that stimulant in her babies. Nursing moms have reported babies who grew suddenly mellow when caffeine was withdrawn from their own diet.

The mother who chooses to breast-feed will begin to nurse her babies shortly after delivery. As we've discussed, approximately 50 percent of twins are delivered at thirty-four to thirty-seven weeks. Babies born at this age may not yet suck vigorously enough to bring in or maintain an adequate supply of their mother's milk. This should not deter a mother from breast-feeding her twins. The babies should nurse first, and then the mother can use a breast pump with a double hookup to begin to express breast milk if necessary. Just as the mother needs to supplement the twins' sucking with the action of the breast pump, the babies may need to have their early nursing supplemented with bottle feedings of breast milk or formula.

Breast-feeding eight to twelve times daily on both breasts for the first couple of days is the very best way to ensure that the breast milk will be in by day three or four. For babies born after thirty-four weeks and feeding by mouth, try to avoid supplementing the babies' nourishment with water or formula unless ad-

Many mothers report success with the "football hold" when feeding their twins.

Particularly with young babies, you may want to hold both babies in your arms, positioning them to cross over each other as they are cradled over your torso.

vised by your doctor, as that is likely to diminish their appetites. It takes hungry babies to bring on their mother's milk supply. It is important to understand that there is no finite supply of breast milk. This is strictly a situation of supply and demand. The more the babies demand through sucking, the more milk a mother's breasts will supply. A breast-feeding mother must be adequately hydrated, drinking at least eight to ten glasses of fluid each day. Cultivating the technique to breast-feed twins requires commitment from a mother, but rest assured that a woman's body is designed to accommodate the nursing needs of both her babies. Finding the time and focus to breast-feed your babies will take support from family, friends, and maybe even colleagues at work. But in the long run, what may seem like an indulgence will prove to have been a highly pragmatic approach.

While the feeding of two babies may appear an overwhelming task at first, it has hidden benefits: Usually, the needs of hungry twins will preclude any possibility of a mother jumping back into a full schedule before she should. Do not underestimate the benefits of enforced rest. Most of us are conditioned to work at an unnaturally overzealous pace, and a new mother is not immune to the seductive lure of a clean house or a stack of completed reports in the "out" basket of her home office. But no mother should settle for an unrested body that staggers through an overbooked day. Remember, no matter how frequently people tell you to rest up before your babies are born, the profound exhaustion experienced in the early weeks or months of your twins' lives can only be remedied by a daily commitment to getting off your feet.

Janet and Christopher Prince are the parents of twin sons, William and Langston. Almost a year after the babies' birth, Janet talks about nursing her sons and shares some strategies for success.

DID YOU START OUT WITH THE IDEA THAT
YOU WANTED TO BREAST-FEED YOUR TWINS?

I always assumed I would at least try breast-feeding. Once I knew I was pregnant with twins, my goal was to try to breast-feed for a year. Our childbirth classes included a breast-feeding course, and the instructor—who did not have twins—had the point of view that babies have their own schedules and she didn't really recommend that I try simultaneous nursing, at least in the beginning. As I was leaving the class, a woman who was attending—she was going to be the coach for her daughter—said she had had twins and that *you had to feed them at the same time or you just go crazy.*

Left to right, Christopher, William, Langston, and Janet Prince.

HOW DID YOU GET STARTED NURSING LANGSTON AND WILLIAM?

They were delivered at thirty-six weeks. And they were really a good size. William was six pounds, four ounces, and Langston was five pounds, thirteen ounces. Now that they are about eleven months old, it is hard to remember exactly how everything went when they were born, but they did have low blood sugar and were given some formula at first. I started trying to nurse them simultaneously in the hospital, almost right away. The hospital staff was supportive. There was a lactation consultant who made herself very available to work with me. The first time I actually tried to nurse, it was with one baby at a time as the consultant showed me how to get each baby to latch on. We definitely had latching problems in the beginning, so it helped to work with one at a time. Langston was not as good an eater at first. He had more problems latching on, and he always took longer. In the very beginning I would have to say there were a handful of days when I did not nurse them at the same time. But I was nursing them together within a day or two. To tell you the truth, I didn't get started pumping at the hospital because it was kind of daunting, even though they were very nice . . . it was just one too many new things. But I had the babies with me in the room and we practiced getting them on the breast a lot. The experience of giving birth to twins is pretty incredible. There is so much to take in, in addition to getting the babies started at nursing. But breast-feeding is so worth it. I don't want anyone to think that if they have a hard time they should give up trying to nurse. I think everyone must have a hard time at first.

CAN YOU TALK A LITTLE BIT ABOUT
GETTING SETTLED IN AT HOME?

We were only in the hospital for two days, and when I came home I had a lot of help. Honestly, I would have to attribute my breast-feeding success to the support I had, at least getting over the hump of learning how to do it . . . sort of getting the babies to the point where they were nursing pros . . . I really needed help at home. They would fall asleep at the breast and it was hard to get them to latch on. But then it got better and better until it seemed they could stay at the breast actually nursing for twenty or thirty minutes—it seemed like they would stay forever if I let them. But now that they're older, for the past couple of months, they seem to want to nurse for about ten minutes at a time.

It was a little crazy because for the first four months, my husband's work took him out of town except for some weekends, and that was really tough. My mother stayed with me for a few weeks and for a time, we were able to have a baby nurse with twin experience who came to lend a hand at night. That really helped ease me through the sleep deprivation because she would bring them to me and then take them away to burp them. I have to say, the burping thing seemed to take ages. One thing that helped to establish their schedule together was that when one of the babies woke up, we'd get the other one up at the same time.

They were born on a Monday, and we just kept nursing so that they were getting the colostrum until my milk came in on Friday. In fact, they were at home under bilirubin lights for jaundice and I nursed them every hour-and-a-half to two hours for the first week or two. It was kind of a brutal schedule but it definitely got my milk flow well established. Actually, because of their low blood sugar and the jaundice, they also got a little bit of formula in a bottle after each nursing session.

WAS IT A CHALLENGE TO GET THEM TO TAKE THE BOTTLE AS WELL AS THE NIPPLE?

Oh yes. I remember even getting them to drink an ounce out of a bottle was like, oh my goodness, we'll never be able to do this . . . but it worked out.

We really had a team. After my mom left, one of my aunts came. Another one of my aunts is an OB/GYN nurse, and she came intermittently and that really helped with the breast-feeding. I started pumping about four days after they were born. I became engorged, so I pumped. Even though it was difficult, the baby nurse encouraged me to pump at least three times a day after nursing. When the baby nurse was there she would occasionally give the babies breast milk from the bottle so I could get some extra sleep. I needed sleep so badly. I did have occasional experiences with a plugged duct and that was very painful, but my baby nurse recommended putting rice in a sock and then briefly heating the sock in the microwave. Placing that over my breast, and also massaging my breast, helped resolve the problem. I know that plugged ducts can cause some women to stop nursing, and there were times I thought I just can't do this anymore, but I'm so glad I stuck with it.

I was almost obsessive about them having only breast milk. I did not want to give them formula. But in hindsight I think I'd be more comfortable now, understanding that it was really okay for them to have a little bit of formula in the very early days when they had jaundice. But after the jaundice resolved, I pretty much tried to give them only breast milk. And that worked out well.

HOW DO YOU MANAGE THE ACTUAL
NURSING TIME AND SCHEDULE?

We kept their room nice and dark at night. Like I said, if one was up and hungry, we always woke the other to feed them together. We immediately tried to establish a bedtime, which in the beginning was nine o'clock, but it eventually became eight o'clock or eight-thirty. I had a friend tell me that she had stopped night feedings at four months for her twins. So at four months I asked Dr. Klein, and he said he thought it was too early—we ended up starting them on solid food at six months. But at four months, we were doing two night feedings—at midnight and four o'clock. And they were up for a morning feeding at seven.

For the first four months, I needed somebody there to help me with nursing them together. I've talked with some of my friends who have twins and they all found that they needed a second person to help them. I needed someone to bring them to me and get them positioned in that "football hold." We tried other positions at first, but somehow it just ended up that the football position was the one that worked the best. It's funny, now, if I have one with me, I go out and we go walking, I go to the store. But when you're nursing two, you're really tied down. I kind of feel now that if I ever nursed one at a time, I could practically do the dishes with the other hand. Another thing is that I made sure to get them both used to both breasts. My right breast has always produced more milk, so I wanted to make sure that one baby wasn't always getting the left side, which wasn't producing as much milk.

NOW THAT YOU'RE BACK AT WORK, HOW IS IT GOING?

The boys are at home with a nanny during the day and I nurse them before I leave for work. When I first went back to work when they were four months old, I pumped three times a day. Now I've cut back to two. Fortunately, I have my own office at work so I can lock the door and have the privacy to pump there. I have to say that when I was home on maternity leave, after the first few weeks, I stopped pumping and just nursed them. The way it has worked out is that I nurse them in the morning; the next time they eat, they have one bottle of breast milk; their third feeding is formula; and then I nurse them when I get home. So since I've gone back to work, they've been getting one formula feeding a day.

CAN YOU TALK ABOUT WHAT NURSING HAS MEANT TO YOU?

It's been absolutely wonderful. But I think all moms of twins feel like there are times when you just wonder how you're making it through each day. Now that they are almost a year old, I'm pretty much ready to stop nursing, but I feel a little conflicted, too. There is really nothing like it. You're so close, and it's so clear they're comforted by it. And to know that I'm the source of their comfort is wonderful. It really is. And this may not be the most important thing, but I definitely attribute nursing to losing my pregnancy weight. Plus all the running around . . .

WHAT WOULD YOU LIKE TO SAY TO NEW
MOTHERS OF TWINS ABOUT NURSING?

I would say it's daunting, but definitely try nursing, and try nursing them at the same time. And I'd say you should think about every possible way you might arrange to get help in the first weeks and even months. I feel so fortunate . . . my boys have gotten such a great start-up for their health. They're hardly sick. In fact, they've only had one cold, I think. The health benefits of breast milk are such that I'd just say to really give it a very serious try. And don't give up after a month. It took me longer than a month to feel like, okay, I've got this. I've talked with other twin moms and they agree that you can kind of hit the wall at a month or two when it still feels really hard, but it definitely gets easier. There are so many things going on. You're dealing with two babies; you're getting to know these people. And unless you've had babies before, and these were my first, nursing is something incredibly new.

I know a lot of women stop nursing when they go back to work. Pumping is no fun. But if you can find a way to work it out, you should, because they grow up so fast and before you know it, the opportunity to breast-feed ends. I would also say, at least for me, simultaneous nursing is absolutely the way to go. I don't see how you find the time any other way. Nursing is such great together time.

WHAT ARE YOUR THOUGHTS ABOUT WEANING THE BOYS?

It was always my goal to nurse for a year, so I'm getting ready to wean them. It's getting harder to simultaneously nurse them for several reasons: They're bigger; they are so interested in what's going on that they look around a lot and don't focus as much on feeding; they're also more aware of each other—

William, left, and Langston show off their ability to nurse on the go! Proud mom, Janet, is preparing to wean the boys at one year of age.

sometimes now, they don't like nursing together. When they're tired, one may reach out and touch his brother who will fly into an absolute fury. I think we'll stop the evening nursing first, because they're not that interested in it anymore. I'm probably not going to give up the morning nursing right away because that's when they seem to want it the most. And there's just a calmness about it.

feeding strategies

Generally, the strategy for feeding twins is to find out what works for you and go with it. If you're breast-feeding, one possibility is to nurse one baby on one breast, then follow with the second baby on the other breast, feeding each for ten to fifteen minutes. At the next feeding, be sure to switch sides to maintain an equal milk supply. One baby may be a more vigorous feeder than the other.

In a second scenario, one baby nurses at both breasts to ensure that one breast does not become engorged due to imbalanced demand. The second baby is then fed expressed breast milk or formula from a bottle. At the next feeding, the babies switch, with the bottle baby taking the breast this time. After breast-feeding is well established, many mothers find it convenient to nurse both babies at the same time, either holding them on a pillow or in a "football hold" under each arm.

Half the battle is won by finding a quiet place where you and the babies are least likely to be distracted. Creating a comfy spot in the babies' room is a good idea: You may decide to have your rocker or easy chair in the nursery. In fact, you may want to provide adequate seating in the babies' room for Mom and Dad to comfortably feed the twins at the same time. Establish a routine that includes having your personal supplies at arm's reach: bottles (if you're using them),

At Three Weeks of Age, You Know Things Are Going Well If . . .

- When seen at 2 weeks by your health-care provider, both twins (born after thirty-four weeks) had reached or exceeded their birthweight.
- You are able to tell the twins apart. (If this is still a problem, nail polish on the big toe of one baby has done the trick for many parents. Of course, this is only appropriate while they're too young to put their feet into their mouths.)
- The twins (and you) are starting to sleep more during the night than the day.
- You are looking for or have found someone to care for the twins while you both go out to dinner.
- Feeding time has become an enjoyable opportunity for either or both parents to bond with the babies.

The Second Law of Survival
There's a Reason They Call Them Pacifiers

When you settle in to feed your babies, you may choose to feed one while the second sleeps beside you. The problem is that there is no guarantee that the other twin won't wake up hungry before you're ready for her. Sucking appears to relax and comfort babies, so this is the moment you don't want to be caught without a pacifier or two.

When you are trying to establish a feeding schedule for the twins of every two to four hours and one or both start clamoring for food after an hour-and-a-half, this is the ideal time to try the pacifier.

Many pacifiers (and bottle nipples) are designed to be orthodontically correct, and their calming properties will simplify things at feeding time.

The Third Law of Survival
Back to Basics

The insistent cries of two hungry babies can compromise your better judgment when it comes to saving your back from undue stress. Particularly when you are just getting your feeding rhythms established, your comfort is as important as the babies'. Get in the habit of sitting smart.

- Even though your babies are not yet heavyweights, lift them as though they were. Bend at the knees and use your arms—not your middle back—to support them.
- Make sure your back is supported when you settle in to feed the babies. Do not sit with an unsupported back and lean in toward your hungry babies.
- Remain conscious of relaxing your neck and shoulders as you hold the babies. This is your time to release, not accumulate tension.

---

your book and reading glasses, the portable phone (with the ringer off), a glass of water, and two pacifiers, for example. Have several spare pillows to support your arms as you cradle one or both of the babies, and be sure to support your back. It is important to see to your own comfort when feeding your twins. Remember, you're in this together, and relaxed parents are a real bonus to hungry babies.

For breast-feeding mothers, once your breast milk is in, the babies are likely to need to nurse every two to four hours during daylight. If you are bottle-feeding, feed each twin two to four ounces every two to four hours during the day. In either case, at nighttime let them sleep until either or both of them awakens, and then feed them. The feeding of twins, whether by breast or bottle, presents the family with a unique set of circumstances. You cannot feed them both on demand, or you will be doing little else but feeding babies for the first few months. (Of course, it may feel like that anyway.) In the beginning, you can let the demands of the first hungry baby dictate the feeding schedule; in other words, feed the first hungry baby, then feed the second baby right away. Even if one baby is sleeping, it should be awakened and fed. When the parents of twins discuss sleeping arrangements for the babies, they often express concern about one baby waking the other. In fact, this may be the good news! You actually want both babies awake so that they can both be fed. While this is in direct opposition to the "if it ain't broke, don't fix it" school of twin care, it is the best way to get your babies on the same schedule.

Different feeding styles are among the first things you'll notice regarding the individuality of your two newborns. You may find that one twin (the squeaky wheel) does indeed regulate herself, and awakens at three-hour intervals demanding to be fed. This baby may be a more vigorous eater than her brother, who is less demanding. The twin who feeds enthusiastically is the natural recipient of your delighted attention. Then, when you go to feed the second, less lively eater, you may not be as persistent in your feeding attempts. There is a tendency to allow the less enthusiastic eater to stop sooner, especially when that baby is the second to be fed. Once you recognize that this behavior exists, you may want to purposely feed the less vigorous eater first. This goes a long way toward assuring both babies an ample opportunity to feed and bond with either parent. Feeding time is a perfect example of an opportunity for a parent's insightful intervention to ensure both babies the bonding time and encouragement they need.

dr. klein on feeding one twin at the breast and one on the bottle

"Some mothers report that one baby seems to prefer the breast, while the other is more enthusiastic about the bottle. If she is content with this situation and both babies are gaining weight and appear to be thriving, then I don't see a problem. If a mom feels uncomfortable about this—if she fears it indicates some disparity in the care or support she is providing her twins—a pediatrician or breast-feeding consultant can look further into the circumstances surrounding feeding time, ranging from the mother's diet to the nursing environment to the order in which the twins are fed. Perhaps the bottle baby will feed vigorously on breast milk from a bottle. A baby who has switched from breast to bottle can still get Mom's cuddling at feeding time. You should feel comfortable about bringing this or any feeding dilemma to your pediatrician."

making it work: a look at the needs of your other children

If there are other children at home, you will want to include them in the lives of the twins in age-appropriate fashion. There are many task-centered moments that are opportunities for older siblings to become acquainted with the new babies. A little one can bring you diapers or sit in her own rocking chair with a baby doll as you feed the twins. An older child can help with many of the household chores. Interestingly, fathers report a renewed pleasure in relationships with children already in the home when newborn twins enter the picture. While siblings are likely to be primed for the arrival of the twins, it is very important to take steps to ensure that they are more invested in than threatened by the newcomers. Just as you have made provisions for the twins, so must you provide for the needs of your other children at this unique moment in your family's life. Siblings, whether they are toddlers or teenagers, will need assurances that their parents are still there for them. This is readily accomplished by providing them with your undivided attention at designated times in their schedules. The certainty of this special time is an invaluable aid, providing parents with a concrete goal to offer their children (and themselves). It is no longer a question of asking a child to wait indefinitely for your attention—the "maybe later" that parents offer guiltily and children hear with dread. Instead, you and your children will come to anticipate the satisfying payoff of a schedule that includes a designated period of time when they (not the twins, or your job, or the house, or anything or anyone else) have your undivided attention. It is equally important for both parents to establish special time with their other children—and whether those children are six or sixteen, to tell them repeatedly that you treasure the time you get to spend one-on-one with them.

The designated time will need to be daily for a young child. In many families, much attention is paid to the fostering of a relationship between the young child with the new babies who are entering the family. Thoughtful family and friends fuss over the child, reinforcing how great it is to be a big brother or sister, and how lucky the twins will be to grow up with such a loving older sibling. But sometimes, lost in the message of the new sibling connection, is the completely *reasonable* resentment a young child is going to feel by virtue of having to share the spotlight of parental attention. It is important to remember that a child's resentment of new siblings is also an expression of the deepness of the bond that child feels with you, the parents. Especially for young children, using your child's name to identify your special time will reaffirm the important bond he or she shares with you. No matter how hectic it has been at the dinner hour, your five-year-old needs to know there is a time in each day that he will have each parent's undivided attention—perhaps it will be Daddy giving him his bath each night. Maybe after bath time, your daughter knows she can count on Mom to read her a story (more likely several stories!) before tucking her in. For your teenager, a weekly event might be more meaningful. It could be going out to lunch with Mom every Saturday, or staying up late one night a week to hang out with Dad and watch a video.

This is not about supplying elaborate treats for your children. It is about providing them with the bedrock knowledge that you are there for them. There are three key elements here: first, that the time be consistent (if you say you'll be putting your daughter to bed each night, then make every effort to make it happen); second, that it be about that child alone; and third, that this is not the time to enlist your child's aid in warming formula for the twins or putting together their cribs. The dramatic entry of twins into the family is a time to rally the troops—and your troops are much more likely to feel generously about meeting the needs of the twins if their own need for love, attention, and guidance is not wanting.

One Mom's Tale
The Twins Come Home

(continued from page 200, Chapter 13)

I delivered my twins by cesarean section at thirty-seven weeks. I had a son and a daughter, Jeff and Molly. Both the babies were able to come home with me, and then the circus really got going! There was no time to ponder what effect my being away for those weeks had on Ben and Emily, my older children at home. I can't say that I felt any guilt at the time . . . but the deficit is more apparent to me now. Every time I see an eighteen-month-old toddler, I realize I came home with two babies when I already had a preschooler and a tiny thing toddling around holding
(continued)

on to my pant leg. Suddenly there were two more. We were really winging it. No nanny, no housekeeper—I was on my own. I nursed at first because I really felt I had to, but it got a whole lot easier when I made a decision to switch to formula. We had a production line and would make twenty-five little feeding bottles at a time. It was great to have Paul able to help feed the babies.

The advice at my twins club was to take it a minute at a time. And as the weeks turn to months, it becomes ten minutes at a time and then half an hour. . . . You just creep along, making a little progress each day. If you insist upon looking at the whole picture, you get overwhelmed. As far as my two older children were concerned, I think we kind of were all together in feeling a little miffed that we were suddenly this big family that required so much work. As soon as the doctor gave me the go-ahead to be out and about with the babies, we were in those car seats and we were gone. I had been isolated for long enough. We got the double stroller, Emily held on, and we were off to the park. In retrospect, with a toddler at home, I'd recommend that parents get a triplet stroller. Emily did kind of get bounced too quickly out of her baby spot. But she adapted by becoming very much the little mommy. She truly helped to care for those babies. She's good at it, and she is also good at letting us know how good she is at it. We are very lucky. I suppose it could have gone the other way, but she loves little children and is wonderful with them. I know there was an impact on Ben, too, but he had already begun to have his own little social life. He had pals and loved to have play dates.

Paul and I worked very hard to make sure everyone was getting attention and that they all got some individual time. But I will tell you they are all very capable and very self-sufficient children. They all seem to make good decisions and I'm very proud of them. But in the first year . . . You know how they always tell you God doesn't give you more than you can handle. . . . My response was that I was sure he had gotten me confused with someone else!

when you don't all come home together: one or both twins remain in the hospital

Pregnancy is a time of heightened emotions for parents. A multiple pregnancy further increases the stakes. You're playing the waiting game. The twins' due date looms large on the calendar—the day the waiting will stop and your family's new life will begin. There is excitement, anticipation, even apprehension. Above all, there is the implicit sense that the birth of the babies will propel you into the next stage of your lives. But if one or both of your twins is unable to leave the hospital, you may find yourselves playing a whole new kind of waiting game.

Medical problems may dictate the need for one or both twins to remain in your hospital's nursery for days, weeks, or even months. This presents logistical and emotional uncertainty for the whole family: How will you bond with both twins? Will you be able to nurse them both? What about the other children at home? Perhaps the most difficult scenario is when only one baby is able to come home with you. There is just no way a mother is going to be able to give those babies "equal" attention, nor should she expect it of herself. There may be days that she is unable to get to the hospital. That is okay. Maybe Father or Grandma can go to the nursery and hold the baby or touch him in his Isolette. The staff in the hospital nursery is highly skilled: They are there to see to your baby's health and to support your needs to love and bond with your baby. If your child's medical condition warrants it, you may be able to hold and feed her. A member of the nursing staff may guide you in the practice of "kangaroo care" (sometimes referred to as "skin-to-skin care"), in which a baby is held to a parent's bare chest for warmth and comfort with wonderfully healthful results. This practice was developed in South America where nurseries lacked adequate numbers of isolettes for warming premature babies. Perhaps what is most extraordinary about this form of care is that in an age of complex medical technology, this low-tech, very accessible method of care is practiced with undeniably positive results, which include less frequent episodes of apnea, increased rate of weight gain, less fitful sleeping, and increased capability to regulate body temperature. Even before the baby is nursing, it is likely that this contact helps to enhance the mother's milk supply.

The technique employed for kangaroo care is simplicity itself: The premature baby, dressed only in a diaper, is held upright between the mother's bare breasts during feeding. And fathers can participate as well. Even though he cannot actually breast-feed, a father can provide warmth and nurturing that will be of great benefit to the baby. The baby will begin to root toward the mother's breast even before being able to latch on and breast-feed. Each neonatal unit will have its particular protocol for initiating kangaroo care, but you can ask the staff about the possibility even before it is mentioned to you. The practice can continue at home after the baby is released from the neonatal unit. Some parents utilizing kangaroo-care sessions with their preemies have reported that the babies began to actually breast-feed at thirty-two to thirty-four weeks.

All parents want to feel they are making their best effort for their babies at this time, but they must have realistic expectations of themselves and each other. The mother who thinks she is going to make it to the hospital, other twin in tow, for every daylight feeding of her baby needs to be counseled about having more realistic expectations. Consult your pediatrician about questions and concerns, not only for the hospitalized twin, but your whole family. Your hospital is likely to have a family support system that may include a family advocate, a social worker, parent support groups, and parent-to-parent programs. Any or all of these resources are there to help your family through a crisis or to provide general information.

There are many things you can do to participate in the life of your baby who remains in the hospital. If it is your intention to breast-feed your hospitalized son, express milk for him. Take your child's picture and keep it with you. Show it to your other children. Call your baby by name. Speak to your daughter when you visit the nursery and let her become familiar with your voice. If hospital regulations permit, bring your other children to see their sister. Answer your children's questions about the twins honestly—reality is preferable to the scary fantasies they'll create if you try to shelter them. Try to stay calm as an individual and united as a couple. Take care of your health and work steadily toward the time you'll all be together.

The Fourth Law of Survival
Compromise

Remember chaos? While chaos may be the prevailing force in your life, compromise is the key to your mental survival. An unmowed lawn or dishes in the sink or even toys all over the living-room floor are a small price to pay for the opportunity to feed your babies in a quiet room away from the chaos.

settling in at home

two weeks and counting

While most adults reach a certain degree of detachment from the anniversary of their own birth (the big "0s"—forty, fifty, and the like—being notable exceptions), having newborn twins at home wrenches you unerringly back to near obsession with noting the anniversary of each of their achievements. You have undoubtedly recognized the miracle of their first twenty-four hours upon the earth, just as you've made careful note of the first smile, the first time they looked into your eyes, the first time they grasped your finger, their first attempts to reach out for each other, even the first dirty diaper.

Making it through each day is a noteworthy accomplishment. By the time you have been home for several weeks, you no longer refer to your babies exclusively as "the twins." Each is likely to have had his own significant moments, her own individual responses to you and to their environment. You know that whereas James likes to be loosely swaddled and startles at the sound of the doorbell, Rebecca can sleep through the "1812 Overture" with the dog barking along. Almost without realizing it, you are transitioning from the dizzying newness of adding two new members to your family to the more reflective examination of what it all means.

What are the ramifications as far as your marriage is concerned? How will you manage financially? Will the demands of family require you to reassess your career or educational goals? The implications of adding twins to the family are further-reaching than the casual observer would imagine. After the joggers in the park admire your two-seat stroller and speculate about your diaper bills, they wish you good luck, and you are the ones who go home to the twenty-four/seven of life with two new babies. Once you have had your babies home with you for several weeks, it is not unusual to find that the stream of well-wishers has dwindled to a trickle of the few steadfast friends and family members who are prepared to hang in there for the duration. We've discussed the importance of accepting the generosity of that support team, but inevitably it is the parents who bear the greatest responsibility in developing successful strategies for the day-to-day life with their children and each other. It is important to return to that primary relationship, because it can and will have such a strong impact on the lives of your twins.

dr. klein on keeping records

"The world can be divided into those who keep records and those who don't. No matter which side you were on before your babies were born, new parents of twins may as well come on board. The purchase of a dry-erase board for the kitchen and a little notebook is a modest investment to make in your twins' care—and your sanity!

The changing of the guard can be a frenetic experience. As Mom, Dad, or a caregiver comes on shift, babies may be cranky, hungry, wet, soiled, in need of medication, or any combination of the above. And there is no guarantee that your parenting/management styles are going to translate easily as one of you takes over for the other. One may have a casual approach to, say, feeding time that drives the other just a little nuts. While Mom may know with certainty just when she fed both babies, and how long it took and how many ounces of formula or expressed milk was consumed by each, Dad, when asked, may glance at the clock and scratch his head, while explaining that the bottles are already in the dishwasher and he doesn't remember *for sure*, but there may have been a little left in the bottle that he figured should be dumped because it ended up staying out on the counter while he was changing the other baby, and . . . you get the picture. As it happens, keeping a record of each baby's feeding, including when and how many ounces they took from a bottle or how long they nursed at the breast, can be an important tool for your pediatrician if there are concerns about one or both babies not gaining adequate weight. I often tell parents to think of it as Weight Watchers in reverse—this time the goal is to put weight on! Maintaining these records will help you to focus on making sure you are taking enough time at feedings. Bring the records with you to your doctor visits, and if one of the babies is not gaining as much as the doctor would like, you can look together at the records to see just how much and how frequently the baby is feeding, and then you can continue to record and monitor your doctor's suggested adjustments. So keep a little notebook with separate records for each twin, and include:

- time of each feeding
- amount consumed
- what was eaten
- time and duration of last nap
- time medication was taken (if applicable)

In order to save time, you might create a template in your computer with the above categories, and print pages that you can fill in and add to a binder. When it comes to the changing of the guard, list the same categories on a dry-erase board and fill in and erase as needed. This is guaranteed to save you time and avoid confusion. If you are not naturally inclined toward keeping records, it may take some effort to get used to this idea, but give it your best shot and you are likely to be pleased with the results.

your couple relationship

The dynamics within the family make a significant impression upon the physical and emotional health of your twins. Each time your physician sees his two, small patients, they are his conduits to viewing the family unit as a whole. Each family has its own threshold of tolerance for such scrutiny. Some parents are extremely receptive to this psychosocial approach to the overall health of the family, while others may view it as an infringement on their privacy. As we have discussed earlier, part of your responsibility in choosing the right pediatrician is to have a grasp of his or her child-care philosophy. You don't need to agree with everything your doctor says, but it is helpful to understand that all pediatricians bring to their practice a point of view honed by their experience as a physician and perhaps as a parent. If you find yourself distinctly at odds with your doctor's outlook over an extended period of time, you may want to look for another pediatrician. But inquiries about your lifestyle are frequently the most effective way to problem-solve where your twins are concerned.

Certainly, the early months of parenting twins are enormously challenging, but does a new mother need to be bone-weary every single day? This is where the team approach can be very helpful. Parents and their pediatrician should take the time to talk about what you laughingly refer to as the twins' sleeping schedule. Or think about what factors are leading to excessive fatigue on your part. What factors, you may ask? Well, how about that you just gave birth to two babies after carrying them around for nine months! Doesn't that pretty much account for all the exhaustion one could ever hope to have? Well, yes and no. The early months of parenting twins is unquestionably one of the most physically draining experiences you are likely to endure. But it does get easier in time, and you can make it a little easier on yourself in the present. In fact, just as people tend to overschedule themselves before they even think about having babies, new parents often have unrealistic expectations of themselves, each other, and even the babies once they are born. That is further exacerbated by the assumption that as new parents of twins, you can kiss the idea of any real relaxation good-bye.

But the truth is that the undeniable joy of having twins does not mean you have to give up having some balance in your life. We've talked about the importance of setting priorities when you come home from the hospital, but the best-laid plans have a tendency to slip away as days turn to weeks and weeks slip into months. What starts as a few hectic days with couples barely seeing each other can turn into a pattern of failed communication. Sometimes your pediatrician is also a detective as you search together for the clues to an improved daily routine for the whole family.

For example: A mother brings her twins in for a checkup and in the course of the examination reveals to the doctor that she is exhausted and at her wit's end. The babies are sleeping most of the day and are up all night. She can't remember the last time she had a discussion with her husband that was not about schedules, and they are both growing eerily familiar with the pizza delivery guy. The first thing the doctor might do is get a detailed description of what goes on in the household in the course of a day:

- When do the babies wake up?
- What do they do when they wake up?
- Are they hungry?
- Who feeds them when they first wake up?
- When do the babies go down for the night?

The outcome is that the doctor realizes these babies are up until 11:00 each night because Dad doesn't get home until late in the evening and that is his only time to be with them. Meanwhile, a pattern is emerging that has Mom frustrated and tired, Dad feeling that his time with the babies is very limited, both parents failing to get any real couple time, and one too many half-eaten pizzas in the refrigerator.

The longer this process goes on, the more difficult it is to change and the greater the frustration all around. Mom is at home, going through the difficult process of establishing a feeding schedule for the babies, while Dad is at work, imagining all the wonderful time he is missing with them. When they are finally together with both babies, they never get around to discussing the reality of both their days. It is not easy to sit there with your milk letting down at the sound of your baby's cry and force yourself to wait an hour until it is time for a feeding. So the blissful time Dad imagines he is missing is not quite the real picture. And the daily interaction he is having in the business world may have frustrations that he no longer feels free to express at home. The essence of the coupledom that brought you together as helpmates and lovers—and gave you the courage and passion to start a family—is under siege. The bottom line is that without effective communication, long-term estrangement between couples sometimes takes root in the tiny shadows of two precious, new lives.

The first recommendation a pediatrician might offer this couple would be to set a bedtime for their babies, and make every reasonable attempt to stick to it.

The benefits of even a little quiet, undistracted couple time in the evening are undeniable to the health of the relationship. We'll talk about this more a little later. Next, a pediatrician might advise these parents to feed the twins every two to four hours during the daytime. That means that if one of the twins seems hungry or cranky an hour after feeding, she may need to be held off. Particularly with twins, you sometimes have to draw that line in the sand and make a commitment to getting them on a feeding schedule. At first glance this may seem too difficult, and maybe even unkind to a hungry baby. But the baby who is always snacking is never really hungry, nor is she ever completely satisfied. Is there someone other than Mom to take the "squeaky wheel" for a stroller ride, cuddle, or play? Being away from the cries of a hungry baby will keep Mom's milk from letting down and perhaps give her some solo time with her other twin, an older child, or even a relaxing bath. If Mom is on call by herself, she might be able to distract the baby with play or a pacifier.

While one parent may be more likely to take the twins for checkups, it is very important to communicate with the absent parent about the guidelines or suggestions your pediatrician offers regarding feeding or sleeping. In the case of the dad who looks forward to his late-evening time with his children, he may need to adjust his expectations—giving up his Saturday-morning basketball game so that he gets weekend time with the babies and uses weeknights to hear about their day in the course of couple time with his wife.

When one twin is still hospitalized several weeks or even months after birth, the strains upon the couple relationship are even greater. This is the time to seek any and all outside support you can. The Family and Medical Leave Act (discussed in chapter 13) is designed for just such a situation. Individual states may have state disability insurance (SDI) that covers family leave for the birth of a child. Speak with an official from the human resource department of your company, or contact your state labor office with your questions about paid and unpaid parental leave. We've talked about the need for flexibility on the part of families with twins, but this same flexibility may need to extend into the workplace. Depending on the medical condition affecting one or both twins, hospitalization could go on for an extended period of time. Parents in that situation are understandably torn as to where they are most needed. That constant anxiety leads to a feeling of distraction that makes you less effective no matter where you are. It's like the old song says: "How can you be in two places at once when you're not anywhere at all?" The neonatal intensive care unit is working twenty-four hours a day to assure the best possible outcome for your baby who is still in the hospital. Truly, the greatest gift you give your baby is to take care of yourself and each other.

dr. klein on sleeping arrangements, bedtime, and keeping the lights out at night

"I know people don't follow it to the letter, but . . . I usually encourage new parents not to have their babies sleeping with them. There is the potential for rolling over on one of the babies, or of having everyone's sleep compromised, and that includes the twins! A baby is highly sensitive to the scent of its mom, particularly if she is breast-feeding. The proximity of Mom's scent as your twins drift in and out of sleep acts as a lure to complete alertness. Consistent with the American Academy of Pediatrics Policy Statement regarding SIDS, I recommend that very young twins sleep in the same room as their parents.

If your twins are several weeks or months old and have no established bedtime, you're not alone. When I ask parents about their twins' bedtime, they usually laugh and tell me that the babies sleep when they're sleepy. Well, establishing a bedtime is ultimately in the whole family's interest. But how, ask the parents, can these little babies understand 'bedtime'? Well, the answer is that they don't have to understand it at first—you do! It is your job to teach the babies that bedtime is that point in their day when they are going to be fed and cared for in the same darkened, quiet environment in which they are learning to sleep for increasingly long periods of time with the lights out. The whole point of establishing a bedtime is to limit stimuli in order to keep the babies from becoming aroused by their environment. Basically, you want to keep your babies 'in the dark.' I suggest that Mom, or Dad, too, if he is feeding one or both of the babies settle into a nice rocking chair or comfortable seat in the darkened room, feed both babies, and then place them in their crib or cribs to sleep. Basically, from bedtime until it is time to get up in the morning, the babies' life should be centered in the room in which they sleep with the lights out. Ultimately, your babies will sleep better if they remain in the same sleep environment. If the goal is to have a nursing mom be able to sleep through a feeding, Dad or another helper can bring the babies expressed milk in bottles.

It is important to keep the room dark, except for the use of a night-light during changing and feeding times. There is very interesting research that shows that for premature babies, starting at about thirty-two weeks, if they are in a darkened hospital nursery at night and have lights on only during the day, their activity levels change—decreasing at night and increasing during the day. They thus are able to begin to develop their own sleep-wake cycles at an early age."

keeping the family healthy

The first thing to remember is that when healthy babies get sick, it is usually because they have been exposed to somebody who is ill. Plain and simple, it is best to keep anybody with the sniffles away from the babies. If either or both parents have a cold, they should be very careful about hygiene. Everyone in the family should wash their hands and wear a mask if they have respiratory symptoms. These masks are available at any drugstore and are very effective. Even if no one is showing signs of illness, people are frequently contagious before they have any symptoms. The simple act of hand washing, and doing it frequently, is often what stands between you and whatever virus happens to be floating around. When brothers and sisters come home from school, they should wash their hands before making contact with the babies. In fact, get the children into the habit of washing their hands thoroughly before and after eating or playing, and certainly after using the bathroom. The antiseptic wipes that are readily available in the grocery store and pharmacy are great for the car or to keep in your purse, but good old soap and warm water should be routine in the house. You should also invest in a stockpile of paper cups. Often members of the family, especially children, leave their empty glasses on the kitchen counter. Another child wanders in for a little orange juice and picks up a sibling's empty, apparently clean glass, and you're well on your way to spreading a virus throughout the family. Use paper cups and have your children toss them directly into the trash or recycling bin after each use. Again, it is impossible to overemphasize the value of hand washing. The child with a cold wipes her nose and touches the baby. Grandma covers her mouth when she coughs, and two minutes later she touches the baby. It might sound almost too fastidious, but when both twins get colds at the same time, you won't think so. A convenient pump bottle of antibacterial soap at the kitchen sink, along with a generous supply of paper towels for hand drying, is a great idea. Young siblings can be encouraged to be attentive to their hygiene with a chart on the fridge that awards them a star when they remember to wash their hands before cuddling their young twin siblings. Encourage children to toss their paper towels in the trash after washing up. A damp, used paper towel left on the counter is an invitation to germs.

Parents also should get used to washing their hands between taking care of one baby and then the other when one of the twins is sick. Realistically, the period of infectivity frequently takes place before you have a hint of illness in either, so colds in babies are not uncommon.

bringing your children at home into the loop

To your children at home, new twins are like a picnic in the rain: the good news and the bad news all in two sweet, but occasionally soggy, packages. One hopes your young children have been exposed to what to expect through pictures, books, hospital tours, and discussion with parents. But all the attention and time that goes into getting your four-year-old ready for her new baby brother and sister cannot fully prepare her for the enormous change that is about to take place in the family dynamic. The firstborn child displaced by the arrival of twins is naturally conflicted by the upheaval. Well-meaning friends and family have tried to make amends for all the attention going to the twins, but after the first rush of little gifts, attention, and words of praise "for such a wonderful big sister," the harsh reality sets in: There is not always a lap for me, because guess who is in it! Older children have been heard to comment, "It's the twins, it's the twins. It's always the twins!"

It is very important to recognize that feelings of jealousy are normal and appropriate. Imagine the reaction of the wife whose husband comes home and says, "Sweetheart, soon I'll be bringing home two new, little wives to be a part

Some Tips for
Your Sibling Teen Sitters

CONSIDER HAVING YOUR TEEN TAKE A BABY-SITTING COURSE.

These classes stress safety, common sense, and, in the case of a medical emergency, how to best respond until trained medical personnel arrive on the scene. Many classes offer certificates of completion that will make your child an attractive baby-sitting candidate to neighbors and friends.

BE CLEAR ABOUT THE TERMS OF YOUR AGREEMENT,
AND STICK TO THEM.

Make sure your child knows that caring for eight-month-old twins does not mean simply having them in the room while she watches her favorite sitcom. And if you've agreed to pay her for sitting, pay up right away!

ALWAYS HAVE EMERGENCY NUMBERS NEXT TO THE PHONE,
OR PROGRAM THEM IN WHERE APPROPRIATE.

Poison control, 911, your pediatrician, and a number where you can be reached should be immediately available.

DON'T HAVE YOUR TEENS SITTING FOR INFANTS
LATE INTO THE EVENING.

They may like to push the limits on their own bedtimes, but young teens get tired and cannot be relied upon to be awake and focused enough to care for two infants at midnight.

of our family. But don't worry, there's plenty of love for everybody and I'll still love you just as much as I ever did and you'll get to love them, too!" Well, it plays just about as well to your four-year-old. As we've said, your children's jealousy about the new babies is also an expression of their bond with you. The lifelong thread of love and attachment between siblings is part of a complex and ever-changing pattern. Your babies are too young to manifest the alliance within the family that is sometimes perceived by other siblings, but they do still have each other in a most basic sense. Mommy and Daddy are together and the twins are together, so the older sibling may very reasonably ask, "Who is my partner?" It is not uncommon for the firstborn to feel lonely in the midst of all the excitement.

Most young children—say, from the ages of three to seven—can be effectively coaxed into showing their "love" for the babies because they are so deeply invested in wanting to please their parents. But the young child constantly asked to kiss the babies, or pat the babies, or tell Grandma how much she loves the babies is essentially playing a role with the expectation that it will make her parents proud of her. There is very little in the way of real affection in that role-playing. The young firstborn child always experiences some displacement, but when twins are on the way, a five-year-old may already have endured several weeks of his mom's need for bed rest. Gone are the outings to the park, and Mom leaning over the side of the tub to make funny shapes with his shampoo-covered hair. By the time the twins have been home for several weeks, it is very important for parents to reestablish a routine with their other children.

Always be sure to keep your child's day-care or preschool teacher apprised of developments at home. And ask the teacher to update you on any changes in the child's behavior at school. Your potty-trained three-year-old may suddenly start having accidents at preschool, and his teacher will be much better equipped to handle it if she knows there are new twins at home. It is very common for young children to ask for a bottle again or to ask to nurse. Parents should be prepared for the full complement of behaviors, from hostility toward friends and family to a hypercritical fixation on "being good" or doing everything right: "Look, Mom and Dad—I never draw outside the lines, and I can tie my own shoes!" Just as adults do not fall instantly in love in the deepest sense of the word, siblings need time to develop affection for one another. Don't underestimate your twins' ability to work their magic upon their older siblings. The early smiles and gurgles from your twins that melt your heart eventually may have a similar defrosting effect on their five-year-old sister.

The rule of thumb is to allow your children to express their feelings about the twins, and expect that they will range from resentment to amusement to the blossoming of real affection. The hard-and-fast rule is that all feelings are fair game, but physical aggression that could hurt the babies is never acceptable.

Your young children may need to channel their feelings through some physical outlet, but overt or covert thumping or pinching is not an option. Be ready to answer questions such as why the singleton is not a twin; whether you love the twins twice as much; and why when their school friends come over, they just want to play with the twins.

Socializing with friends or organized activities outside the orbit of the twins can be helpful, but try not to change your children's current care any more than necessary. If you were considering sending them to a new preschool at a time that coincides with the birth of the twins, you might want to rethink making such a substantial change. The first six months may be the most difficult for your young children. Conversation that elevates their status without diminishing the twins can be very successful in fostering good sibling relationships. Offer ample opportunity for commiseration and support: "It's fun feeding the babies, but it sure can take a long time." Some parents report the beginnings of real kinship once the babies begin to be more fun to play with. Let your children take pride in the skills they are sharing with their little siblings. Just as your focus shifts from seeing "the twins" to seeing two individuals, your children are likely to have similar feelings. They may experience greater rapport with one twin. That's okay. Try, where possible, to engineer opportunities for older siblings to have outings with one twin at a time, even if it is half-an-hour of play in the living room. And most important, give your children the gift of patience with their questions, feelings, and behavior.

Many scouting, community, and first-aid organizations are offering baby-sitting safety programs for preteens and young teens. Certainly you want your older children to pitch in and pull their fair share in the family without financial compensation, but hiring your older children (sometimes in tandem with a responsible friend) to care for your twins can be a real win/win situation. Older siblings love having an opportunity to earn money while providing you with an opportunity for some couple time—and their baby brothers and sisters with a loving caregiver. Teens report typical earnings of four to ten dollars per hour, and they appreciate the chance to be recognized in their roles as helpmates to hard-working parents.

Preteens, ages ten to twelve, can be hired as "mother's helpers"—on hand to entertain the twins for an hour or two during the day when a parent is at home but would like some uninterrupted time to work or rest. However, even the most competent preteen sitters are not recommended for twins under school age. Older siblings may be very capable of helping out with infants when necessary.

One Family's Story
One Twin in the Hospital
and One at Home

Carol and Vince's twin boys, Alex and Nicky, were born at thirty-one weeks. They are now twelve-and-a-half, and Carol says she is trying to adjust to becoming the mother of teenagers. She spoke about her experience with having one son in the hospital for two weeks and the other transferred by ambulance to a neonatal intensive care unit nursery at another hospital, where he remained for five months.

My first recollection is that it was so odd coming home from the hospital empty-handed . . .

I didn't really get to see either of them at first. They were both delivered by C-section and I remember a nurse sort of showed me these two little, green bundles and said, "Here they are!" and then whisked them away. I had all these expectations of cuddling them and it just wasn't like that. The next time I got to see them was about four-and-a-half hours later. They wheeled Alex into my room in his Isolette. . . . I remember hearing his little monitor beeping as it rolled down the hall. I saw him before they transported him to another hospital with an NICU, but I never got to hold him. I didn't see Nicky until after that. He was in an Isolette, too. He was a little jaundiced and ended up staying in the hospital for the first two weeks. Vince went to see Alex right away at the hospital he had been transported to, and I remember they told him at the NICU to get a Polaroid camera and take pictures of Alex to bring to me. I had them with me the whole time Alex was hospitalized.

I was released from the hospital after four days and I remember telling Vince I wanted to go home at night because I just didn't want to see anyone. I was not ready to talk to anybody right away. But soon, a very natural pattern emerged. . . . My mother would take me to the hospital to nurse Nicky and then we'd drive over the hill to the hospital that Alex had been transferred to. After a few days I got a double breast pump and started pumping and freezing breast milk for Alex in sterile bottles. It actually reached a point where there was no more room in the freezer.

(continued)

But if anyone touched my milk supply in the freezer I would flip. . . . It was like our hoard of gold.

As it happens, Alex never did nurse, but in a way that gave Vince an excellent opportunity to really connect with him. After two weeks Nicky came home, and that was wonderful. Once Alex was ready to take nourishment by mouth, Vince would feed him my breast milk from a bottle. That time with Alex was very, very important to my husband. It was difficult, but eventually I came to look at our situation in a more positive light. Alex had the benefit of my breast milk and the benefit of wonderful time with his father. They developed a closeness that has never changed. In fact, once Alex came home, we tended to kind of pair up that way. If we were going out, Vince would tend to have Alex and I would take Nicky. I remember becoming aware of that and trying to sort of impose a conscious change, but for the most part we did kind of follow the path that had been established early on.

Alex's care felt very collaborative . . . and from the beginning, the communication from the hospital was fantastic. There was the neonatologist, our pediatrician, the thoracic surgeon, the head NICU nurse assigned to Alex's case, all the other nurses, and several specialists who were brought in to consult.

I found that I only wanted to communicate positive things with friends and business associates. After the first month, the hospital really encouraged us to bring friends and family to scrub in and get as close to Alex as they and we felt comfortable with. We developed a real camaraderie in the NICU with other parents whose babies were having a difficult start. There was a Korean family that spoke no English, but we became friends and exchanged gifts as our children's conditions improved enough for each to be moved from the most serious-level NICU to an interim care unit, where Alex actually spent the most time.

Eventually time kind of lost all meaning. At first you really sort of lived for it. In the first few hours of Alex's life they told us he'd have to be in intensive care for ten to twelve days, and it sounded like an eternity. At twelve days he was still in there and looked like he was almost worse off, and they told us it would be ten to twelve weeks. By the time we hit twelve weeks we had stopped asking. We knew there was no way his medical team could really assess that. . . . He was very slow coming along. It was a roller coaster every day. There wasn't a time I wasn't thinking of Alex and wanting the boys together, but we just worked at projecting a pos-

itive outlook . . . just knowing that he would be home with us eventually. And there were times I felt very torn that I could not be in two places at once. But I just could not see exposing Nicky to everything at the hospital. . . . They certainly worked at providing the most sterile environment possible, but we both picked up colds there. Other people did, too. It was not the place I wanted to bring a healthy child. We had one at risk, and we felt that was all the risk we were willing to take. But except for a time that Vince and I were both sick, I don't think he missed a day of visiting Alex.

Vince and I were somehow balancing each other's emotional needs. When I was losing it he would really come through with a very positive outlook, and when it reversed I could do the same for him. Though I didn't think of it at the time, I have to say that it was the hand of God, or whatever you want to call it, that lifted us up and kept us caring for each other. As the weeks turned into months, there was just something that carried us forward and kept us from becoming completely unglued, because both of us were wrung dry. . . .

Connecting with Alex was a little hard when he came home. But I'll never forget those first twenty-four hours. My parents were with us and I remember turning to Vince and saying, "I don't think he's ready to come home. I think we have to bring him back." I remember feeling he had caregivers who were better equipped than I was to help him. [Alex] could not relax that first night. . . . We were so thrilled to have him with us, but you could just feel the tension in his little body. His back would arch and he'd scream. I really felt like I was not the best person to care for him. And we'd been through colic with Nicky, so we were used to crying. . . . But of course, it was really just a matter of time.

And as far as their relationship within the family, I've never really second-guessed how things might have been different if Alex had not had so many problems when he was born. But I do remember thinking around the time they turned three that they seemed to kind of discover each other. Sort of this realization that "I've got a buddy here." Suddenly they got very engaged with each other for long periods of time. And their communication with each other was remarkable. We'd really sit back and marvel. And it's interesting that Alex has always been comfortable with our leaving to go out as long as he had Nicky there. But Nicky seemed more attached . . . less willing to let go.

As far as Alex's development, we came to trust our pediatrician's judgment
(continued)

that he was doing fine. I'm sure it can be different for every child, but our doctor reassured us that in Alex's case there was no timetable that we had to follow . . . that as long as he was developing one skill after the next in an appropriate sort of developmental order he was doing really well. But by the time he started reading really early, ahead of everybody else, we felt a sort of amazing confirmation that his mind was certainly okay and his body, his physical aptitude, just needed its own pace to catch up, which it has.

If I were to offer advice to any parents going through the experience of having one baby at home while one was hospitalized, I'd say this is going to teach you the meaning of patience, and it is the most important thing you can learn. Your baby will come along at his or her own pace. You have to care for the one at home and take comfort that he is at home. You really have to let go of your expectations and the sooner you do that, the better off you'll all be. Think of it as a roller-coaster ride, and just make sure you and your husband strap yourselves in with one seat belt.

your twins from birth to two months

your growing twins

correcting for early delivery

After your twins are born, your pediatrician will begin to plot their growth on a growth chart. The growth chart is a graph of the range of normal height, weight, and head circumference and may be broken down into two charts: one from birth to three years, and the second from two to eighteen years. In appendix B you will find sample growth charts for three sets of twins. We have limited the age range in those charts to eighteen months for the purposes of this book.

Two of the important concepts to understand when discussing babies born prematurely are *gestational age* and *corrected age*. What exactly do those terms mean, and how do they relate to each other? Let's take the hypothetical example of twins who are born six weeks before their due date:

- The full-term pregnancy is considered to be forty completed weeks of gestation.
- Teddy and Erin are born six weeks (one-and-a-half months) prematurely, giving them a gestational age of thirty-four weeks.
- Today is two months past the date of their birth and approximately two weeks past their due date.

- Their *corrected* age, based on their due date, is *two weeks*, while their chronological age based on their actual birth date is two months.

So we describe Teddy and Erin as being born at a gestational age of thirty-four weeks, and at two months of age we plot them on their growth curve at both their actual chronological age of two months and their corrected age of two weeks. Parents of premature babies, particularly those who must remain hospitalized, sometimes get very tuned in to the plotting of these curves, particularly if their twins' weight appears to be below average for an infant of its age.

This tendency to focus on your babies' weight is understandable, particularly in the anxious early weeks of a premature infant's life, because there is so little that a parent can feel is concrete evidence of the baby's increasing well-being. But it is easy for a parent to grow obsessed with weight gain and we know that particularly in the case of a premature baby in the hospital, we will see weight fluctuate from day to day. There are two important factors to remember:

- You still need to correct for your twins' age. They may have been born two weeks ago, but if they were born six weeks early, there is still a need to correct for their gestational age.
- While the babies are being weighed daily, a single measurement of weight loss does not have much significance. Only a trend of weight loss or gain over time is helpful in assessing each of your twins' health.

Parents of significantly premature babies are well advised to relax their concern with weight gain from day to day, especially once the babies get home. It is usually not a good idea to have an infant scale at home. There are stories of concerned parents walking into a butcher shop and weighing their babies on those scales. The pediatrician is likely to be closely monitoring the babies' progress with checkups every week or every other week at first. The twins will be weighed and measured and have their head circumference recorded on their charts. In the case of one baby who has been discharged several months after his twin, there is likely to be a real disparity in size as well as development. This is part of the continuing challenge of supporting each twin's right to his or her own distinctive size, temperament, and range of skills.

dr. klein on infant stimulation programs

"I am most likely to recommend an infant stimulation program for babies who are significantly premature, usually born under thirty-two weeks. If this is the case with your twins, you might ask your pediatrician for his recommendation. These programs are offered by occupational or physical therapists, or other health-care professionals who specialize in the developmental needs of premature babies. It can be very rewarding for parents to work with a specialist who is trained to teach you gentle exercises, positioning, and other ways to interact with your babies that will help to advance their development."

• *Your Very Young Baby*

If the hospital has discharged your twins at thirty-four weeks corrected age or older, they should have a normal startle reflex, be able to suck and swallow, and have normal breathing capabilities. They may look at your face but not really be tracking yet; they may smile in their sleep, but not responsively; and they will probably start making sounds other than crying, though those sounds may not be too distinct yet.

There will be some ability to lift and turn their heads, though that really varies. As far as muscle tone is concerned, babies born at less than thirty-four weeks may not yet be quite on par with the term baby. Premature infants born at less than thirty-four weeks have low muscle tone. As they lie on their backs, their arms and legs are in extension. As babies develop in utero from the second trimester to term, they begin to assume the fetal position with arms flexed and legs drawn into the abdomen, like little balls. Your premature twins may not have completely developed this ability in utero, so you need to become their personal trainer. Your goal is to work gently but steadily to help your babies into that flexed position, particularly when they are on their tummies. The current pediatric recommendations are for your babies to sleep on flat surfaces (no pillow) on their back. They need to practice being placed on their tummies (*tummy time*) at least two to three times a day for a ten-minute session with their knees and arms tucked gently under their bodies. Remain with them while they are in this position. Talk to them from a position slightly above their heads. This will encourage each baby to push up and to work at lifting his or her head.

The Social Smile

There are few things in your life that compare to the first time you get a smile of recognition and pleasure from your babies. This is different from the reflexive smile that you have watched play across their faces in sleep. This is the smile that tells you they are happy to see you, or that something has truly tickled their fancy. This is the looking-around smile that is a response to all the smiling and singing and cooing you have used to reach out to your twins. This milestone usually occurs by six to eight weeks of age (corrected age for premature babies).

Sleeping More at Night

Contrary to what many say, there is no correlation between your twins' eating solid food and sleeping through the night. Your eight-week-old babies are likely to be taking in ample nourishment by bottle or breast, and as a result are ready to go a little longer between feedings. One of the first challenges faced by you and your babies is the development of a rhythm that will eventually lead to all of you sleeping through the night. Your babies had many months of daily movement (yours) before their birth to lull them into a restful state. By the time they are six or eight weeks old, they are beginning to learn how to quiet themselves.

If you hear the babies whimper or gurgle a bit, don't rush to them. Babies, like adults, wake and fall asleep again several times throughout the night. One of their biggest jobs is to learn to comfort themselves back to sleep. So don't entertain them, and change them only if they are really wet or soiled.

Looking From Side to Side

Your babies will begin tracking your close movements and will look into your eyes. In the early weeks they will have the ability to focus approximately the distance from their head to your face while nursing or being held for a bottle. At about eight weeks, your twins will start to follow a moving object within a visual radius of 180 degrees.

parental questions and concerns

• *Fevers*

If one or both of the twins feels warm to the touch and you suspect a fever, take a temperature under the arm with a mercury or electronic thermometer. Other means of temperature taking are not as reliable. Place the thermometer in the baby's armpit for five minutes. With an uncomfortable or crying baby, simply hold the thermometer in place as you cuddle or rock the baby to provide comfort. If the temperature is above 99 degrees Fahrenheit, then you will need to take a rectal temperature. This is easily done with your baby on his or her back, legs held gently up and together. Put a little petroleum jelly on the tip of a rectal thermometer and insert it about one inch into the baby's rectum for three minutes. Hold the thermometer gently in place by letting it rest between your index and middle fingers as your hand lies outstretched across the baby's bottom. If the rectal temperature is 100.4 degrees Fahrenheit or higher and your baby is less than two months of age, seek medical attention immediately. When reporting on your baby's temperature to your pediatrician, describe it precisely as it appears on the thermometer.

• *Breathing Sounds*

By the time babies are four weeks of age, they will have begun to secrete mucus in the lining of the nose. The airway is so small that even if there is just a little mucus in there, they can start to make a lot of noise when they breathe. Parents may mistake this for a cold or think there is some other problem. If there are other symptoms, such as a runny nose, cough, or fever, then one or both of your babies may indeed have a cold. Observe them while they are feeding: If they have to stop sucking to take a breath, that is the strongest indication that the nasal passage is clogged. Saline nose drops, which can be purchased over the counter, usually relieve the clogging.

• *Feeding*

Once you've made it to the two-week mark at home with your babies, you have probably grown more confident about their overall care and feeding. If your twins go in for a checkup after two weeks at home and they are both gaining weight adequately, it is a pretty safe assumption that they are both eating well.

Your doctor may ask how much the babies are eating. Term infants—as well as babies born at thirty-four to thirty-six weeks, and eating well enough to be discharged from the hospital—should nurse ten to fifteen minutes or more at both breasts at every feeding.

Even after a few weeks, your twins born at thirty-four weeks may not nurse vigorously enough to maintain an adequate milk supply. In that case, nurse first and pump immediately afterward. As the twins get closer to term, this problem usually corrects itself, but not always. Start with the side that you stopped with the time before. Nurse or bottle-feed every two to four hours during the day, timing from the start of one feeding to the next. During the day if the babies are asleep four hours after the start of their last feeding, wake them even if they've been asleep for just ten to fifteen minutes and feed them. Nursing both twins should take thirty to forty minutes each, or approximately half that time if you are nursing them simultaneously. At night, feed the babies when they wake up. If one awakens for a feeding, rouse the other to feed as well. If the mother does not have enough breast milk, she can try switching breasts every five minutes for a full thirty minutes of nursing both babies. She might also try to nurse every two hours for just a few days until the milk supply has improved. The rule of thumb is to switch breasts frequently to increase milk supply, but not increase the length of time you nurse at each feeding.

If Mom feels that all she is doing is breast-feeding, that will eventually have an effect on Dad. Soon nobody is happy, and Mom may stop breast-feeding sooner than she had hoped. In fact, if a father supports the mother's desire to breast-feed the twins, nursing is likely to go on longer than it otherwise might. Your pediatrician can root like mad from the sidelines, but a doctor's encouragement is far less significant than the father's support in the long run. There is an increased time factor in feeding your twins no matter what method you use. There is no data that gives an average length of time that mothers nurse their twins. The goal here is to have two thriving babies who are gaining weight, and a successfully functioning family.

• Your Noisy Babies

Babies at this age are beginning to make a whole barnyard of sounds: They are gasping, snorting, grunting, cooing, and sucking loudly. By now you have probably come to recognize a whole litany of cries from each of your babies. If your noisy baby becomes unusually quiet, you should mention it to your pediatrician. But for the most part, you can sit back and enjoy the show.

• The Facts About Immunization

Immunization is one of the most important elements of pediatric care. There are numerous illustrations of how the introduction of immunization practices are linked to the decline of a given disease. The introduction of the Haemophilus B conjugate vaccine (Hib) has almost wiped out this bacteria as a major cause of meningitis. Rubella, once a major cause of birth defects, has been almost completely obliterated.

Vaccines, like all drugs marketed in the United States, are required by law to be tested before they are licensed for production, sale, and use. The Food and Drug Administration, along with other federal agencies, continues to monitor vaccine safety even after licensing. Over the years, concern about a possible relationship between autism and thimerosal—a mercury-based preservative that was used in minute amounts in many vaccines—has motivated much research on the subject. Currently, almost all immunizations used in infants under two years of age are thimersol-free. In 2004, the Immunization Safety Review Committee—established by the Centers for Disease Control and Prevention (CDC), the National Institutes of Health (NIH), and the Institute of Medicine (IOM)—published its eighth and final report *rejecting the hypothesis of a causal relationship between thimerosal-containing vaccinations and autism.* We have also seen data from other countries indicating that where thimerosal has been absent from vaccinations for at least ten years, there is no corresponding decrease in autism. Speculation regarding a connection between autism and the MMR (measles/mumps/rubella) vaccine, which does not contain thimerosal, has also been found to be without any foundation.

Parental understanding of vaccination practices is vital to the public safety and the ongoing success of infant and childhood vaccination programs. Pediatricians throughout the country have discussions on a daily basis with parents who are concerned that we are giving their babies too many vaccinations. It is helpful to consider that while the number and variety of vaccinations has increased, the amount of *antigen* (the actual protein to which the body reacts) is less than it was twenty years ago and is in a purer state. Parents are often surprised to learn that their twins are exposed to five hundred to a thousand different antigens a day just from what they put in their mouths! The following information about thimerosal, issued by the American Academy of Pediatrics, offers an excellent overview of the facts.

What Parents Should Know About Thimerosal

Used with permission of the American Academy of Pediatrics,
copyright © 2002, revised August 2004.

What is thimerosal?

- Thimerosal is an organic mercury-based preservative used in vaccines.
- Thimerosal has been used as an additive to vaccines since the 1930s because it is very effective in preventing bacterial and fungal contamination, particularly in opened multi-dose containers.
- Thimerosal is also found in other medicines and products including some throat and nose sprays and contact lens solutions.

Does thimerosal cause autism?

- There are no valid studies that show a link between thimerosal in vaccines and autistic spectrum disorder. A 2004 report from the Institute of Medicine, Vaccines and Autism concluded that the available evidence is against the existence of a causal relationship between thimerosal-containing vaccines and autism.
- The CDC examined the incidence of autism in relation to the amount of thimerosal a child receives in vaccines. They found no change in autism rates relative to the amount of thimerosal a child received from vaccines in the first 6 months of life. In other words, a child who received more thimerosal was not more likely to be autistic.

Have any studies shown thimerosal in vaccines causes health problems in children?

An early CDC study suggested a possible weak connection between the amount of thimerosal given and certain neurodevelopmental disorders, such as ADHD, speech and language delays, and tics (but not autism). Further review by independent experts led many to feel this study was flawed in parts of its design that favored a connection when none may have existed. Later studies did not show any connection. Researchers will continue to look at this question.

Which vaccines contain thimerosal?

- Since 2001, all routinely recommended vaccines manufactured for administration to infants in the U.S. have been either thimerosal-free or have contained only extremely small amounts of thimerosal.

- In 2004, the AAP recommended that children 6–23 months of age receive an annual influenza vaccination. Some thimerosal-free influenza vaccine is now available for infants under 3 years of age. Thimerosal-preserved influenza vaccine contains only small amounts of thimerosal (12.5 micrograms per dose).

- Many routinely recommended childhood vaccines never contained thimerosal: measles/mumps/rubella (MMR), polio (IPV), varicella/chicken pox. Some of the Haemophilus influenzae type b (Hib) and diphtheria/tetanus/pertussis (DTaP) vaccines never used thimerosal as a preservative.

Why was thimerosal removed from vaccines if there is no danger?

- Even though there's no evidence that thimerosal in vaccines is dangerous, the Public Health Service and the American Academy of Pediatrics believe the effort to remove mercury-based preservatives from vaccines was a good decision. Mercury exists in a different form in our environment (such as in some fish), so children will be exposed to it in other ways. We can't always remove mercury from the environment. But we can control the mercury used in some vaccines. So, by taking thimerosal out of vaccines, we are lessening the amount of mercury a child will be exposed to early in life.

What risks does mercury pose to an infant's health?

- Studies of mercury ingested from fish and other sources have shown that in high doses, mercury can cause brain damage. Mercury can also affect the kidneys and immune system. Mercury in vaccines (ethyl mercury) is in a different form than mercury in food products (methyl mercury). It is difficult to predict adverse effects of ethyl mercury exposure based on studies of exposure to other forms of mercury. Experts have differing opinions.

Have any adverse reactions to thimerosal ever been reported?

- When vaccines containing thimerosal have been administered in the recommended doses, allergic-type reactions (hives, shock) have been noted on rare occasions. No other harmful effects have been reported.

Should parents have their children who have received vaccinations with thimerosal be tested for mercury?

- No. Infants and children who have received thimerosal-containing vaccines do not need to have blood, urine, or hair tested for mercury. The body eliminates a mercury dose completely within 120 days—it doesn't stay in your child's body.
- Screening children for mercury exposure will likely result in more questions than answers. Mercury in the urine is a measure of inorganic mercury exposure, not the organic form found in thimerosal. Mercury found in blood, hair, or fingernails can come from any mercury source. It is more likely to come from dietary and environmental mercury sources than from thimerosal. Children who are suspected to have had environmental exposures (from broken thermometers or excessive fish consumption) may be appropriately tested.

Who should be concerned about exposure to large amounts of mercury?

- Pregnant women, nursing mothers, and young infants should be especially careful about mercury exposure. Some fish contain high levels of organic mercury. State health, environmental, and conservation officials have information about which fish to avoid in your state. Pediatricians can also give parents advice about avoiding exposure.

Immunizations have already been successful at nearly wiping out many diseases, so why should children continue to get vaccinated when these diseases barely exist anymore?

- Although vaccine-preventable diseases are at record low numbers, the organisms that cause these diseases are still present. Unvaccinated children continue to be at risk of serious, even deadly diseases. We are only one airplane ride away from many parts of the world where these diseases are still rampant and where immunization is not available. We cannot afford to let down our guard.

visiting the doctor

dr. klein describes a well-baby visit

"When I see a family with twins, one of the things we discuss is the importance of looking at their babies as individuals. Each twin has come into the world with a partner but is still unique. During the course of the well-baby visit I try to ask my questions as they pertain separately to each baby. Then we speak in a more general way about "the twins." Early on, it is not unusual for parents to come in and begin talking about their experience, saying "the twins are this . . ." or "when should we expect the twins to do that." I always try to steer the conversation to their observations about first one baby and then the other.

First we take the measurements for height, weight, and head circumference of each baby and record them on their individual growth chart. I prefer to initially observe each baby in its parents' arms, so I ask Mom or Dad to sit in a chair holding one baby at a time. If the mother needs to stand with her baby so she can rock her, that's fine; we do what is comfortable. At the first visit, I explain to my families that I like to begin the visit with the baby on his parent's lap. If I observe that at each subsequent visit a mother with twins walks into the examination room with one baby held by her caregiver, and she puts the other baby down in its carrier and sits down alone, I may begin to think that this mother is feeling a little overwhelmed, even depressed and detached from her babies. I'll try to steer our conversation to a discussion of what is happening at home. Maybe she is in need of more support than she is getting, and we can brainstorm a little bit about finding her some help.

If both parents are not available, it is helpful if there is another adult at the visit to help out. I have a form that I use as a guideline for the visit, but I don't let it rule our conversation. As we talk, I put the appropriate notes in the baby's chart. I ask about questions or concerns that they want to address and we may go into detail right then, unless their question involves the physical exam. If it doesn't happen to come up in the course of the conversation, I'll always ask about how the baby is feeding and sleeping and the life of the family in general.

Then we go on to discuss development. We talk about what the baby has done so far and what to expect in the future. I may make suggestions about feeding or sleeping, and it is not unusual to inquire about what kind of support is available to the family. If I feel there are unexplored options as far as help for tired parents, we may talk about them. We discuss what immunizations, if any, are going to be given at the visit, and what the complications might be. I have parents sign forms giving permission for their baby's immunization.

If the baby is on medication, we review that and talk about any past medical history, where appropriate. If there was some problem or issue discussed at a prior visit, I will bring it up to see what resolution, if any, there was. Of course, each progressive visit encompasses additional elements of the baby's development.

I talk about safety issues at almost every visit. Sometimes I think I may repeat things too frequently, but I feel it is important to stress everything from car safety to pool safety to baby-proofing the house. I begin to talk about baby-proofing at the four-month visit, because that is when babies will usually start to reach for things that they invariably put in their mouth. I like to give parents a sheet of paper with the telephone number for the national poison control center so they can keep it near their telephone. By the nine-month visit, when babies are likely to be crawling around, I am really hoping that all the twin-proofing of the house is complete.

Then I move on to the complete physical examination of the baby: top to bottom, stem to stern. At four or five months, and sometimes before that, I begin the exam with the baby on its mother's lap. I like to take a little time to play as we start the physical. When the baby is old enough, I may hand him one or two tongue depressors to hold and then we'll play with them. Play is instructional for me and tends to be calming for the baby. I begin the exam by listening to the chest because I want to make sure I get to that, even if the baby becomes restless or upset during the exam. I listen to their lungs to make sure there is no wheezing—no questionable sounds. I listen to the heart to make certain there are no abnormalities there. I then listen to the abdomen and examine it with my hands.

While the baby is on the parent's lap, I remove the diaper and examine the baby's genitalia, and also the hips to make sure they are moving correctly. I stretch out their legs to make sure they are of equal length, and put the diaper back on. I ask the parent to hug the baby by placing their arms over the baby's arms. While the baby is comfortably restrained, I look at the ears, nose, and throat. I look in the mouth to see if teeth are coming in.

Depending on the age, I may hold the baby upright in order to make sure that he can support his weight on his legs. In an older baby, I may ask to see how she is walking. At this point, the typical examination of one baby is pretty much completed and I go on to the second twin.

At the end of the visit, we will discuss any problems that are the result of prematurity if that is the case; we'll talk about any referrals to specialists when needed; and discuss any medicine that needs to be prescribed or refilled. At that point, my nurse will follow up with the appropriate immunizations, hemoglobin measurement, or tuberculosis testing as needed."

the well-baby visit: birth to two months

The checkup, or well-baby visit, is an important opportunity for your pediatrician to assess your twins' health on an ongoing basis. Each doctor has an individual approach, but you can count on several components being present in any pediatrician's routine: Your twins' height, weight, and head circumference will be plotted on a growth curve that is a permanent feature of each baby's medical chart. They will be plotted for their actual age, and for their corrected age if need be. There are likely to be inquiries about eating and sleeping and an opportunity for you to ask any questions you have about your babies' progress.

immunizations: birth to two months

You will find a detailed immunization chart from birth to preadolescence at the back of this book. Look there for specifics regarding each immunization.

The first hepatitis B (Hep B) vaccine is given anytime between birth and two months of age, with a second dose given between one and four months of age (at least four weeks after the first dose), and the third dose between six and eighteen months of age (at least eight weeks after the second dose).

The first diphtheria, tetanus, acellular pertussis (DTaP) vaccine is given at two months of age.

The first Haemophilus influenzae type B (Hib) vaccine is given at two months of age.

The first poliovirus (IPV) vaccine is given at two months of age.

The first pneumococcal vaccine (PCV) is given at two months of age.

the growth curve

The growth curve is a tool that your pediatrician uses as a measure of your twins' health. Invariably, a baby who is growing well is fundamentally healthy. If one or both of your twins are not growing well, your doctor may not immediately know why, but examination of the growth curve over time will definitely suggest the need for further evaluation.

Each of your babies will be weighed and measured for height and head circumference. These three measurements will be plotted on a graph that is called the growth chart. Your pediatrician can share that information with you so that you can have a visual impression of each baby's growth relative to him or herself over time as well as relative to other babies. It is important for parents of twins, especially if they are fraternal, to anticipate different rates of growth. The curves differ for boys and girls, so if your son and daughter are of equal weight, that does not mean they are at the same point on the growth curve. As your pediatrician assesses your twins' growth patterns over time, any number of patterns may emerge. The plotting of the growth curve is a sort of jumping-off point for discussions regarding all aspects of your babies' lives, including feeding, sleeping habits, and their individual temperaments. This book's appendix includes growth charts for three sets of twins born at twenty-seven weeks, thirty-four weeks, and at term.

safety

Safety issues for your twins will grow more complex as increasing mobility makes their world larger. To start, you must look at the world of the very young baby and make immediate adjustments to that environment. Keep these same issues in mind when visiting a friend's home or traveling with your young twins.

twin-proofing your home

As we said in chapter 13, by the time your babies come home, you need at least the following safety precautions:

- Keep emergency phone numbers next to every phone.
- Place cribs and changing tables safely away from electrical wires, cords, and curtains.
- Observe rules of pet and plant safety.
- Store all toxic substances in a high, locked cabinet.
- Never leave the twins unsupervised at bath time or near any water.
- Keep all small objects such as coins, buttons, nuts, popcorn, grapes, and small toys (like Legos) away from your twins' grasp. Older siblings should be instructed never to leave their own toys in the twins' increasing reach.
- Be very careful about choking safety. Never place jewelry chains around the neck of an infant. Do not tie pacifiers on a ribbon or string to pajamas or other clothing.
- Do not leave your twins unattended on any surface. They may surprise you by rolling over for the first time, and you don't want it to be onto the floor from their changing table!
- Never leave your infant in a playpen that has one side down.

• *Poison Control*

Until recently, parents were advised to keep syrup of ipecac in the home to induce vomiting in the event of a baby or child swallowing poison. There was always the proviso that ipecac was to be used only under the guidance of a doctor or poison control center, yet there was widespread evidence that this recommendation was not always followed. In a reversal of its longstanding position on the use of ipecac, the American Academy of Pediatrics no longer recommends that parents keep ipecac in the home, citing three reasons: the possibility of resultant lethargy and drowsiness that could complicate diagnosis and treatment, prolonged vomiting that might result in the loss of other antidotes, and the possibility that the stomach might not be emptied of all the poison ingested. If your baby swallows poison, contact a poison control center for further information. The universal poison control number in the United States is (800) 222-1222.

In the Car

There are numerous consumer publications that can help you decide on the right car seats for your twins. While convenience and aesthetics play a part in this purchase, safety is your primary concern. When you have twins, you will need to strap one car seat into the center position of the rear seat and the other in the right, rear passenger area. This will enable you to have at least some access and visual contact with both babies. The car seats face back for babies that are this young, and are securely strapped in place. You can purchase special mirrors that clip to the visor in the front and attach by suction to the rear window, allowing a great view of front- or rear-facing car seats.

Babies should never be held on a lap in a moving car, even for a few seconds. And of course, you must not leave them alone in the car even to run into the gas station while you are at the pump. Police stations in towns all across the United States have received calls from panic-stricken parents who have locked their keys inside the car with an infant. Also, consider buying a sunshade that will protect your young babies from overheating while riding in the car. (See the Resource Guide at the back of the book for information about choosing and using car seats.)

Tender Skin

If either of your twins has a diaper rash, it will usually respond to a zinc oxide cream. If diaper rash does not respond to zinc oxide, ask your physician for further suggestions. There is no need to apply any other lotion, oils, creams, ointments, talc, or cornstarch to your babies' sensitive skin. Both talc and cornstarch can clog your babies' pores and can be breathed in through the nose. It is also a good idea to turn down the hot water temperature in the house to 120 degrees Fahrenheit or below. Just in case there is an accident, you will be very thankful that the water was no hotter. Also, keep your young twins out of direct sunlight. If you are out on a sunny day, be sure they have on hats or are in a shaded area. Infants under six months of age should be protected from direct sunlight and have their heads and bodies protected from the sun when they are out and about with you. For babies and infants older than six months, be sure to choose a barrier sun block containing titanium dioxide or zinc oxide with a sun protection factor (SPF) of at least fifteen. Barrier sunscreens sit on the surface of the skin and create a barrier that keeps the sun's rays from penetrating the covered areas. The labels on water-proof sunscreens may indicate coverage of up to eight hours, but reapply generously every two hours regardless of the directions. Sunscreen is not recommended for general use on babies younger than six months, but in the event that babies that young are going to be exposed to any prolonged periods of sun, a titanium dioxide or zinc oxide sunscreen can be used sparingly on parts of the body, such as the backs of the hands, that are not covered by clothing and are most exposed.

• Smoke

Babies should not be exposed to cigarette smoke. Smokers should smoke outside your house, and they should wash their hands and face and remove their outer clothing before holding the baby. Ideally, babies should never be in a room, car, or enclosed area where anyone has smoked.

dr. klein on the dangers of cigarette smoke

"We know that smoking during pregnancy is hazardous to mother and baby. But the parent who smokes around young babies continues to jeopardize the children's health as well as their own. There are numerous risks to infants: increased colds, ear infections, sudden infant death syndrome (SIDS), and other breathing problems are all associated with exposure to cigarette smoke. I cannot overstate the importance of raising your twins in a smoke-free environment."

• Foods to Avoid

Babies under one year of age should not be given honey, as it has been known to cause botulism in the immature digestive system. Whole milk, fish, citrus fruits, and egg whites should also be avoided, as there seems to be a higher likelihood of developing allergic reactions to these foods if they are introduced too early. We'll discuss food allergies in greater detail later on.

• Sleep Positioning

The Back to Sleep initiative (as discussed in chapter 14) has been very successful in reducing the incidence of SIDS in the United States, yet the placement of babies in the supine, or back, position has resulted in an increase in a condition called *positional plagiocephaly*, or flattening of the head, which while creating what may be a significant cosmetic problem, poses no medical consequences. (Look in the Resource Guide at the back of this book under Health and Medical Concerns.) The malleable nature of an infant's skull leaves it vulnerable to flattening as a result of continued external pressure from the crib mattress during sleep hours. It is also possible for positional plagiocephaly to commence in singleton or multiple births in utero. Uterine constraint—the result of limited space in utero being shared by twins—may be a cause of an increased incidence of plagiocephaly in twins at birth. There is also some thinking that the twin with the lower in-utero placement is more likely to develop plagiocephaly.

Of course, there is nothing that can be done to address plagiocephaly while the babies are in utero. But it is a condition that can almost always be successfully addressed after the babies are born. The following steps will be helpful in alleviating this condition should it be present in either or both of your babies. Remember that unless your doctor tells you otherwise, your twins should still be positioned on their backs to sleep:

- Discuss with your doctor any concerns you may have about the shape of each baby's head. Your doctor may initiate a discussion to alert you to the condition and the steps you can take to alleviate it. Positional plagiocephaly is usually diagnosed without X-ray or other laboratory tests.
- In the early weeks of your twins' lives, they are unable to turn their heads

and will remain in the sleeping position in which they are placed. Unless your doctor suggests a different strategy, alternate the head position—left side one night, right side the next—and repeat until advised to do otherwise.

- As your twins develop the capacity to turn their heads, the use of a "sleep positioner" will help you to maintain this approach.
- During supervised playtime, while the babies are on their tummies, stimulate them to lift their heads, strengthening their back and neck muscles. Encourage them to look to either side by positioning yourself in the room, or using a toy to get their attention.
- At feeding time, give the babies an opportunity to turn their heads by nursing both twins on both breasts. If bottle feeding, hold each baby in the crook of one arm and then the other.
- Be aware that swing and car-seat times are also opportunities for your babies' heads to rest on an external surface, as well as a chance to look in only one direction. Use the stimulus of your voice, a toy, or perhaps each other to encourage them to turn their heads in the other direction.
- When carrying the babies in front-carry slings, be aware of varying head positions as suits their needs.

Torticollis is another condition that appears to have increased in frequency since parents have been advised to place their babies on their backs to sleep, though medical researchers are not yet absolutely certain about the relationship between torticollis and back sleeping. What is known is that there is an association between uterine constraint and positioning and torticollis, and that torticollis is a risk factor for plagiocephaly. Torticollis—which comes from two Latin words meaning "twisted neck"—refers to tightening of the muscles on one side of the neck, resulting in babies tilting their head in one direction while looking the opposite way. If this condition is present, you and your doctor will most likely observe it within the first two to six weeks. It can be quite obvious, or so mild as to be almost imperceptible. If torticollis is diagnosed, physical therapy, consisting of gentle stretching motions, will be recommended. The steps we've outlined above will also be helpful in treating this condition.

Roundtable Talk

PRESENT AT THE DISCUSSION ARE:
Dr. Connie Agnew
Jill Ganon
Tom & Sarah
Laura & Nick
Joan & David
Robert & Grace
Kate & Matt

TOPIC FOR DISCUSSION IS:
Managing Day-to-Day

JILL: Okay. So tell me a little about the day-to-day. . . . How do you manage?

KATE: All I can say is that if we ever had another one, it would be a piece of cake. Thank goodness my mom has come down from Canada. I'm a twin, and my mother has a lot of experience. My sister who lives near her has had two kids in the last five years, so my mother has plenty of recent experience, too.

MATT: But this is her first out-of-town assignment . . .

JOAN: I think it might be different if our friends were having babies now. I've felt kind of isolated. . . . I was on bed rest for a long time as well as being home recovering with the twins after their birth. I didn't know a whole lot about baby care, and I'm in the medical field [Joan is a psychiatric nurse]. Now I'm on leave from my job, and I've found it very hard to find someone who is "twin capable" to give me a break. We end up mostly having friends and family come in to sort of help out while we're there. The days can get pretty long.

LAURA: The day-to-day. . . . Let's just say I've been doing my marketing on Fridays at midnight. Sometimes it feels like people just don't understand. A friend will say, "Come on over with the babies." If I plan to be there at noon, I have to be up at 5:00 A.M. to be there on time. Christmas Day was a perfect example. We didn't make it to brunch until 1:30, and that was with both of us getting ready. You really do need to get some help once in awhile.

NICK: The first few weeks were great. Laura's mom took off a week and my folks came in from Ohio. But since then . . . Laura's mom takes a day off here and there. I take off in the morning and get home at 7:30 or 8:00 P.M. It would be nice to afford a nanny, but we can't. And we kind of thought people in the old days pulled it off. We don't have to buy in to this more pampered—no pun intended—society. But I should say that Laura's parents will come any evening we need them. But we still never get anyplace on time.

LAURA: And my parents know the routine. They can walk in and take over in an instant. This is just normal to us. I've never been the mother of just one child. And I also really get a lot of support from the twins club. Meetings alternate between having speakers and support groups. You can break into a smaller group of moms with twins the same age as yours and you just talk about what the babies are doing: Mine aren't sleeping throughout the night, etc. You get some questions together and go back into the larger group and ask those moms how they've handled things, what stroller works for you. And it is a great resource for buying used clothes and things that you need in twos! I knew there was a national club, so I just called information and eventually found two local L.A. clubs.

TOM: Our relatives are all in New York. When it comes to getting help we advertise, but it is rough. We've hired people from agencies at ten to fifteen dollars an hour and they are incompetent. You'd think that someone who is supposed to be able to care for twins would be able to change a diaper without getting poop all over the blanket. . . . We really try to get at least a few hours a week for each other. I'm a musician and it was always my intention to stay at home during the day but, honestly, this situation with our babies being so premature has pretty much done in my business.

Fortunately, Sarah makes a lot more money than I do. So we're squeaking by, and I figure we'll recover sometime later on.

ROBERT: We felt so fortunate that we were able to take the boys home from the hospital with us. Grace's mom came to help. Grace was breast-feeding, so I was just a shuttle service . . . from mom to the crib and from the crib to mom. But we also made a conscious decision that we wanted to be the ones to raise our children. Sometimes it's nuts. But every Saturday, no matter what, we go out. Except last Saturday we decided we'd rather sleep than go out. . . .

But you know how you always hear about how the stress of twins can just make your marriage fall apart? We've become more focused around our kids and our marriage is just better.

18

your twins from three to four months

your growing twins

• *Exploring Their Environment*

The amount of stimuli coming into your twins' world is far greater than their ability to send signals back out. By the time they are three months old, they are already trying to mimic your voices and speak back to you. They are learning to use their limbs in a more coordinated fashion, and are likely to stare at their own hand. Both babies are probably indicating interest in more of their environment. They are working hard and can become cranky or even appear bored in reaction to overstimulation at this age. The American Academy of Pediatrics discourages television viewing for children under the age of two, including scheduled programming and videos that target this age group. Trying to limit or control television viewing for young babies is difficult, especially if there are other children in the house, so you should consider making a clear-cut rule for the family: no television on when the twins are in the room. We all know how effortlessly the television manages to insinuate its way into our lives, and we also know how easy it is to allow it to baby-sit for our children. In large part, the reason for the AAP recommendation is the understanding that time spent by young children and babies watching TV is time they are not spending interacting with other people as well as the rest of their environment. These interactions are vital to your babies' social, cognitive, and emotional development. In addition, this is a very important time for your twins' brain development. The "wiring" of your babies' brains develops in direct response to what is going on in their environment. There is concern that television has an adverse effect on this process. Certainly, this recommendation may take planning and effort to accomplish when you have other children at home, but it may also serve as an opportunity to reevaluate the entire family's television viewing habits.

• *Babbling and Laughing*

Babies learn speech by imitating—that is why it is so important to talk with your twins. Their responsive smiles are now accompanied by cooing, babbling, and the use of sounds to get your attention. Your twins may laugh as a sign of pleasure or amusement. There is a tremendous range of expression in these beginnings of speech. The impression that your twins are mimicking you sometimes is probably pretty accurate.

• *Drooling*

Somewhere around four months, babies will start drooling. It's not a sign of teething, but is occurring because their salivary glands are now making more saliva. And since it's also the time when, from a developmental perspective, they can get their hands into their mouths, they'll chew on their hands—which causes them to drool even more.

• *Hearing*

The AAP has endorsed universal newborn hearing screening programs (UNHSP) for infants before they leave the hospital after birth. While such screening is not yet in place in every state and in every hospital throughout the country, it is growing closer and closer to becoming a nationwide policy. Before you bring your babies home, find out whether or not they have received a hearing screen. If they have not, discuss it with your pediatrician. Undetected hearing loss in newborns is likely to impede their speech, language, and cognitive development. Infants with normal hearing almost always produce well-formed, single-syllable sounds (though they sometimes repeat), such as "da," "na," "bee," and "ya," before eleven months of age. If either of your twins does not begin to make these or similar sounds before eleven months, this should be considered a sign of possible impaired hearing and an audiologic assessment should be made. Your twins may begin to pay attention to and show pleasure at music.

• *Purposeful Grasp and Voluntary Release*
At three months, your twins are likely to grab a tiny fistful of your hair and give a mighty tug, but it is still strictly hit-or-miss from a developmental standpoint. By four to five months they will be able to voluntarily release their grasp of held objects. They will purposefully reach for, swing at, or grasp for objects but are not yet efficient enough to reliably grab an object that interests them.

• *Bring Hands Together into the Midline*
By three to four months you may notice your twins bringing their hands together over their tummies and then to their mouths. Previously, they may have inadvertently found their hands, but this marks a more purposeful ability to control motor skills. If your babies have not yet begun to put their hands in their mouths for comfort or exploration, they are likely to do so now. At four months they may also start to transfer objects from hand to hand.

parental questions and concerns

• *Diaper Rash*
Diaper rash is a common problem for babies of any age. It usually responds well to over-the-counter ointment containing zinc-oxide. If there is a lot of discomfort, place the baby in lukewarm water for five or ten minutes at a time, several times a day. Most infants find that very soothing. Some parents prefer to use cloth diapers due to environmental concerns. However, parents—especially parents of twins—need to consider the additional work and possible added expense of diaper service for two infants. Today's disposable diapers, particularly the overnight diapers that contain a gel that soaks up the urine, do an excellent job of keeping babies dry. Sometimes, parents call the pediatrician with a concern that their baby has awakened with some kind of unknown gel-like substance in the diaper, but that is just the gel used to absorb hours of urine accumulation. So while these diapers may disintegrate a bit after a long night, they are generally very effective.

Babies are also inclined to get yeast infections or monilial dermatitis in the diaper area. It classically shows up as a very bright, red area of skin that is surrounded by little, red spots. This can be treated by an over-the-counter antifungal medication or a prescription medication ordered by your doctor.

• *Different Temperaments and Different Development*

In just one day, a pediatrician seeing several sets of twins is going to hear one parent's concern that the babies are not sleeping enough. The next parent will be concerned that the babies appear to be sleeping too much. What's a doctor to say? The answer is that there is no such thing as the perfect set of twins: We have no perfect baby model. There is a broad range of normal when it comes to babies. As long as your twins are eating, healthy, and growing well, whatever they're doing is okay. Of course, what is perfectly swell for each of them may not make life particularly easy on the rest of the family!

There are certain temperaments that babies may exhibit at particular moments in their development: the crying or the cheerful baby; the anxious or the placid baby. While we like to look back and draw a straight line from the sunny baby to the relentlessly optimistic ten-year-old, we may be imposing our subjective viewpoint more than we realize. The baby who could bring down the nursery walls with her cry can become a remarkably composed five-year-old. For the parents of twins, this may be of particular interest. The implications for twins are obvious. There is an understandable, even an inevitable, tendency to compare and label: the leader and the follower; the big one and the little one; the bright one and the physical one. The reality is far more fluid, or at least it should be. The twin who is labeled "the good eater" is going to have certain expectations thrust upon her so that even when Grandma comes to visit, she will be expected to settle in for a whole bottle at a feeding. If Grandma is feeding the twin who has been labeled "the fussy one," she has the reasonable expectation that this twin won't feed as enthusiastically. And so a cycle of self-fulfilling prophecy begins. The twin with the greater large-motor skills chases the ball while the other twin has quiet time. The quieter baby waits for the new diaper every time because he just doesn't make such a fuss. The temptation to label any child can come from the most loving impulse: the desire to know deeply what your child is about. But the consequences of doing this with your twin infants can also have an impact on how they will relate to each other in years to come. You are into the first year of a lifetime of inevitable comparisons: It is more or less built into the system when you have twins. You do your twins and yourselves a great service by trying to remain flexible in the way you perceive and relate to each of them. This is not easy to do, but it is a gift that you can give to your twins on a daily basis.

• Sweet Dreams

As your twins grow larger, they may start to interfere with each other if they are in the same crib. It is not unreasonable to expect them to wake for a changing and feeding once during the night. If one or both is still waking two or three times a night, you may want to think about how you can help your babies learn to comfort themselves back to sleep. This is the point where parents need to consider that they may be going to the babies too soon, denying them the op-portunity to learn how to wake up and feel secure enough to go back to sleep without any attention from Mom or Dad. Your pediatrician may ask you about your babies' daily feeding schedule. By the time they are three months old, they should be eating less frequently, as they can consume more at each feeding. If they eat too frequently during the day, every time they wake up they may as-sume it is time to eat. Parents sometimes inadvertently set themselves up for difficulties by allowing their babies to fall asleep during the day in their auto-mated swings. A swing can be a wonderful tool when it comes to soothing one or both of your twins—getting through a fussy time or even occupying them safely while you are busy with a task in the same room. But babies are creatures of habit, and if they get used to falling asleep in their swings, you may be in for a tough time getting them to doze off in their cribs. Speak with your pediatri-cian about guidelines to help your twins develop the rhythm of daytime wake-fulness and nighttime sleeping.

dr. klein on sleeping through the night

"Like adults, babies will awaken several times in the course of the night. If they have not yet learned to fall asleep inside the crib and are used to falling asleep in their parent's arms, they will not be able to go back to sleep when they wake up inside their crib. I usually recommend the use of a transitional blanket for helping babies to comfort themselves and learn to fall back to sleep. I can't say it is completely successful every time, but many parents have had great results.

At some point—when the babies are about four months of age and starting to reach for and grasp things—each baby can be given a small, flannel blanket (about 18" × 18"), maybe with a border of soft satin which will feel wonderful to the touch. For the first week, Mom sleeps with the blanket to give it her comforting scent. The following week, when Mom or Dad holds the twins while nursing or giving a bottle, the babies get their blankets to hold on to while they fall asleep. *As soon as the baby is asleep,* she is placed (on her back) in the crib, with the blanket either still held in her grasp or right next to her. Remember, this blanket goes into the crib *next to* your baby, *not under* her. The third week, Mom or Dad should watch each twin intently and place them in their cribs *just as they are about to fall asleep.* The fourth week, let your babies be a little more awake when you place them in their cribs with their blankets after their feeding. For several subsequent weeks, allow your baby to be even more awake before you put her in the crib with her blanket. The object, of course, is to have your twins associate falling asleep with this soft, wonderful-smelling, transitional blanket. So, in the middle of the night the baby wakes up, grabs the blanket, and is self-comforted back to sleep."

Should the Babies Be Separated If One Is Sick?

The period of incubation for most viral infections is quite variable, ranging from a few days to several weeks. Trying to separate your twins when one shows symptoms of a cold is usually a case of too little too late. Very young babies, even in the same crib, are not likely to interact with each other that much, and you can certainly put them at either end of the crib to ensure that they won't be touching each other's faces or grasping for each other's toys. Be sure to wash your hands after caring for each twin, especially when one is ill.

Cradle Cap

The dry, scaly crust that can often occur in a baby's hair with an associated rash on the face is thought to be caused by a yeast infection in the scalp. Cradle cap is the body's reaction to that infection. You can lightly rub mineral oil into your baby's scalp, comb out the flakes, and then wash the hair immediately with baby shampoo. Do not use baby oil, which is absorbed by the skin. Cradle cap also responds very well to over-the-counter medicated shampoo, or your pediatrician can prescribe a special shampoo as well as a medicated cream to put on the rash if needed.

dr. klein on keeping little babies clean in the big, dirty city

"It may be different in other areas of the country but here in a large, urban center with so much dust and smog, I recommend that parents bathe their babies every day. The layer of dust you see daily on your furniture also coats your babies' skin. A daily bath helps to keep your babies' skin soft and clean and without rashes. It is important to remember that, even in parts of the country where the winters get very cold, you can bathe your babies daily without worrying about their catching a draught or a cold. You catch colds from germs, not from being cold!"

visiting the doctor

immunization: three to four months

The second hepatitis B (Hep B) vaccine is given between one and four months of age.

The second diphtheria, tetanus, acellular pertussis (DTaP) vaccine is given at four months of age.

The second Haemophilus influenzae type B (Hib) vaccine is given at four months of age.

The second poliovirus (IPV) vaccine is given at four months of age.

The second pneumococcal (PCV) vaccine is given at four months of age.

safety

basic twin-proofing

- *Security Gates*

Although your twins will not be crawling until much later, now is the time to prepare your house for their increased mobility. Be sure to use security gates at the top and bottom of the stairs, as well as to cordon off any area in the house to which your twins should not have access. This is particularly important with twins, because you cannot guarantee that they will both be doing their exploring in the same area of the house at the same time. In fact, you can almost guarantee that they won't!

- *Corner Covers*

This is a simple way to make all those sharp corners a lot less lethal. Mount on cabinets, tables, corners, etc.

- *Electrical Outlet Covers*

Be sure to cover all outlets to which your twins have access, including the surge protector strips that many people use with their computers. You can purchase outlet caps or swivel covers that automatically cover the outlet when you pull the plug.

- *Doorknob Covers*

These flexible covers slip on to doorknobs and prevent children from turning them, while keeping them easy for adults to squeeze and turn.

- *Drape and Blind Cord Windups*

We've already discussed the importance of not placing the crib next to exposed cords, but these devices can prevent a real tragedy in the world of your increasingly curious twins. Use them throughout your home.

- *VCR, DVD, and TV Locks or Covers*

Save your entertainment center from prying fingers.

• *Scatter Rugs*

Tack down scatter rugs to prevent slipping on hard floors.

twin-proofing your bathroom

• *Toilet Lock*

The toilet is often of great curiosity to exploring babies and must be locked closed from your twins, who might easily topple into trouble. The toilet lock installs and detaches easily for adults or older children in the house. The basic rules for water safety apply here: Do not allow your babies access to this or any standing pool of water.

• *Non-slip Mats for the Tub or Shower*

Safety mats provide traction in slippery tubs or showers and are important for the whole family.

• *Bath Spout Cover*

This soft cover can adapt to most tub spouts. It cushions and insulates against bumped heads. This is especially effective for the twin tub time that can get a little hectic.

twin-proofing your kitchen

• *Stove Guard*

Protect your twins from reaching out and touching a hot burner, even though it has been turned off. Stove guards mount easily and remove for cleaning or when not in use.

• *Oven Lock*

Made from material that can withstand the heat of the oven, this lock will prevent your twins from opening the oven at any time but still allow for easy access by an adult.

• Drawer and Cabinet Latches

These are a must for keeping two sets of hands away from sharp knives, glassware, and cleaning supplies. Remember that dishwasher soap and even regular dish soap could be dangerous to your babies. Keep them locked away.

twin-proofing the twins' bedroom

We've already discussed basic crib and changing-table safety. The following items may be helpful as you work with your twins to establish longer sleeping patterns:

• The Nursery Monitor

Many parents find the nursery monitor reassuring. There are monitors on the market today that have wrist receivers so you can hear the babies while you're in any room of the house.

• Night-Light

Be sure to have a low light source in the bedroom—enough light to change a diaper, but not so much as to entice your babies into activity. Some night-lights feature a silent switch and will shut off automatically after giving your babies time to drift off to sleep. Place the light near the door to the bedroom.

dr. klein on the importance of twin-proofing and general safety

"At the four-month well-baby visit, as babies are beginning to grab items and put them into their mouth, I discuss the implications of that developmental milestone as far as the babies' environment is concerned. I like to go into greater detail about baby-proofing the home and other aspects of safety.

As a physician, I have had to treat infants who were injured, some severely, in accidents that could have been prevented through baby-proofing in the home. It can be a terrible tragedy that I'd love to see all families spared. And I must stress to parents of twins that by the time those babies are mobile, scooting off in opposite directions, you will find great comfort in having prepared a safe environment for them.

Every home is different. Some families choose to call a professional baby-proofing company to go through the entire house and develop a list of recommendations that they can implement, or in some cases hire the same company to do the whole job. You can also adopt a twin's-eye view of the world by crawling about your home and seeing what looks inviting: an edge of a tablecloth to tug, the fishbowl on a low bookshelf, the books themselves, a coffee table that showcases your treasured ceramics.

If you have not yet done so, this is the time to choose a closet with a lock to provide a twin-proof (as well as teen-proof, and holiday and birthday gift–proof) spot for toxic substances, dangerous objects, and certainly any firearms that are in your home."

Roundtable Talk

PRESENT AT THE DISCUSSION ARE:

Dr. Connie Agnew

Dr. Alan Klein

Jill Ganon

Tom & Sarah

Nick & Laura

Joan & David

Robert & Grace

Kate & Matt

TOPIC FOR DISCUSSION IS:

The Financial Impact of Parenting Twins

JILL: Can we talk a little about financial implications of having twins?

JOAN: Our finances . . . we go back and forth from being in denial . . . sort of we'll be okay once I get back to work . . . to "Oh my God! What are we going to do?" . . . And just when you think you're getting out from under, something comes up. This week it was an emergency with our dog . . . two hundred dollars a day for intensive care.

NICK: We love our doctor but medical costs are a concern, particularly with Laura not working. Now that we only have my insurance, for some bizarre reason it doesn't seem to be covering well-baby care, immunizations, and things like that. Is anybody else experiencing that?

JOAN: Our insurance stopped paying on one of the babies because they kept asking, "Why are you sending one baby to the doctor twice in one day?"

LAURA: Our insurance company kept complaining that we were submitting duplicate charges.

NICK: It is mass confusion since the boys were born five months ago. It is amazing that the insurance companies just don't comprehend twins.

ROBERT: I find it helpful to keep very strict records and to really scrutinize all bills. I have definitely found billing errors. It's really crazy. You make too much money to qualify for low-income help, but suddenly you're down to one income and your expenses skyrocket.

TOM: You learn really quickly that the computer doesn't think.

SARAH: You really have to read your policies. I knew our situation would be complicated, so I got a second policy. We find that we get a lot of denied claims at first because the babies go to the doctor so frequently.

TOM: It is still rough because our second policy has turned out to be our primary [one] because I am older, and that seems to be the way they work it. The only way we could manage a second policy was with a huge deductible. But we also have California Children's Services [CCS] and Medi-Cal. In California, any baby born under 1,200 grams may qualify for both. You do have to qualify through diagnosis and financial screening. Our babies also qualify for SSI [Social Security Income] due to their low birth-weights. But there is an income factor there, too.

DR. KLEIN: I was under the impression that even someone with a substantial income would qualify at least for CCS because the health-care bills, especially hospital bills, are so staggering.

TOM: That is true, but there is a level beyond which they do not cover.

DR. KLEIN: In general, I counsel couples to put significantly premature twins, born at less than thirty-three weeks or so, on both their policies if possible. I know it is difficult. The cost of their care is usually so high that even your 10 or 20 percent responsibility can amount to a lot of money.

TOM: I don't know if people understand that there are caps to what insurance companies will pay. You really need to research that ahead of time if you can, especially with the potential for enormous costs with a multiple birth.

DR. KLEIN: Another option no one has mentioned yet is the possibility of asking for a discount. . . . I can't remember anyone here ever approaching me.

JOAN: But you can bet we will now!

DR. KLEIN: Well, you should ask. I have families who do, and a lot depends on their insurance. It used to be that I could give everyone who had twins a discount. Now, a lot of insurance already grants a discount over my usual charge, so it is not as easy to discount it further. But depending on your personal financial situation, it can be reasonable to ask.

ROBERT: I asked for discounts. The worst they can do is say no. In many cases, when you have twins they will either write off the balance or discount it. We'd start with the business office and they would put us through to the supervisor or sometimes directly to the doctor. We were not turned down, and the least we received was a discount. It depends on what the insurance pays and what the original discount was. If insurance has paid 90 percent

of a $1,200 [bill], chances are they'll write off the balance or most of it.
Sometimes it really feels like a matter of survival.

DR. KLEIN: In my practice, I try to offer discounts to anyone who has real financial hardship. Sometimes we work out long-term payment plans. But it is
important to understand that there is a clause in the insurance contract
that doctors agree to that says if there is no charge to the patient, there can
be no charge to the insurance company. So a complete discount is difficult.

JOAN: As a nurse, I always ask doctors if they give professional discounts. It is
less likely now than it used to be. In retrospect, I wonder if it was wise to
have dropped my insurance to go on my husband's policy. I thought I was
paying this unnecessary fee for my own coverage, but we might be better
off if I'd kept it. It just was not something I thought through prior to becoming pregnant.

your twins from five to six months

your growing twins

• *Teething*

The appearance of your babies' first teeth can happen anywhere from three to eighteen months. If your twins are identical, you can expect to see similar dental characteristics between them. Your pediatrician will be looking to see that the teeth are appearing in an appropriate order. Resist the temptation to let your babies go to sleep with a bottle of milk or juice as either will promote tooth decay, even in young babies, after the teeth have erupted.

• *Changes in Growth Patterns and Growth Rates*

At five or six months, you are likely to see that the rate of growth as indicated in your twins' growth charts is going to decrease. In other words, they are not going to grow quite as fast. As a rule of thumb, your pediatrician will expect the weight gain in the first six months to round out to approximately an ounce a day. After six months, that drops to an ounce every other day for the rest of the first year.

In the case of premature twins, we may still be correcting for the expected date of delivery: Your five-month-old babies who were born four weeks early will be at a four-month range in growth and development. Generally, over time their growth and developmental capabilities will go into the range that no longer needs correcting. The degree of prematurity is a factor: Once your twins move into the normal growth range, and are growing at a normal rate for their actual age, your pediatrician may decide it is no longer necessary to correct. If your twins are two months premature, that two months is very significant when we are looking at a baby who is five months old. However, as your twins grow up, those two months grow less meaningful. By the time your twins are five years old, those two months will have become inconsequential.

dr. klein on the use of growth hormone

"Biosynthetic growth hormone (GH) has been available for prescription use in the United States since 1985. It has been an important therapy to stimulate adequate growth in various clinical situations including growth hormone deficiency, kidney failure, and several other specific abnormalities such as idiopathic short stature, Turner's syndrome, and Prader Willi syndrome, with both of these syndromes being associated with specific chromosomal anomalies.

Recently, the Food and Drug Administration approved the expanded use of GH for children born small for gestational age (SGA)—a weight or length below the tenth percentile for gestational age—if they have failed to reach the normal height range by two years of age. Because the in-utero growth rate drops off during the last ten weeks, twins are more likely to be among those small-for-gestational-age babies that are born each year in the United States and may not catch up to their peers in growth by age two.

Concerns about a child's height are very understandable in our society, where we have grown culturally accustomed to associating a person's individual stature with their overall attractiveness and stature in society. There are long-held perceptions that a short child, particularly a boy child, may be psychosocially disadvantaged by being considered "the short kid." Interestingly, there is increasing evidence culled from more recent studies that children, adolescents, and adults are largely on par with their taller peers insofar as their psychosocial functioning in society is concerned. Certainly, as parents, it is understandable that we want to seek the best of all possible outcomes for our children. But we need to consider the possibility that we bring our own biases to the examination of our children's height. If you have questions about the growth of either one or both of your twins and you want to consider growth hormone therapy, your pediatrician will direct you to have an expanded discussion with a pediatric endocrinologist."

• Increased Social Behavior

By the fifth month, laughter may be a regular feature as your twins show great pleasure in playing with you. Your babies are increasingly interested in sustained social contact, and may show their displeasure loud and clear if contact is broken before they are ready. Babies at this age are also beginning to show excitement at the sight of food.

• Sitting Unassisted

The six-month-old baby won't get to a sitting position unassisted but, placed in position, may sit unaided for a while. Of course, placed side by side, your twins may grab at each other and tend to support or topple each other over. They begin to sit on their own with their backs rounded, supporting their weight on their hands, which are placed palm down in front of them.

• Transferring Objects from Hand to Hand

Sometime after four months, babies begin to transfer objects from hand to hand. Your baby is likely to observe and compare held objects.

parental questions and concerns

• Starting Solid Foods

Your babies will be ready for the introduction of solid foods sometime between their fourth and sixth months. The recommendation is that babies who are being breast-fed not be started on solid foods until six months. If additional foods are introduced too early, they may interfere with breast-feeding. The introduction of solid foods at this point is only to give new flavors and textures, not to provide nutrition. In actuality, if breast-feeding moms want to go eight or nine months without starting solid foods and their babies are growing well, that is fine. Bottle-fed babies are often started on solid foods as young as four months. But if they are not that interested in solids at that point, it is fine to wait and try again each week or so until they show some interest, which is most likely to occur by six months of age.

If solids are introduced too early, there is a greater likelihood that an infant will become allergic to them. Don't succumb to pressure to start solids too soon because you think it will help your babies sleep through the night. The introduction of solids depends on the readiness of each baby's digestive tract. Term babies are usually ready by five months, but this is certainly something that parents will want to discuss with their own pediatrician. For the premature baby, a corrected age of between four and six months is usually appropriate.

You are likely to perceive your twins' increased interest in watching you eat. Once again, the wonderful power of babies to mimic is at work as they watch you chew and begin to imitate the chewing motion. Introduce one food at a time so you will know what food isn't working if either twin has a reaction to it. It is also a good idea to feed both babies the same foods to simplify your already complicated world. If one of your twins doesn't like squash but both like carrots, feed them carrots for now.

dr. klein on introducing solid foods

"I recommend that when introducing solid foods, parents think in terms of breakfast, lunch, and dinner—feeding their babies first at the breast or bottle and then offering solid food immediately thereafter, so that the whole feeding event is considered a meal. Many times, parents hesitate to offer solid food right after their baby has nursed, for fear that once sated with milk or formula, the baby will not be interested in the solid food. I explain that the method I recommend avoids establishing a pattern in which babies become accustomed to eating all the time—a practice that can lead parents to using food to control behavior. I also think that once babies are ready for solid food, continual snacking throughout the day conditions them to expect to eat frequently, which limits their capacity to sleep through the night. Really, it is three meals a day and a bottle or the breast at bedtime.

I suggest that you pick one day of the week to introduce new foods. Start with rice cereal for the morning and evening meals—just one to two teaspoons twice a day—and build up to a total of three to four tablespoons at each feeding by the end of the week. The following week try a yellow vegetable, like squash, after the noon bottle or breast-feeding and offer three to four tablespoons of rice cereal, plus squash, after the evening breast- or bottle-feeding. This will have you well on your way to establishing a schedule of three meals a day.

Remember to give a bottle- or breast-feeding first, followed immediately by the solid food.

During the second half of your twins' first year of life, they are still getting most of their calories from formula or breast milk, so solids should supplement, not supplant, that important nourishment. If your pediatrician feels that the babies are putting on weight a little too fast, he may recommend that you reverse the order and give the solid food first. In the third week of solid foods try another cereal, like barley or oatmeal. In the fourth week try sweet potatoes and, if all is going well, slowly introduce other appropriate foods, one new food per week. Stay with single-ingredient items as you introduce the other food groups: green vegetables, fruits, and meats. Hold off with fruits until your twins are enthusiastic about several other foods. Fruits are sweet, and one or both of your twins may have a sweet tooth and resist other foods once he realizes sweet tastes are an option."

• Help with Feeding

If there is any time that help is important, it is at feeding time. The more organized you are, the better off you'll all be. If you have to prepare the cereal after nursing one or both babies, so much time goes by that it is as though you were into another feeding. Have the solid foods ready before you sit down to nurse or offer a bottle. Each baby should have his or her own spoon and bowl in order to minimize the spread of illness. If you're nursing, of course you'll be holding one or both babies, but if they are taking a bottle, now is a good time for them to be in a high chair.

Even with young babies, it is important to begin to establish meal and snack times so that food does not become a tool of behavior modification. Mealtimes for your twins can be an organizational challenge, but they can also be an opportunity for wonderful time with each baby.

• Allergies

It is helpful to understand that there can be a genetic predisposition toward developing allergies. If Mom is allergic to walnuts, that does not necessarily mean that either twin will be allergic to walnuts, but they may be inclined to develop allergic reactions. If you have a history of respiratory allergies in the family, it is wise to try to create a dust-free environment for your children. Eighty percent of children who do have allergies are allergic to dust or dust mites, and it is possible to delay the onset of allergy to dust by limiting early exposure.

• *Most Common Food Allergens*
(limit exposure before one year of age)

berries	chocolate
citrus fruits	egg white
milk	shellfish
tomatoes	wheat

peanuts and also tree nuts (should not be given before four years of age due to choking hazard)

• *Least Common Food Allergens*
(customary beginning foods for young babies)

apples	apricots
barley	cooked carrots
oats	peaches
pears	plums
rice	squash

• *The Child-rearing Taboo: Favoritism*
While nobody wants to acknowledge it, the bottom line is that parents frequently do have favorites. This is the case where any siblings are concerned, and it can certainly be the case with twins. (There, we've said it.) As your children grow and develop and their temperaments change, the child who was the favorite of one parent may lose that status as the parent finds reason to favor another. A parent's choice of a child as a favorite may take place on a conscious level, but it is just as likely to be subconscious. Often, a parent singles out a child for reasons that are not clear. Other times the reasons are painfully appar-

ent, though parents may be uncomfortable with what such favoritism says about them. Parents can easily find themselves charmed by a strikingly beautiful or wonderfully kind child. Sometimes a parent's fierce protection of the child who seems less gifted or less obviously endowed can lead to favoritism. Sometimes the reasons are far more subtle and fluid and never rise to the level of consciousness. The parents of twins are likely to choose different favorites, and they may shift their positions. Talking with your mate about your feelings may provide you with revelations that ultimately enhance your parenting of both babies. But remember that however infrequently such feelings are acknowledged, they are very common. The parents who anticipate them are better equipped to handle them when they arise.

Negotiating the World with Your Twins

Remember to leave plenty of time. Parents of one young child are often troubled by how long it takes to get out of the house. As far as trying to rush anywhere, twins are double trouble. Your best bet is to leave yourself plenty of time to accomplish even modest goals. Just know that there is no such thing as running to the market for a minute if you're doing it with your twins. Give yourself an extra hour just to account for getting in and out of the car at either end of your travels. You are going to have many happy moments out and about with your beautiful babies, so be sure to give yourself lots of time to enjoy them.

Vomiting and Diarrhea

Diarrhea is often difficult to distinguish from regular bowel movements in breast-fed babies, since their movements are typically quite loose. An increase in the volume and/or frequency of bowel movements may indicate that your baby has picked up some kind of "stomach flu." In most cases, both vomiting and diarrhea are self-limiting and require no specific medication.

Blood in the bowel movement is reason for extra concern and you should call your pediatrician. It may indicate the presence of a bacterial infection.

What we used to refer to as the BRAT diet—bananas, rice, applesauce, and toast—is no longer recommended to treat diarrhea. It has been replaced by diets that contain complex carbohydrates such as pasta, rice, and mashed potatoes. Even milk is no longer considered something that needs to be withheld in children with diarrhea. Unless your doctor tells you otherwise, there is no reason to stop breast-feeding if your child has loose stools or diarrhea, but you should avoid anything containing a lot of sugar, such as apple juice, sports drinks, and certainly, soda.

If your baby vomits, withhold feeding for at least two hours from the time of vomiting. For the baby who is breast-feeding, you can try nursing for no more than five minutes at a time, every fifteen minutes. For babies taking a bottle, offer half an ounce of Pedialite (an electrolyte replacement solution), either straight or mixed half-and-half with flat ginger ale, breast milk, or formula, every fifteen minutes for the first hour, then an ounce every fifteen minutes for the next hour, then two ounces every fifteen minutes for the third hour. Continue to feed small amounts throughout the day—no more than three to four ounces at a time. If a nursing baby is not tolerating breast milk in small amounts, switch over to Pedialite. The focus is to keep your baby safely hydrated.

The primary concern with vomiting and diarrhea is dehydration. The signs of dehydration are a lack of tears, dryness of the mouth, decreased urination, and, in extreme cases, dehydration can result in skin that can becomes "tented," or remains as though still held between your thumb and forefinger after you are no longer gently compressing your baby's skin. Call your physician for specific instructions at the first sign of dehydration. Usually, dehydration can be treated or prevented with electrolyte replacement solutions that are readily available in your supermarket or pharmacy.

visiting the doctor

• *Immunization: Five to Six Months*
  The third hepatitis B (Hep B) vaccine is given between six and eighteen months of age.
  The third diphtheria, tetanus, acellular pertussis (DTaP) vaccine is given at six months of age.
  The third Haemophilus influenzae type B (Hib) vaccine is given at six months of age.
  The third poliovirus (IPV) vaccine is given between six and eighteen months of age.
  The third pneumococcal vaccine (PVC) is given at six months of age.

An annual influenza vaccine is recommended for all children between six and twenty-three months of age. Discuss this with your doctor.

safety

• *Burn Safety*

As previously stated, parents of young babies should turn their hot-water heaters below 120 degrees Fahrenheit so that if the baby is burned, the burn will be less serious than it would at a higher temperature. When running a bath for the twins, run the cold water first, then the hot. When turning the water off, do the opposite, never allowing only hot water to run into the tub. Before putting your babies in the water, be sure to swish the water around to avoid any hot spots. Never add hot water with the babies in the tub.

Be very conscientious about keeping babies away from hot beverages at home and certainly in a restaurant, where a server could inadvertently spill hot coffee or tea on one of your twins.

When using the stove, use the back burners first, and turn all pan handles away from the front of the stove if you use the front burners. If your baby does get burned, place the burned area under cold running water for at least five minutes.

• *Choking*

Although it may seem early to discuss this, be very careful about the dangers of choking. Children should not have raw carrots, raw celery, bacon, peanuts, nuts, or popcorn until they are four years old. Grapes and hot dogs that are skinned and cut into tiny pieces are acceptable for your babies once they are at least one year of age.

• *Sunburn*

As discussed in chapter 17, babies' tender skin should not be in direct sun if they are under six months of age. At six months, choose a titanium dioxide or zinc oxide sunscreen with a sun protection factor (SPF) of at least fifteen and apply it generously. It is a good idea to dab a bit of sunscreen on an arm or leg of each baby and wait several hours to make sure there is no adverse reaction.

Avoid PABA sunscreens, which can irritate your babies' delicate skin. If you are going to be out in the sunshine, don't expose the babies to the strongest sun of the day.

Roundtable Talk

PRESENT AT THE DISCUSSION ARE:
Dr. Alan Klein
Tom
David
Robert
Matt

TOPICS FOR DISCUSSION ARE:
Do Husbands Feel Acknowledged for Their Role?
Do You Have a Favorite?

TOM: I have to say that sometimes I feel like their butler. . . . But I just put those feelings away because I'm always their advocate and I'll always do what needs to be done. Friends and family would send cards and call, and in my situation it was kind of crazy. We had three babies [premature triplets born at twenty-six weeks], and they were so small and in the NICU. I couldn't hold them except for putting my hand in through the porthole of the Isolette. We'd been trying for so long to have a baby. . . . Well, I had a friend whose wife had also just given birth and I finally asked him, could I come over and hold your baby? I needed grounding. . . . I needed a goal of what to feel when you hold a child. It was wonderful.

ROBERT: It can feel like a thankless job. . . . But we wanted so badly to have a baby. As fathers we are really out there doing all the legwork. Our wives are there with the babies, really needing to be served by us. We'd been trying for so long to get pregnant. We'd had a miscarriage and we really both wanted these babies. We were very excited and wanted to take every precaution. I was there for all of it. I went to every doctor appointment . . . everything.

DR. KLEIN: I think I'm hearing that even though you were involved, I'm not sure you were acknowledged.

ROBERT: I was acknowledged by my wife but nobody else. She has told me she could never have gone through it without me. Unless you've been through it you cannot understand. Especially with infertility and then multiple babies. I set up every appointment and asked every question. I didn't want my wife to go through anything but labor. Bed rest was crazy. . . . I'd get her out to an appointment, then home and in bed, then I'd get back and make her dinner and then it would start all over again. I kept track of all the billing, and it was complicated. People don't realize. It was extremely nerve-racking.

TOM: Since you'd had a miscarriage, you sort of had that fear. It never occurred to me. I just had faith. But when the kids were finally born, and they were so premature and we were told we'd probably lose all of them [they had triplets, one of whom died at eleven days], I had so many feelings, and one of them was terror at starting all over.

MATT: My wife was on bed rest for two weeks. She is pretty mentally tough and I don't think she was looking for me to do that much. I think she found it pretty frustrating because she couldn't get around. I suppose I did try to wait on her because I didn't want her to do anything. She didn't seem to need a lot of support . . . or maybe she did and I didn't realize it. I felt very involved, but I never felt like she was going to break down. I tend to worry more than she does anyway, so I was kind of prepared for anything she might have needed. And we called the doctor with the slightest problem. I think I felt appreciated to the degree that it was relevant to me. Actually, some of my friends thought it was odd that I went with her to the doctor appointments. But I was sensitive to the fact that there was risk associated with her pregnancy and I have a very low tolerance for uncertainty. I felt better being there.

DR. KLEIN: I think there is a sense among the general public that pregnancy is very much an experience that is owned by women. But with all of you having wives on bed rest, you were very much involved. You played a much

bigger role, and I'm wondering if other people—your friends and family—
knew the extent of your involvement.

DAVID: If I was acknowledged by anyone at all, it was my wife, Joan. I worked
with a guy who told me that the day his child was born, he and his wife
got out of bed and she fixed his breakfast and then they went off to the
hospital and he waited in the waiting room. But that was a while ago.

DR. KLEIN: Do you guys have a favorite?

MATT: We don't. But I think it might be because my wife was a twin and she
always had the sense that her sister kind of got more attention . . . always a
little wilder . . . the squeaky wheel kind of thing. So we really work to make
sure that doesn't happen. I mean, one has a couple of irritating points and
the other has different irritating points and we just deal with it.

DAVID: I had a thought that while I see them as individuals I also see them as
parts of a whole, and if one weren't there I'd really feel that something was
missing. Even when we look at them and try to see who seems to have the
physical characteristics of my side of the family, it doesn't feel like an issue
of favoritism. . . . Not like I'd prefer that one.

ROBERT: I'll just say I don't have a favorite. . . . I cannot imagine one without
the other. But one of them just grabbed me. It's funny. One of them looks
like her and one of them looks like me. I seem to favor the one that looks
like her and she seems to spend more time with the one that looks like me.
I have a few theories. Maybe subconsciously I feel I'm afraid to get too
close to the one that looks like me. Or maybe the same way I'm attracted
to my wife, I'm drawn to the boy that looks like her.

DAVID: We named the boys after their grandfathers, and my family appears to
favor the child named after their side of the family.

TOM: Well, there's one I definitely have more fun with. You don't love your kids
the same . . . but you love them the same amount. They just do different

things to me. I couldn't say which I love better. My son is into everything and I love that about him . . . although I try to discipline him and he just laughs at me. Yet my daughter melts my heart. She is more needy, but she snuggles into me. . . . I love them differently.

DR. KLEIN: With families with two children one frequently is identified as the mother's child and one as the father's, and in my practice it isn't static: It really tends to move back and forth. It will be interesting to see how it develops with your twins.

TOM: Well, I think if you put it in those terms, Samantha is more mine because my wife, at least in my mind, seems to favor Michael. He looks like her father, and Sarah lost her father when she was very young. There is just some bond she has. She has such warm and loving memories of her father.

MATT: Maybe it is a question of who you bond more with. My son John didn't have serious problems, but he had a problem with eating enough. He was smaller and needed more attention. And I think that my wife thinks I can get John to eat more than she can, so it ends up that I spend more time with him.

TOM: There are times I feel more affection for one than the other, but it does go back and forth.

ROBERT: It seems like we all have in common the fact that we were ready and we all really wanted our kids. And with twins, if you aren't ready for it, I can't imagine how you would cope.

your twins from seven months to one year

your growing twins

- *Thumb Finger Grasp and Voluntary Release*

At about eight months your babies will begin to grasp objects between thumb and forefinger, as well as discover the thrill of uncovering a hidden toy. By one year of age, babies will have the ability to turn the pages of a book. They will also be able to release an object when another person requests it.

- *Responding to Requests*

At seven to nine months, your babies are likely to respond to your verbal request ("Give me the block") if it is accompanied by the gesture of your outstretched hand. By twelve months, your verbal request ("May I have the block?") will be responded to without any need for accompanying gestures.

- *Your Social Babies*

At seven months of age your twins may show a preference for one parent over the other, but both parents should be assured that it is only temporary. Babies will show real individuality now, and have their own personal responses to each social contact with family, friends, and other babies. Around this time, your babies may get a lot of enjoyment from play with a mirror. By about ten months your twins will be responding to their names, waving bye-bye, and playing responsive games like peek-a-boo and patty-cake. Your year-old twins may be engaging in make-believe play, such as pretending to drink from a cup or read a book.

First Words

At seven months you will hear the beginnings of polysyllabic vowel sounds, and between ten and twelve months you may hear words with repetitive consonant sounds like "mama" and "dada." Your year-old twins may have some additional words in their vocabularies.

Motor Skills

By seven months your babies may support most of their own weight, and you can observe them bouncing actively. Not every baby learns to crawl. Some babies lift themselves to a standing position and eventually begin to just walk. But if your twins are going to crawl or creep, they are likely to be pretty mobile by ten months. Walking readiness continues to advance as one or both babies begin to pull themselves to a standing position and then walk or "cruise," holding on to furniture for support. Next, they will begin to walk with you holding one of their hands, until taking one or two unassisted steps.

parental questions and concerns

Putting Twins in Day Care

Children in a day-care setting outside the home are definitely exposed to more colds, but each baby's world must grow larger at some point and whenever that happens, the baby is vulnerable to whatever bug happens to be out there. Although it may seem that all the sick time is hard on young bodies, rest assured that your babies' immune systems can easily handle the load. In addition, recent studies have shown that children in day care are less likely to develop allergies when they get older. Decisions about day care should be made keeping several factors in mind: parents' work situations, the family's finances, and the availability of help to come to your home.

Motor Development

By six-and-a-half to seven months of age, your twins are probably rolling from their tummies onto their backs and from their backs onto their tummies. By seven to eight months they are sitting without support. They are working at pulling together the elements of control over their bodies in order to attain the next developmental milestone. You'll see them beginning to rock back and forth on all fours in preparation to crawl. Again, some babies will take their first steps at ten months after only several weeks of crawling, while some will pull to a stand and just start walking at twelve months without ever having crawled. It is the appropriate connecting of each of these activities that tells you your babies' development is as it should be.

Questions from Strangers

We are all captivated by twins. As parents, you have now entered a segment of the population that is more knowledgeable about, and sensitive to, twin issues than your average shopper in the checkout line. Along with admiring looks and pleasant comments, parents report remarks from "Wouldn't you just know that the boy would be the more beautiful baby?" to "Gee, they look tiny. Are they okay?" It is important to develop your own protocol for dealing with remarks from strangers, or even casual friends. If your twins were premature and you get tired of hearing about how small they are for their age, don't hesitate to tell the inquiring stranger that your seven-month-old twins are five months old.

Weaning

Sometimes, one or both twins will wean themselves spontaneously. In that case, the mother may need to express milk to avoid engorgement. But if the mother is making the decision to begin weaning, it should be done in a manner that spares her the discomfort of engorgement.

Weaning can be most effectively accomplished if done over a period of several weeks. The first week, stop the noontime feeding; the second week, stop the early-evening feeding; the third week, stop the bedtime feeding; and, finally, stop the morning feeding. The morning feeding is saved for last because that is when the mother is likely to have the greatest milk supply and risks engorgement.

It is often easier to have the father or another caregiver give the bottle when Mom is attempting to wean. While mothers often worry that their babies will go hungry, they almost never do. With Mom not there, they simply become hungry enough to accept a bottle and will soon be quite content with the new arrangement. If the mother is the only one available at feeding time, putting the baby in a high chair rather than cuddling in the recognized nursing position may make the baby more receptive to accepting a bottle.

visiting the doctor

- *Immunization: Seven Months to One Year*
    The third hepatitis B (Hep B) vaccine is given between six and eighteen months of age.
    The fourth Haemophilus influenzae type B (Hib) vaccine (if needed) is given between twelve and fifteen months of age.
    The third poliovirus (IPV) vaccine is given between six and eighteen months of age.
    The first measles, mumps, rubella (MMR) vaccine is given between twelve and fifteen months of age.
    The first varicella zoster virus (chicken pox) vaccine is given between twelve and eighteen months of age.
    The fourth pneumococcal vaccine (PCV) is given between twelve and fifteen months of age.
    An annual influenza vaccine is recommended for children between six and twenty-three months of age and for older children with certain risk factors. Discuss this with your doctor.

safety

- *Finalize Twin-proofing for Your Active Babies*
Now that your babies are getting around and beginning to explore, you can see why it is important to be a few steps ahead of them when it comes to safety. With their increased mobility, you can no longer tell yourself you have an eye on them: There is no guarantee they will stay where you put them!

dr. klein on baby walkers

"Baby walkers present a particular danger because they move so fast and can allow babies to scoot their way into trouble really quickly. *This is especially true with twins, when they are more than likely to take off in two directions at once!* The best-intentioned and most diligent parent is no match for twins in baby walkers. There are wonderful stationary centers you can buy for your twins with plenty of stimulation but no wheels."

• *The Perils of Exercise Equipment*

The treadmill that is designed for your health can be very dangerous to your twins. This is another case where two tiny explorers can get into real trouble. Babies should have absolutely no access to treadmills, stationary bikes, workout stations, hand weights, or barbells. These fitness tools are very enticing to babies, perhaps because they are attracted to your physical activity when you use them.

• *Pool and Jacuzzi*

If you are fortunate enough to own a pool or Jacuzzi, it should be in a gated, enclosed area. Even then, there should always be a protective pool cover securely anchored in place whenever the pool is not in use. Inflatable wading pools are no exception: Never allow your twins to play in the yard with a filled wading pool unless they are supervised by an adult. A baby can drown in only a few inches of water.

• *Windows, Balconies, and Porches*

Windows are very dangerous to babies who like to hoist themselves up for a better view. Remember, a screen is not an adequate barrier for an enthusiastic infant, and your twins can create better access than the singleton baby, whether by happy accident or collaboration. Keep windows closed unless they are blocked by baby-safe window guards.

Roundtable Talk

PRESENT AT THE DISCUSSION ARE:
Dr. Connie Agnew
Dr. Alan Klein
Jill Ganon
Tom & Sarah
Nick & Laura
Joan & David
Robert & Grace
Kate & Matt

TOPICS FOR DISCUSSION ARE:
Out in the World with Your Twins
Reflections on a Year with Your Twins

NICK: Our boys are identical and you just don't ever really forget that they are twins. They are fourteen months now, and they tackle each other and go back and forth doing the same things. And I have to say they get an enormous amount of attention when we just go out to the mall.

LAURA: In talking to lots of other parents with twins, it seems that identical twins seem to reach developmental milestones very close to the same time . . . more so than fraternal twins. These guys were walking within a week of each other . . . they stood unassisted on the same day.

NICK: You can sort of identify with celebrities, though I think it's maybe more difficult with twins. People stare at celebrities but they stay away. But put identical twins in a stroller and nobody has any qualms about coming right up to you and asking a million questions. It's kind of flattering, but sometimes you're really in a hurry. Of course, if you just have one or if we take separate strollers and split up when we get to the mall, no reaction whatsoever. But the double stroller is a sideshow.

TOM: We'll have Sammi in pink and Michael in jeans and people will still come up to us and say, "Wow, twins . . . boy and girl. Are they identical?" [laughter]

JILL: Do you give a lot of thought to how they are dressed?

LAURA: Our boys usually wear similar things. Overalls, but each one has a different color shirt. It's kind of fun at a family party or something. But knowing my family and not wanting to deal with "who is who?" all day, I'll make sure one is in white socks and one in red, or something like that. And also, if we're at home and I want to know which one is running off, I can't see their faces, but I can look at the socks and know—there goes Kevin!

JILL: Do they communicate in a special way with each other?

TOM: I don't know if they use their own language, but we have their cribs end to end and they sort of grab at each other. You can hear them laughing. They only do it when they are by themselves. If they catch me poking my head in, it's over. Whatever it is they are communicating, they both find it really funny sometimes.

MATT: I think our guys are communicating. They are not yet a year old. They look at each other and make all sorts of noises, they fight over toys, roll over each other. They will literally shake each other sometimes . . . they are very funny.

LAURA: We have their cribs end to end. If by some miracle they are napping at the same time. I'll hear giggling when they wake up and I'll peek in their room, and they are in their cribs looking like jailed inmates. And in the high chair . . . God forbid one starts laughing. They'll look at each other and start to howl. Forget trying to feed them.

JILL: So how would you sum up the year?

MATT: For us, I'd say that other than the fact that we now have two kids, everything was the same for us. I travel a lot, so when I get home I like to stay home. It's like Joan said, sometimes you look at them and say, "How did we do that?" Especially now that they are ten months old—out of the slug stage. . . . Now they really know you and each other and are doing things. It's incredibly exciting. If anything, our relationship is better.

KATE: Like Matt says, things haven't changed that much. I'm just more tired than before.

TOM: I'm incredibly aware of how much they've developed and how different they are from each other. My son is very independent, but my daughter will really pull and cry if she wants my attention.

JOAN: I've gone back to work part-time, so now we have sitters who come in. That is a big step. Sometimes they scream when I leave, sometimes they don't. They are going through some separation issues. Sometimes David will walk into the bathroom and they're just outside the bathroom door, crying and crying. Of course, now Paul can reach the knob, so he'll just open the door and see if his dad's in there.

MATT: Now I say we never get to go to any of the parties that we never went to anyway. . . . This is the greatest thing we've ever done. If anything, our relationship is better. We have someone living in to help with the kids, and it's been strange getting used to having somebody living with us. But she goes her own way on the weekends. Once the kids are in bed, our life is the same as it always was, except we're much more tired. I think it's great.

JOAN: The boys are such an important part of our family, and my marriage is more important to me now. It's sort of like everything is more important in a balanced way. I'm not sure if it's because we had twins but I think it is. Having twins stopped us from being these two little people with big jobs. If we'd just had one, I think I would have pretty much taken care of the baby, and David would have done his thing at work and of course loved the baby. But we wouldn't have become the kind of team we are now.

LAURA: At first, I didn't have the self-confidence as a mother to do it alone and was always asking for help. But now, fourteen months have passed and there is the sense that if we can do two [babies], we can do anything. It's so much fun, there's so much love, and now they are at the point where they're really responding. They'll hug me . . . sometimes I have to laugh at what it must look like as I walk across the living room with one on each leg . . . or else they are following me around like ducklings.

TOM: So much has happened since we first knew we were pregnant. We're so involved with Samantha and Michael, and they are making such incredible progress. You don't necessarily realize how much Brian [their third son, who died eleven days after birth] is a part of our lives until we think about maybe leaving L.A. and we realize it would feel like we were abandoning him. . . . He's a sort of a guardian angel. We had to make the decision to take him off life support and it was excruciating. We still wonder if we did the right thing because we went through the process with our daughter, too. We were ready to take her off life support. You have to understand, they were so tiny. . . . Sarah was holding her one last time, and Samantha just wouldn't stop staring at Sarah. We finally decided to do a CAT scan, and that gave us hope that at least her condition wasn't deteriorating. And now she is a little behind her brother but she is growing and doing really well. And she was almost taken off life support. That's as heavy as it gets. It's hard not to feel that maybe there could have been a miracle for Brian, but his problems were so much more severe. . . . He's a big part of our prayers. . . . He'll always be a part of our family.

NICK: On some level, I kind of look at it like a job. There are times all of us in the work world don't like our job, but you learn to have some perspective. Laura is a full-time mom and I know how incredibly hard she works. She is the one on call for these boys Monday through Friday, and it might mean sometimes she's up through the night, but I'm there with her and the boys on weekends. I know it is tough on Laura.

LAURA: It's absolutely worth the bloodshot eyes, and I wouldn't trade it for anything. As a couple, we've learned so much.

Appendix A

immunization schedules

Recommended Childhood and Adolescent Immunization Schedule   UNITED STATES • 2005

Vaccine ▼ \ Age ▶	Birth	1 month	2 months	4 months	6 months	12 months	15 months	18 months	24 months	4–6 years	11–12 years	13–18 years
Hepatitis B[1]	HepB #1	HepB #2				HepB #3				HepB Series		
Diphtheria, Tetanus, Pertussis[2]			DTaP	DTaP	DTaP		DTaP			DTaP	Td	Td
Haemophilus influenzae type b[3]			Hib	Hib	Hib	Hib						
Inactivated Poliovirus			IPV	IPV		IPV				IPV		
Measles, Mumps, Rubella[4]						MMR #1				MMR #2	MMR #2	
Varicella[5]						Varicella				Varicella		
Pneumococcal[6]			PCV	PCV	PCV	PCV			PCV	PPV		
Influenza[7]						Influenza (Yearly)				Influenza (Yearly)		
	Vaccines below broken line are for selected populations											
Hepatitis A[8]										Hepatitis A Series		

This schedule indicates the recommended ages for routine administration of currently licensed childhood vaccines, as of December 1, 2004, for children through age 18 years. Any dose not administered at the recommended age should be administered at any subsequent visit when indicated and feasible.

▓▓▓ Indicates age groups that warrant special effort to administer those vaccines not previously administered. Additional vaccines may be licensed and recommended during the year. Licensed combination vaccines may be used whenever any components of the combination are indicated and other components of the vaccine are not contraindicated. Providers should consult the manufacturers' package inserts for detailed recommendations. Clinically significant adverse events that follow immunization should be reported to the Vaccine Adverse Event Reporting System (VAERS). Guidance about how to obtain and complete a VAERS form is available at www.vaers.org or by telephone, 800-822-7967.

☐ Range of recommended ages   ▨ Only if mother HBsAg(–)
▓ Preadolescent assessment   ▓ Catch-up immunization

 DEPARTMENT OF HEALTH AND HUMAN SERVICES
CENTERS FOR DISEASE CONTROL AND PREVENTION

The Childhood and Adolescent Immunization Schedule is approved by:
Advisory Committee on Immunization Practices www.cdc.gov/nip/acip
American Academy of Pediatrics www.aap.org
American Academy of Family Physicians www.aafp.org

Footnotes Recommended Childhood and Adolescent Immunization Schedule

United States • 2005

1. **Hepatitis B (HepB) vaccine.** All infants should receive the first dose of HepB vaccine soon after birth and before hospital discharge; the first dose may also be administered by age 2 months if the mother is hepatitis B surface antigen (HBsAg) negative. Only monovalent HepB may be used for the birth dose. Monovalent or combination vaccine containing HepB may be used to complete the series. Four doses of vaccine may be administered when a birth dose is given. The second dose should be administered at least 4 weeks after the first dose, except for combination vaccines which cannot be administered before age 6 weeks. The third dose should be given at least 16 weeks after the first dose and at least 8 weeks after the second dose. The last dose in the vaccination series (third or fourth dose) should not be administered before age 24 weeks.

    Infants born to HBsAg-positive mothers should receive HepB and 0.5 mL of hepatitis B immune globulin (HBIG) at separate sites within 12 hours of birth. The second dose is recommended at age 1–2 months. The final dose in the immunization series should not be administered before age 24 weeks. These infants should be tested for HBsAg and antibody to HBsAg (anti-HBs) at age 9–15 months.

    Infants born to mothers whose HBsAg status is unknown should receive the first dose of the HepB series within 12 hours of birth. Maternal blood should be drawn as soon as possible to determine the mother's HBsAg status; if the HBsAg test is positive, the infant should receive HBIG as soon as possible (no later than age 1 week). The second dose is recommended at age 1–2 months. The last dose in the immunization series should not be administered before age 24 weeks.

2. **Diphtheria and tetanus toxoids and acellular pertussis (DTaP) vaccine.** The fourth dose of DTaP may be administered as early as age 12 months, provided 6 months have elapsed since the third dose and the child is unlikely to return at age 15–18 months. The final dose in the series should be given at age ≥4 years. **Tetanus and diphtheria toxoids (Td)** is recommended at age 11–12 years if at least 5 years have elapsed since the last dose of tetanus and diphtheria toxoid-containing vaccine. Subsequent routine Td boosters are recommended every 10 years.

3. *Haemophilus influenzae* **type b (Hib) conjugate vaccine.** Three Hib conjugate vaccines are licensed for infant use. If PRP-OMP (PedvaxHIB® or ComVax® [Merck]) is administered at ages 2 and 4 months, a dose at age 6 months is not required. DTaP/Hib combination products should not be used for primary immunization in infants at ages 2, 4, or 6 months but can be used as boosters after any Hib vaccine. The final dose in the series should be administered at age ≥ 12 months.

4. **Measles, mumps, and rubella vaccine (MMR).** The second dose of MMR is recommended routinely at age 4–6 years but may be administered during any visit, provided at least 4 weeks

have elapsed since the first dose and both doses are administered beginning at or after age 12 months. Those who have not previously received the second dose should complete the schedule by age 11–12 years.

5. **Varicella vaccine.** Varicella vaccine is recommended at any visit at or after age 12 months for susceptible children (i.e., those who lack a reliable history of chickenpox). Susceptible persons aged ≥ 13 years should receive 2 doses administered at least 4 weeks apart.

6. **Pneumococcal vaccine.** The heptavalent **pneumococcal conjugate vaccine (PCV)** is recommended for all children aged 2–23 months and for certain children aged 24–59 months. The final dose in the series should be given at age ≥ 12 months. **Pneumococcal polysaccharide vaccine (PPV)** is recommended in addition to PCV for certain high-risk groups. See *MMWR* 2000; 49(RR-9):1–35.

7. **Influenza vaccine.** Influenza vaccine is recommended annually for children aged ≥ 6 months with certain risk factors (including, but not limited to, asthma, cardiac disease, sickle cell disease, human immunodeficiency virus [HIV], and diabetes), health-care workers, and other persons (including household members) in close contact with persons in groups at high risk (see *MMWR* 2004; 53[RR-6]:1–40). In addition, healthy children aged 6–23 months and close contacts of healthy children aged 0–23 months are recommended to receive influenza vaccine because children in this age group are at substantially increased risk for influenza-related hospitalizations. For healthy persons aged 5–49 years, the intranasally administered, live, attenuated influenza vaccine (LAIV) is an acceptable alternative to the intramuscular trivalent inactivated influenza vaccine (TIV). See *MMWR* 2004; 53(RR-6):1–40. Children receiving TIV should be administered a dosage appropriate for their age (0.25 mL if aged 6–35 months or 0.5 mL if aged ≥ 3 years). Children aged ≤ 8 years who are receiving influenza vaccine for the first time should receive 2 doses (separated by at least 4 weeks for TIV and at least 6 weeks for LAIV).

8. **Hepatitis A vaccine.** Hepatitis A vaccine is recommended for children and adolescents in selected states and regions and for certain high-risk groups; consult your local public health authority. Children and adolescents in these states, regions, and high-risk groups who have not been immunized against hepatitis A can begin the hepatitis A immunization series during any visit. The 2 doses in the series should be administered at least 6 months apart. See *MMWR* 1999; 48(RR-12): 1–37.

Appendix B

growth charts

Boys: Birth to 18 Months Physical Growth Percentiles

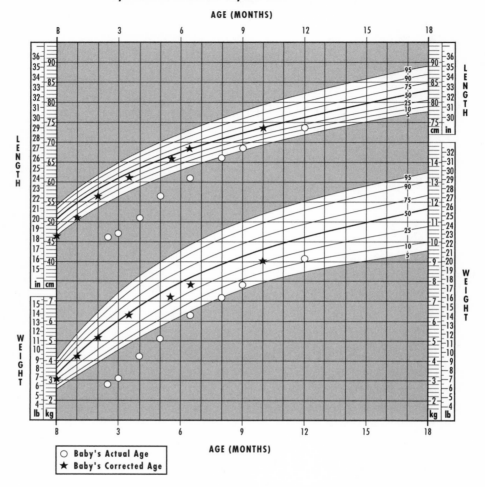

AGE (MONTHS)

○ Baby's Actual Age
★ Baby's Corrected Age

TWIN BOY "A" BORN AT 27 WEEKS GESTATION

*Adapted from Hammill PVV, Drizd TA, Johnson CL, Reed RB, Roche AF, Moore WM: Physical growth: National Center for Health Statistics percentiles.
AM J CLIN NUTR 32:607-629, 1979. Data from the National Center for Health Statistics (NCHS), Hyattsville, Maryland.
© 1982 Ross Laboratories

Boys: Birth to 18 Months Physical Growth Percentiles

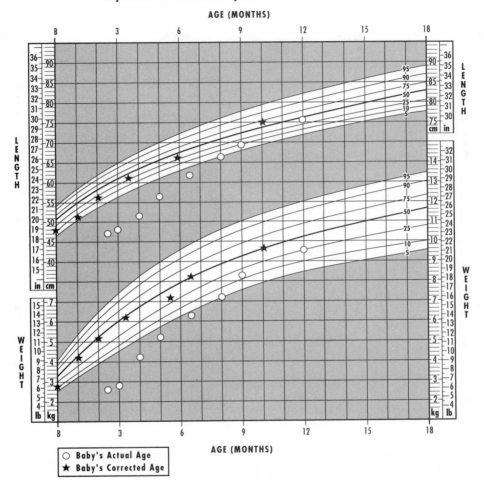

AGE (MONTHS)

- ○ Baby's Actual Age
- ★ Baby's Corrected Age

TWIN BOY "B" BORN AT 27 WEEKS GESTATION

*Adapted from Hammill PVV, Drizd TA, Johnson CL, Reed RB, Roche AF, Moore WM: Physical growth: National Center for Health Statistics percentiles. AM J CLIN NUTR 32:607-629, 1979. Data from the National Center for Health Statistics (NCHS), Hyattsville, Maryland.
© 1982 Ross Laboratories

Boys: Birth to 18 Months Physical Growth Percentiles

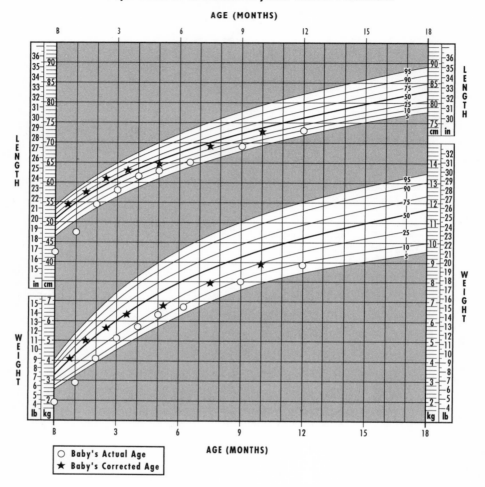

○ Baby's Actual Age
★ Baby's Corrected Age

TWIN BOY "A" BORN AT 34 WEEKS GESTATION

*Adapted from Hammill PVV, Drizd TA, Johnson CL, Reed RB, Roche AF, Moore WM: Physical growth: National Center for Health Statistics percentiles.
AM J CLIN NUTR 32:607-629, 1979. Data from the National Center for Health Statistics (NCHS), Hyattsville, Maryland.
© 1982 Ross Laboratories

Boys: Birth to 18 Months Physical Growth Percentiles

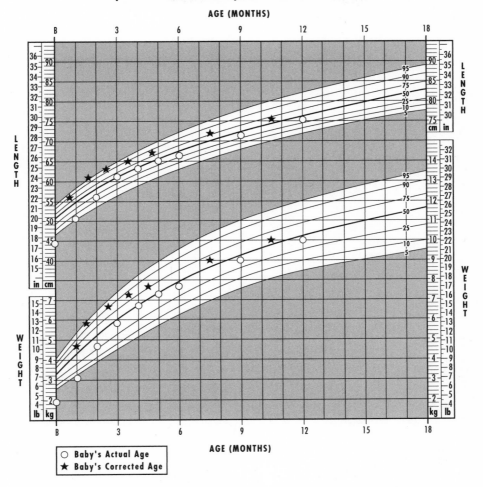

- ○ Baby's Actual Age
- ★ Baby's Corrected Age

TWIN BOY "B" BORN AT 34 WEEKS GESTATION

*Adapted from Hammill PVV, Drizd TA, Johnson CL, Reed RB, Roche AF, Moore WM: Physical growth: National Center for Health Statistics percentiles. AM J CLIN NUTR 32:607-629, 1979. Data from the National Center for Health Statistics (NCHS), Hyattsville, Maryland.
© 1982 Ross Laboratories

Boys: Birth to 18 Months Physical Growth Percentiles

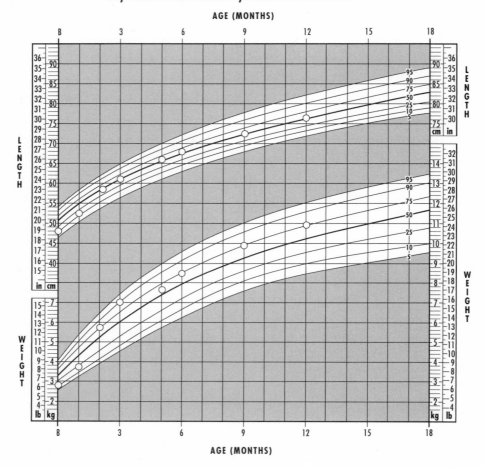

FULL-TERM TWIN BOY

*Adapted from Hammill PVV, Drizd TA, Johnson CL, Reed RB, Roche AF, Moore WM: Physical growth: National Center for Health Statistics percentiles.
AM J CLIN NUTR 32:607-629, 1979. Data from the National Center for Health Statistics (NCHS), Hyattsville, Maryland.
© 1982 Ross Laboratories

Girls: Birth to 18 Months Physical Growth Percentiles

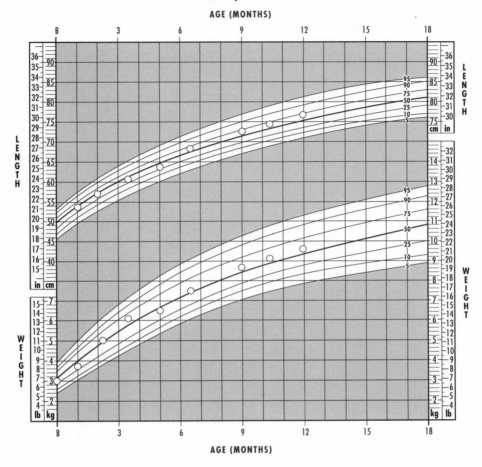

FULL-TERM TWIN GIRL

*Adapted from Hammill PVV, Drizd TA, Johnson CL, Reed RB, Roche AF, Moore WM: Physical growth: National Center for Health Statistics percentiles.
AM J CLIN NUTR 32:607-629, 1979. Data from the National Center for Health Statistics (NCHS), Hyattsville, Maryland.
© 1982 Ross Laboratories

Appendix C

midtrimester risk for chromosome abnormalities

Maternal Age	Risk For Trisomy 21	Risk For Trisomy 18
15	1:1215	1:4734
16	1:1210	1:4716
17	1:1205	1:4695
18	1:1198	1:4668
19	1:1189	1:4632
20	1:1177	1:4584
21	1:1160	1:4521
22	1:1140	1:4443
23	1:1114	1:4341
24	1:1081	1:4212
25	1:1040	1:4053
26	1:990	1:3858
27	1:930	1:3624
28	1:862	1:3357
29	1:784	1:3054
30	1:700	1:2727
31	1:613	1:2388
32	1:526	1:2049
33	1:442	1:1722
34	1:365	1:1422
35	1:296	1:1152
36	1:236	1:921
37	1:186	1:726
38	1:146	1:567
39	1:112	1:438
40	1:86	1:336
41	1:65	1:255
42	1:50	1:195
43	1:38	1:147
44	1:28	1:111
45	1:22	1:84
46	1:16	1:63
47	1:12	1:45
48	1:8	1:33
49	1:6	1:24
50	1:5	1:18

The numbers provided in this table are approximate risks based on data currently available. These numbers are **population-based** risk estimates, and should not be presented as a woman's individual risk.

These numbers represent the estimated risk for a fetus with Down syndrome or Trisomy 18 at **midtrimester**.

Approximately 23% of Down syndrome fetuses and 70% of Trisomy 18 fetuses will be lost between midtrimester and term.

MIDTRIMESTER RISK FOR CHROMOSOME ABNORMALITIES

Appendix D

immunization
during pregnancy

Table 1. Immunization During Pregnancy

Immunobiologic Agent	Risk from Disease to Pregnant Woman	Risk from Disease to Fetus or Neonate	Type of Immunizing Agent	Risk from Immunizing Agent to Fetus	Indications for Immunization During Pregnancy	Dose Schedule*	Comments
			LIVE VIRUS VACCINES				
Measles	Significant morbidity, low mortality; not altered by pregnancy	Significant increase in abortion rate; may cause malformations	Live attenuated virus vaccine	None confirmed	Contraindicated (see immune globulins)	Single dose SC, preferably as measles–mumps–rubella[†]	Vaccination of susceptible women should be part of postpartum care. Breastfeeding is not a contraindication.
Mumps	Low morbidity and mortality; not altered by pregnancy	Possible increased rate of abortion in first trimester	Live attenuated virus vaccine	None confirmed	Contraindicated	Single dose SC, preferably as measles–mumps–rubella	Vaccination of susceptible women should be part of postpartum care.
Poliomyelitis	No increased incidence in pregnancy, but may be more severe if it does occur	Anoxic fetal damage reported; 50% mortality in neonatal disease	Live attenuated virus (oral polio vaccine) and enhanced-potency inactivated virus vaccine[‡]	None confirmed	Not routinely recommended for women in the United States, except women at increased risk of exposure	*Primary:* Two doses of enhanced-potency inactivated virus SC at 4–8 week intervals and a third dose 6–12 months after the second dose

Immediate protection: One dose oral polio vaccine (in outbreak setting) | Vaccine indicated for susceptible pregnant women traveling in endemic areas or in other high-risk situations. |
| Rubella | Low morbidity and mortality; not altered by pregnancy | High rate of abortion and congenital rubella syndrome | Live attenuated virus vaccine | None confirmed | Contraindicated, but congenital rubella syndrome has never been described after vaccine | Single dose SC, preferably as measles–mumps–rubella | Teratogenicity of vaccine is theoretic, not confirmed to date; vaccination of susceptible women should be part of post-partum care. |
| Yellow fever | Significant morbidity and mortality; not altered by pregnancy | Unknown | Live attenuated virus vaccine | Unknown | Contraindicated except if exposure is unavoidable | Single dose SC | Postponement of travel preferable to vaccination, if possible. |

Disease	Effect on Pregnancy	Effect on Fetus/Neonate	Vaccine	Risk to Fetus from Vaccine	Indications During Pregnancy	Dose Schedule	Comments
Varicella	Possible increase in severe pneumonia	Can cause congenital varicella in 2% of fetuses infected during the second trimester	Live attenuated virus vaccine	None confirmed	Contraindicated, but no adverse outcomes reported if given in pregnancy	Two doses needed with second dose given 4–8 weeks after first dose. Should be strongly encouraged	Teratogenicity of vaccine is theoretic, outcomes reported 4–8 weeks not confirmed to date. Vaccination of susceptible women should be considered postpartum.
OTHER							
Influenza	Increase in morbidity and mortality during epidemic of new antigenic strain	Possible increased abortion rate; no malformations confirmed	Inactivated virus vaccine	None confirmed	All women who are pregnant in the second and third trimester during the flu season (October–March); women at high risk for pulmonary complications regardless of trimester	One dose IM every year	—
Rabies	Near 100% fatality; not altered by pregnancy	Determined by maternal disease	Killed virus vaccine	Unknown	Indications for prophylaxis not altered by pregnancy; each case considered individually	Public health authorities to be consulted for indications, dosage, and route of administration	—
Hepatitis B	Possible increased severity during third trimester	Possible increase in abortion rate and preterm birth; neonatal hepatitis can occur; high risk of newborn carrier state	Purified surface antigen produced by recombinant technology	None reported	Pre-exposure and postexposure for women at risk of infection	Three-dose series IM at 0, 1, and 6 months	Used with hepatitis B immune globulin for some exposures; exposed newborn needs birth dose vaccination and immune globulin as soon as possible. All infants should receive birth dose of vaccine.
Hepatitis A	No increased risk during pregnancy	—	Inactivated virus	None reported	Pre-exposure and postexposure for women at risk of infection; international travelers	Two-dose schedule 6 months apart	—

Immunobiologic Agent	Risk from Disease to Pregnant Woman	Risk from Disease to Fetus or Neonate	Type of Immunizing Agent	Risk from Immunizing Agent to Fetus	Indications for Immunization During Pregnancy	Dose Schedule*	Comments
INACTIVATED BACTERIAL VACCINES							
Pneumococcus	No increased risk during pregnancy; no increase in severity of disease	Unknown, but depends on maternal illness	Polyvalent polysaccharide vaccine	None reported	Recommended for women with asplenia; metabolic, renal, cardiac, pulmonary diseases; smokers; immuno-suppressed. Indications not altered by pregnancy.	In adults, one SC or IM dose only; consider repeat dose in 6 years for high-risk women	—
Meningococcus	Significant morbidity and mortality; not altered by pregnancy	Unknown, but depends on maternal illness	Quadrivalent polysaccharide vaccine	None reported	Indications not altered by pregnancy; vaccination recommended in unusual outbreak situations	One SC dose; public health authorities consulted	—
Typhoid	Significant morbidity and mortality; not altered by pregnancy	Unknown	Killed or live attenuated oral bacterial vaccine	None confirmed	Not recommended routinely except for close, continued exposure or travel to endemic areas	Killed *Primary:* Two injections SC at least 4 weeks apart. *Booster:* Single dose SC or ID (depending on type of product) *Booster:* Schedule not yet determined	Oral vaccine preferred
Anthrax	Significant morbidity and mortality; not altered by pregnancy	Unknown, but depends on maternal illness	Preparation from cell-free filtrate of *B anthracis*; no dead or live bacteria	None confirmed	Not routinely recommended unless pregnant women work directly with *B anthracis*, imported animal hides, potentially infected animals in high incidence areas (not United States) or military personnel deployed to high-risk exposure areas	Six-dose primary vaccination SC, then annual booster vaccination	Teratogenicity of vaccine theoretical

Table 1. Immunization During Pregnancy

Immunobiologic agent	Risk from disease to pregnant woman	Risk from disease to fetus or neonate	Immunizing agent	Risk from immunizing agent to fetus	Indications for immunization during pregnancy	Dose schedule	Comments
TOXOIDS							
Tetanus–diphtheria	Severe morbidity; tetanus mortality 30%; diphtheria mortality 10%; unaltered by pregnancy	Neonatal tetanus mortality 60%	Combined tetanus–diphtheria toxoids preferred: adult tetanus–diphtheria formulation	None confirmed	Lack of primary series, or no booster within past 10 years	*Primary:* Two doses IM at 1–2-month interval with a third dose 6–12 months after the second. *Booster:* Single dose IM every 10 years after completion of primary series	Updating of immune status should be part of antepartum care.
SPECIFIC IMMUNE GLOBULINS							
Hepatitis B	Possible increased severity during third trimester	Possible increase in abortion rate and preterm birth; neonatal hepatitis can occur; high risk of carriage in newborn	Hepatitis B immune globulin	None reported	Postexposure prophylaxis	Depends on exposure; consult Immunization Practices Advisory committee recommendations (IM)	Usually given with hepatitis B virus vaccine; exposed newborn needs immediate postexposure prophylaxis.
Rabies	Near 100% fatality; not altered by pregnancy	Determined by maternal disease	Rabies immune globulin	None reported	Postexposure prophylaxis	Half dose at injury site, half dose in deltoid	Used in conjunction with rabies killed virus vaccine.
Tetanus	Severe morbidity; mortality 60%	Neonatal tetanus mortality 60%	Tetanus immune globulin	None reported	Postexposure prophylaxis	One dose IM	Used in conjunction with tetanus toxoid.

Immunobiologic Agent	Risk from Disease to Pregnant Woman	Risk from Disease to Fetus or Neonate	Type of Immunizing Agent	Risk from Immunizing Agent to Fetus	Indications for Immunization During Pregnancy	Dose Schedule*	Comments
Varicella	Possible increase in severe varicella pneumonia	Can cause congenital varicella with increased mortality in neonatal period; very rarely causes congenital defects	Varicella–zoster immune globulin (obtained from the American Red Cross)	None reported	Should be considered for healthy pregnant women exposed to varicella to protect against maternal, not congenital, infection	One dose IM within 96 hours of exposure	Indicated also for newborns of women who developed varicella within 4 days before delivery or 2 days following delivery; approximately 90–95% of adults are immune to varicella; not indicated for prevention of congenital varicella.
STANDARD IMMUNE GLOBULINS							
Hepatitis A	Possible increased severity during third trimester	Probable increase in abortion rate and preterm birth; possible transmission to neonate at delivery if woman is incubating the virus or is acutely ill at that time	Standard immune globulin	None reported	Postexposure prophylaxis, but hepatitis A virus vaccine should be used with hepatitis A immune globulin	0.02 mL/kg IM in one dose of immune globulin	Immune globulin should be given as soon as possible and within 2 weeks of exposure; infants born to women who are incubating the virus or are acutely ill at delivery should receive one dose of 0.5 mL as soon as possible after birth.

*Abbreviations: ID, intradermally; IM, intramuscularly; PO, orally; and SC, subcutaneously.

†Two doses necessary for adequate vaccination of students entering institutions of higher education, newly hired medical personnel, and international travelers.

‡Inactivated polio vaccine recommended for nonimmunized adults at increased risk.

Data from General recommendations on immunization. Recommendations of the Advisory Committee on Immunization Practices (ACIP) and the American Academy of Family Physicians (AAFP). Centers for Disease Control. MMWR Recomm Rep;51(RR-2):1–35. Available at http://www.cdc.gov/mmwr/preview/mmwrhtml/rr5102a1.htm. Retrieved October 11, 2002.

Appendix E

resource guide

baby slings and carriers

BabyBjörn
www.babybjorn.com

The Better Baby Sling Company
http://www.betterbabysling.freeserve.co.uk/

Didymos
http://www.didymos.de/english/index_e.htm

Over The Shoulder Baby Holder
http://www.earthbaby.com/overtheshoulderbabyholder.html

Sling-Ezee
Parenting Concepts
P.O. Box 1437
526 Grizzly Road
Lake Arrowhead, CA 92352
(800) 727-3683 in U.S. & Canada
http://www.parentingconcepts.com

Tot Tenders Inc.
(800) 634-6870
http://www.tottenders.com/

breast-feeding, breast pumps, nursing bras, and pillows

Big Girls Bras
http://www.biggerbras.com/collection_maternity_nursing_bras.cfm
Nursing bras and bras for plus-size women

Birth and Beyond
1810 14th Street
Suite 208
Santa Monica, CA 90404
(310) 458-7678
birthandbeyond.net
Breast-feeding instruction and mothers support group

Breastfeeding.com
http://www.breastfeeding.com/
Breast-feeding information and support

Breastfeeding.com
http://www.breastfeeding.com/reading_room/nursing_bras/basics.html
Photos and descriptions of nursing bras

Breastfeeding World
http://www.breastfeedingworld.com/
Breast-feeding products and information

Cozy Cuddles Nursing Pillow
(416) 299-5507
http://www.cozycuddles.com/
Nursing comfort pillows with convenient washable covers

La Leche League International
1400 North Meacham Road, Schaumburg, IL 60173-4808
(847) 519-7730
TTY: (847) 592-7570
http://www.lalecheleague.org/
Breast-feeding information and support

Lact-aid International Incorporated
P.O. Box 1066
Athens, TN 37371-1066
(866) 866-1239
http://www.lact-aid.com/
Supplemental feeding system provides oral sucking therapy for infants, as well
as nutritional supplementation

Medela
E-mail:customer.service@medela.com
http://www.medela.com/
Breast pumps and nursing aids; directs customers to most convenient rental
station and/or breast-feeding consultant

Two-At-A-Time Nursing Pillow
(416) 248-1109
http://www3.sympatico.ca/kjkennedy/pillow1.html
E-mail: two_at_a_time_nursing_pillow@hotmail.com
Pillow designed to comfortably support two nursing babies

car safety seats

Airline car seat restrictions (by carrier)
www.mommyguide.com

American Academy of Pediatrics
www.aap.org/family/carseatguide.htm

Auto Safety Hot Line
Car seat recall
(888) 327-4236

National Highway Traffic Safety Administration
www.nhtsa.dot.gov
Car seat inspection centers by zip code
Child passenger safety
Child seat safety recalls
Child seat ratings

child-proofing and safety

KidCo
(800) 553-5529

Office of Information and Public Affairs
Publication #202 ("The Safe Nursery—A Buyer's Guide")
http://apartments.about.com/library/articles/bl_babychecklist.htm

One Step Ahead
(800) 950-5120

Rev-a-Shelf
(800) 762-9030

The Right Start
(800) 548-8531

The Safety Zone
(800) 999-3030

childbirth education

Birth and Beyond
1750 Ocean Park Boulevard
Suite 206
Santa Monica, CA 90405
(310) 458-7678
birthandbeyond.net
Childbirth preparation and parenting resources

The Bradley Method of Natural Childbirth
http://www.bradleybirth.com/
(800) 4 A BIRTH

Lamaze International Childbirth Educators
http://www.lamaze.org/

Marvelous Multiples
http://www.marvelousmultiples.com/
A resource for families expecting multiples

clothing, bedding, and general baby care

Jan's Custom Knits
http://www.elucidations.us/JansCustomKnits/home.htm
Baby blankets for multiples

The Natural Baby Catalog
7090 Whipple Avenue
North Canton, Ohio 44720
(800) 922-7397
http://shop.store.yahoo.com/naturalbaby/info.html
Bedding, slings and carriers, strollers, diapers, covers, knapsacks, footwear, lambskin, books, and more

The Natural Baby Company
E-mail: info@naturalbabycompany.com
http://www.naturalbabycompany.com/
Eco-friendly diapers

The Preemie Store
1682 Roxanna Lane
New Brighton, MN 55112
(800) 676-8469
http://www.preemie.com/
Clothing for smaller babies

health and medical concerns

Craniosynostosis And Positional Plagiocephaly Support (CAPPS)
E-mail: CAPPSORG@aol.com
www.cappskids.org

Kangaroo Care
http://www.prematurity.org/baby/kangaroo.html
The many benefits of skin-to-skin care for premature babies

National Center for Complementary and Alternative Medicine
NCCAM Clearinghouse
P.O. Box 7923
Gaithersburg, MD 20898
Toll-free in the U.S.: (888) 644-6226
International: 301-519-3153
TTY: 866-464-3615
E-mail: info@nccam.nih.gov
NCCAM web site: nccam.nih.gov

National Cord Blood Program
E-mail: ncbp@nybloodcenter.org
(866) 767-6227
http://www.nationalcordbloodprogram.org

National Immunization Program
Centers for Disease Control and Prevention
http://www.cdc.gov/nip/

Sidelines National Support Network
P.O. Box 1808
Laguna Beach, CA 92652
(888) 447-4754 (HI-RISK4)
Fax: (949) 497-5598
http://www.sidelines.org/cont_01.htm
E-mail for National Office: sidelines@sidelines.org
A nonprofit organization providing education, referral information,
support, and advocacy services for women experiencing complicated
pregnancies.

Sudden Infant Death Syndrome (SIDS)
Back to Sleep Campaign
P.O. Box 29111
Washington, DC 20040
(800) 505-2742

Sudden Infant Death Syndrome (SIDS)
National Institute of Child Health and Human Development
http://www.nichd.nih.gov/sids/sids.cfm

Torticolliskids.org
www.torticolliskids.org
Information and support for families dealing with torticollis

Twin-to-Twin-Transfusion Syndrome (TTTS)
Mary Allen, RN, Fetal Therapy Coordinator
St. Joseph's Women's Hospital
Fetal Therapy Department
3001 West Martin Luther King Boulevard
Tampa, FL 33607
(888) FETAL-77

(813) 872-3982
Fax: (813) 872-3794
mallenrn@aol.com

The Twin to Twin Transfusion Syndrome (TTTS) Foundation, Inc.
411 Longbeach Parkway
Bay Village, OH 44140
(800) 815-9211 or (440) 899-8887
http://www.tttsfoundation.org/
A nonprofit organization providing educational, emotional, and financial
support to families before, during, and after pregnancies diagnosed with TTTS

magazines, newsletters, and books

The Browne Twins Series
by Patricia Frechtman
goldengma@nvbb.net

Caring for Your Premature Baby
by Alan H. Klein, MD, and Jill Alison Ganon
Available at your local bookstore and at amazon.com and other online book-
sellers

Carrying a Little Extra: A Guide to Healthy Pregnancy for the Plus-Size Woman
By Paula Bernstein, Ph.D., MD, Marlene Clark, RD, and Netty Levine, MS,
RD
Available at your local bookstore and at amazon.com and other online book-
sellers

Lose Your Mummy Tummy (and other maternity fitness books and DVDs)
by Julie Tupler, RN
www.maternalfitness.com

Raising Twins
by Eileen Pearlman, Ph.D., and Jill Alison Ganon

Available at your local bookstore and at amazon.com and other online book-sellers

The Twins Foundation
P.O. Box 6043
Providence, RI 02940
(401) 729-1000
http://www.twinsfoundation.com/pubs4sale/twins_letter.htm

The Twins Letter (published quarterly)
subscriptions and back issues
www.simpleshop.net/catalog.mv?1086

TWINS magazine (published bimonthly)
11211 East Arapahoe Road, Suite 101
Centennial, CO 80112-3851
(888) 558-9467
E-mail: twins.editor@businessword.com
http://www.twinsmagazine.com/

maternity needs

girdles and support hose

Gottfried Medical
P.O. Box 8966
Toledo, OH 43623
(800) 537-1968
Custom vascular support hose; prescription required

Healthy Legs
Jobst Support Hose, Medi Support Hose
6342-A SW Macadam Avenue
Portland, OR 97239
(888) 495-0105
http://healthylegs.com/jobstsupport.html

Vascular support hose available at retail outlets; custom maternity girdles and support hose with prescription

IEM Orthopedics
P.O. Box 592
Ravenna, OH 44266
(330) 297-7652
Custom maternity lumbo-pelvic support

strollers

Baby Jogger
http://www.babyjogger.com/
Side-by-side jogging stroller

Runabout Strollers
http://www.bergdesign.net/runabout.htm
Double, triple, and quad strollers

Stroller World
http://www.strollerworld.com/Perego/index.html
Twin and triplet Perego strollers

Yahoo Shopping
http://shopping.yahoo.com/b:Twin%20Strollers:36065392
Comparison shopping for twin strollers; side-by-side and tandem models available

support for families with twins

Center for Loss In Multiple Birth, Inc. (CLIMB)
c/o Jean Kollantai
P.O. Box 1064
Palmer, AK 99645

(907) 746-6123
E-mail: climb@pobox.alaska.net

Family and Medical Leave Act (FMLA)
www.dol.gov/esa/whd/fmla

To Buy Two (The Auction Website for Multiples)
www.tobuytwo.com

Twin Services
http://home.ix.netcom.com/~rtnews1/index.html
E-mail:twinservices@juno.com
Helps twin families to maintain their health and sanity

Twinless Twins Support Group
P.O. Box 980481
Ypsilanti, MI 48198
(888) 205-8962
http://www.twinlesstwins.org/
E-mail: contact@twinlesstwins.org
A support group serving twins (as well as multiples) who suffer from the loss
of companionship of their twin

twinsight
Eileen M. Pearlman, Ph.D., Director
1137 2nd Street, Suite 109
Santa Monica, CA 90403
(310) 458-1373
Fax: (310) 451-8761
http://www.twinsight.com/
E-mail: epearlman@twinsight.com
Dr. Pearlman, who is an identical twin, works with multiples of all ages and
their families. Twinsight offers counseling, psychotherapy, workshops, and
consultations via phone or in person. Dr. Pearlman is the coauthor, with Jill
Alison Ganon, of *Raising Twins*.

teratogens, poisons, occupational and reproductive hazards

Environmental Protection Agency (EPA)
(202) 382-2080
www.cdc.gov/epa/homepage.html

National Capital Poison Center
www.poison.org
(800) 222-1222

National Institute of Occupational Safety, Guide to Chemical Hazards
(800) 35-NIOSH
www.cdc.gov/niosh/homepage.html

National Lead Information Center
(800) 424-5323
www.epa.gov/lead

Occupational and Environmental Reproductive Hazard Center
University of Massachusetts Medical Center, Department of OB/GYN
Worcester, Massachusetts 01655
(508) 856-2818

OTIS: Organization of Teratology Information Services
www.otispregnancy.org/otis_find_a_tis.htm
(866) 626-6847
online site for locating local teratogen information service throughout the
fifty states and Canada

Poisonous plants
www.ansci.cornell.edu/plants/alphalist.html

poisonprevention.org
www.poisonprevention.org
(301) 504-7908

Reprotox
http://reprotox.org/
Information regarding environmental hazards to human reproduction and development

travel

Federal Aviation Administration
http://jag.cami.jccbi.gov/cariprofile.asp
Formula to calculate radiation received in flight

twin organizations and research

Center for Study of Multiple Birth (CSMB)
Suite 464
333 East Superior Street
Chicago, IL 60611
(312) 266-9093
http://pubweb.acns.nwu.edu/~1gk395/csmb.html
E-mail:1gk395@nwu.edu (Dr. Louis Keith, director)
A public charity organized in 1977 in support of medical and social research in the area of multiple births

The International Society for Twin Studies
http://www.ists.qimr.edu.au/
An international, multidisciplinary organization established to further research and social action in all fields related to twin studies

International Twins Association (ITA)
c/o Lynn Long or Lori Stewart
6898 Channel Road, NE
Minneapolis, MN 55432
(612) 571-3022

http://www.intltwins.org/
A nonprofit agency promoting the spiritual, intellectual, and social welfare of
twins throughout the world

The Louisville Twin Study
University of Louisville
Health Sciences Center
Room 20, MDR Building
Louisville, KY 40292-0001
(502) 852-5140
Fax: (502) 852-1093
http://pediatrics.louisville.edu/resident/childdev-unit.htm
E-mail: mlriese@gatekeeper.1ts.louisville.edu
In its fifth decade, this program is one of the oldest and largest twin-family
studies of child development in the world

Minnesota Center for Twin and Adoption Research
University of Minnesota
Department of Psychology
75 East River Road
Minneapolis, MN 55455

Mothers of Supertwins (MOST)
MOST
P.O. Box 306
East Islip, NY 11730
(631) 859-1110
http://www.mostonline.org/
E-mail: info@MOSTonline.org
A nonprofit organization serving the needs of families expecting multiples
and parents who have triplets, quadruplets, or quintuplets

Multiple Births Canada
P.O. Box 432
Wasaga Beach, Ontario Canada

L9Z 1A4
(705) 429-0901
(866) 228-8824
http://www.multiplebirthscanada.org/english/index.php
E-mail: office@multiplebirthscanada.org
An organization to improve the quality of life for multiple-birth individuals
and their families in Canada

The National Organization of Mothers of Twins Clubs, Inc. (NOMOTC)
http://www.nomotc.org/
E-mail: nomotc@aol.com
A nonprofit nationwide network of parents-of-multiples clubs sharing
information, concerns, and advice

Twin Days Festival
Twin Days Festival Committee
P.O. Box 29
Twinsburg, OH 44087
(330) 425-3652
http://www.twinsdays.org/
An annual festival for twins of all ages in Twinsburg, Ohio

The Twins Foundation
P.O. Box 6043
Providence, RI 02940
(401) 751-8946
http://www.twinsfoundation.com
E-mail: twins@twinsfoundation.com
A nonprofit membership organization and research information center on
twins that includes a national twin registry and a quarterly newsletter

index